D1106525

ROBERT B. RAY

# THE
# AVANT-GARDE
# FINDS
# ANDY HARDY

HARVARD UNIVERSITY PRESS

CAMBRIDGE, MASSACHUSETTS

LONDON, ENGLAND    1995

*Library of Congress Cataloging-in-Publication Data*

Ray, Robert B.
  The avant-garde finds Andy Hardy / Robert B. Ray.
    p.   cm.
  Includes bibliographical references and index.
  ISBN 0-674-05537-3 (cloth : alk. paper).—ISBN 0-674-05538-1 (pbk. : alk. paper)
  1. Motion pictures—Philosophy.   2. Avant-garde (Aesthetics)   3. Andy Hardy films.   I. Title.
  PN1995.R38   1995
  791.43'01—dc20

  95-13646

I dedicate this book to two generations: to my mother and father, who introduced me to the Andy Hardy movies on Saturday morning television, and to my daughters, Margaret and Eleanor, with whom I watch them now.

CONTENTS

# The Movies of the Andy Hardy World

· · · · · · · · · · · · · · · · · · · · · · · ·

*Ah, Wilderness!* (1935)

*A Family Affair* (1937)

*You're Only Young Once* (1938)

*Judge Hardy's Children* (1938)

*Love Finds Andy Hardy* (1938)

*Out West with the Hardys* (1938)

*The Adventures of Huckleberry Finn* (1939)

*The Hardys Ride High* (1939)

*Andy Hardy Gets Spring Fever* (1939)

*Babes in Arms* (1939)

*Judge Hardy and Son* (1939)

*Young Tom Edison* (1940)

*Strike up the Band* (1940)

*Andy Hardy Meets Debutante* (1940)

*Andy Hardy's Private Secretary* (1941)

*Life Begins for Andy Hardy* (1941)     *Babes on Broadway* (1941)

*The Courtship of Andy Hardy* (1942)

*Andy Hardy's Double Life* (1942)

*The Human Comedy* (1943)

*Girl Crazy* (1943)

*Andy Hardy's Blonde Trouble* (1944)

*National Velvet* (1944)

*Love Laughs at Andy Hardy* (1946)

*It's a Wonderful Life* (1946)

*Andy Hardy Comes Home* (1958)

*Chapter One*

. . . . . . . . . . . . . . . . .

INTRODUCTION:

REINVENTING FILM STUDIES

This book proposes using the avant-garde arts as models for new ways of writing and thinking about the movies. To experiment with this hypothesis, I have taken as my principal subject matter (although, for the sake of illustration, I will include others) a series of popular films made at MGM in the 1930s and 1940s. Since this book concerns both the movies and the methods we have for studying them, I might introduce it in several ways. Indeed, those who remember Italo Calvino's *If on a winter's night a traveler*, with its multiple beginnings, can probably imagine dozens of ways to start.[1] Since, however, I am writing this introduction on the first day of fall, let us say that if on an autumn night, a traveler were to open this book about the avant-garde and Andy Hardy, he or she might find it beginning in this way:

*In 1939 . . .*

In 1939—the *annus mirabilis* of what has come to be known as the Classical Hollywood Cinema, the year of, among others, *Gone with the Wind, Stagecoach, The Wizard of Oz, Ninotchka, Mr. Smith Goes to Washington, Wuthering Heights, Destry Rides Again, Young Mr. Lincoln,* and *The Roaring Twenties*—something strange happened. An actor, who had not previously been taken very seriously by either his studio or the public, became the movies' number-one box-office attraction, a position he would hold for the three years during which the Studio System, at the peak of its power and inventiveness, would produce such films as

*Only Angels Have Wings*
*Goodbye, Mr. Chips*

*You Can't Cheat an Honest Man*
*Mr. Smith Goes to Washington*
*Intermezzo*
*The Hunchback of Notre Dame*
*The Great Dictator*
*The Shop Around the Corner*
*The Mortal Storm*
*His Girl Friday*
*The Grapes of Wrath*
*The Philadelphia Story*
*Rebecca*
*Kitty Foyle*
*Foreign Correspondent*
*Gunga Din*
*The Great McGinty*
*The Letter*
*Pride and Prejudice*
*My Favorite Wife*
*All This and Heaven Too*
*Citizen Kane*
*Suspicion*
*How Green Was My Valley*
*Meet John Doe*
*Sergeant York*
*The Maltese Falcon*
*High Sierra*
*The Lady Eve*

The box office champion for the years during which these movies appeared was not Gable, Garbo, Cooper, Grant, Tracy, Hepburn, Garland, Stewart, Davis, Bogart, Power, Flynn, Crosby, or Cagney. In 1939, 1940, and 1941, the most popular performer in the American cinema was Mickey Rooney. While Rooney starred in a dozen movies during this period, his success rested primarily on a low-budget series initiated by MGM as a way of profiting from the surprising success of *Ah, Wilderness!*, the studio's 1935 version of Eugene O'Neill's small-town comedy. The series, whose first film, *A Family Affair*, appeared in 1937, quickly came to focus on Rooney's character, Andy Hardy.

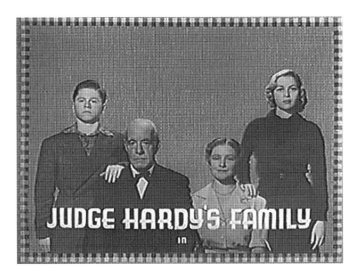

The problem posed by this event (Rooney's succeeding Gable as the King of Hollywood) begins with the vehicle that made it possible. Between 1937 and 1946, MGM made fifteen Andy Hardy movies, seven in 1938 and 1939 alone.[2] From our point of view, more than fifty years later, the striking thing about these films is their *ordinariness*. Expecting a correlation between box office appeal and starring roles in "major motion pictures," we are surprised to find Rooney's success depending on what his own studio classified as B pictures. But what makes the Hardy movies significant is precisely their typicality. Because film history concentrates on masterpieces, we forget that when the studios were releasing almost five hundred movies a year, most of them had far more in common with the Hardy pictures than with *Citizen Kane*. Thus, if we want to try to understand the Hollywood Studio System, the prototype of all twentieth-century media apparatuses, we might do well to start with its *average* product. When two out of three Americans went to the movies at least once a week, they were, after all, likely to see something resembling an Andy Hardy movie.

Since we are not used to studying (or even seeing) ordinary studio pictures, their appeal seems not precisely specifiable.[3] Indeed, to the extent that certain of their charms have receded from us, the Andy Hardy movies (and their enormous popularity) have become slightly odd, illegible, *mysterious*. How to account for the immense success of stories whose reliance on stock situations (Andy's fights with Polly Benedict, sister Marian's amorous misadventures, Judge Hardy's always imminent financial ruin), overt moralizing (the "man-to-man talks"), and fortuitous coincidences (the map-found-in-the-attic that legitimizes a claim) must have seemed anachronistic even to thirties audiences?

We can always mount the obvious explanation: the Hardy series as Escape-from-the-Depression. We could also suggest (emphasizing the uncanny connections) that even while working quickly and sticking to a formula, the Andy Hardy filmmakers had accidentally plugged into the main tradition of American culture. The mischievous good/bad boy, Andy descended from Huck Finn (played by Rooney in 1939). On the other hand, his entrepreneurial energy identified him with Huck's chief rival, Tom Sawyer, and with the line of American promoters, impresarios, and inventors: Horatio Alger, P. T. Barnum, Booth Tarkington's Penrod, and most important of all, Edison (also played by Rooney in 1940's *Young Tom Edison*). The Hardy movies themselves belonged to a group of films about American small-town families whose productions influenced each other: *The Magnificent Ambersons, It's a Wonderful Life, Meet Me in St. Louis, Since You Went Away, The Human Comedy, Babes in Arms*. In many of these cases, the influences were explicit. From Booth Tarkington, O'Neill derived his own *Ah, Wilderness!*, which in turn prompted the Hardy series. The Hardy movies influenced *Meet Me in St. Louis*, which starred Judy Garland, who had appeared in three Hardy films. *Meet Me in St. Louis* was based on stories by Sally Benson, who subsequently adapted Tarkington's *Seventeen* for Broadway, and then scripted the strangest of the small-town movies, Hitchcock's *Shadow of a Doubt*. The most important film of the group, *It's a Wonderful Life*, appears in hindsight as a dark Andy Hardy movie, summarizing and making overt themes which the Hardy series had swept under the rug: money, prostitution, suicide, hopelessness.[4]

The Hardy films' success represents a phenomenon peculiar to modern life: a popular entertainment, made without aesthetic ambition, can gain an unprecedented hold on the collective consciousness. It would, in fact, be almost impossible to find someone who had reached movie-going age in the years 1937–1946 who had not at least heard of Andy Hardy. Nevertheless, almost nothing has been written about the Hardy movies.[5] They continue to be mentioned, however, as the principal source of television's family sitcoms (from *Ozzie and Harriet* and *Father Knows Best*, the series most obviously derived from the Hardy series, to

*Family Ties* and *The Cosby Show*), but have themselves seemed beneath the attention of contemporary film scholars, ideological semioticians after bigger game.

. . .

That would be one way of beginning this book, a way that corresponds to the protocols of academic writing, which require a justification of method and subject matter: someone analyzing, for example, *Bleak House* usually begins by arguing for the novel's significance (or neglect: the two amount to the same thing). I have made such arguments about the Andy Hardy series, perhaps as a token gesture, designed to conceal my real reasons for writing about them: first, for my own interest (does even my childhood liking for these movies bespeak a founding nostalgia? can a child be nostalgic?); second, for their ideological obviousness (demythologized by the passing of time alone); and third, for the provocation inherent in linking Andy Hardy with the term "avant-garde." But one can imagine, of course, other entrances into this subject.

Here, then, would be another way to begin:

*film studies is . . .*

If on an autumn night, a writer began to write a book called *The Avant-Garde Finds Andy Hardy,* he might start by saying that film studies is dead. That would be the most dramatic way to characterize the situation, useful in conversation perhaps, hyperbolic in writing, where I might put it this way: there is now an increasingly widespread sense that after over twenty years of exhilarating work, film studies has stagnated. The discipline whose beginnings coincided with the flowering of structuralist, semiotic, ideological, psychoanalytic, and feminist theory has evolved into another professional specialty (like Romanticism or Eighteenth-Century Poetry), with all the routinized procedures of any academic field.[6] Indeed, what "theory" overthrew (New Critical interpretations based on close readings of individual texts), film studies became. Cinema journals and conferences brim over with papers rounding up the usual suspects for hermeneutical interrogation. Indeed, the typical title in film studies has become "Barthes, Brecht, Bakhtin, Baudrillard, and all those other people, and *Robocop*." Here, for example, are some representative titles from a recent conference of the Society for Cinema Studies:

"The Three Stooges and Derrida: Notes on Deconstructive Comedy"
"Oedipal Drama and the Post-Vietnam Hollywood Film"
"Hollywood and Vietnam: John Wayne and Jane Fonda as
    Discourse"
"*Cheers* and the Mediation of Cultures"
"Textual Pleasure and Transgression in *The Thorn Birds*"
"Female Desire in *All This and Heaven Too*"
"Masochism and Male Hysteria in *The Naked Spur*"
"Gendered Readings of *The Newlywed Game*"
"*Thirtysomething,* Polysemy, and Intertextuality"
"Gender Relations and Popular Culture in Mayberry"
"Ideological Crisis: *Robocop,* Video, and the Reconstitution of
    Subjectivity"

I want to make clear in this introduction that I am not against theoretical analyses of popular culture; I am not against the application of sophisticated semiotic, ideological, and psychoanalytic methods to the study of popular forms. I am not against writing about *Mayberry RFD* or *The Newlywed Game.* My point is that, in effect, they already *have* been written about. The extraordinary contagiousness of contemporary theory lies precisely in its generalizing power: the old model of scholarship, which relied on a specialized, scrupulous coverage of a field of study, insisted that the right to speak about, for example, fiction or narrative accrued only to those who had read all the major novels in a given literature (hence such books as Wayne Booth's *The Rhetoric of Fiction,* which seems to mention every important English novel). Contemporary theory, on the other hand, finds its representative model in Barthes's *S/Z,* which uses one Balzac novella (and a minor one at that) to make an argument about narrative in general. Having seen that approach in action, academics have ignored its lesson and insisted on using it as a new model for case-by-case analyses. But if you understand Barthes's points about storytelling, you do not need to see them worked out with a hundred other examples: that procedure may be useful for beginning students, as a way of apprehending Barthes's approach, but surely it should not be the model for advanced scholarly work.

Why not? Simply because we know in advance where such analyses will lead, and thus even the most skilled of such efforts will achieve very little "information," if we define "information" (as cybernetics does) as a function of unpredictability (a definition I will clarify later in this chapter). How does this problem apply specifically to film studies? Having committed itself to a particular way of doing business (which we might call "semiotic," using that term to stand for the amalgam of structuralist, psychoanalytic, ideological, and feminist methodologies), film studies has, since 1970, constructed an enormously powerful theoretical machine for exposing the ideological abuse hidden by the apparently natural stories and images of popular culture. That machine, however, now runs on automatic pilot, producing predictable essays and books on individual cases.[7]

New Criticism, which arose in the 1930s, maintained its dominance for over thirty years. Why has the semiotic paradigm grown stale so quickly? That question's answer also amounts to a reply to those who, while granting the predictability of much recent semiotic/ideological work on mass culture, insist on retaining the approach for political reasons. In fact, however, although the method originated in a political impulse coinciding with the 1960s' increased ideological sensitivity, it now seems to serve more an immediate institutional politics of academic tenure and promotion.[8] Thomas Kuhn (The Structure of Scientific Revolutions), of course, would have predicted exactly this development: normal scientists, by virtue of their role, have far less intense commitment to their discipline's founding impulses than do its progenitors. Why? Because they don't need such continuously conscious pledges of allegiance: born into the paradigm, they take it for granted and pursue its immediate rewards. While Darwin, Newton, and Einstein were devout missionaries, most biologists and physicists are just men and women with jobs, thinking about paychecks and day-to-day research puzzles. In an academic climate, whose vast oversupply of Ph.D.'s has fostered a concomitant oversupply of publications ("nearly one million articles and three hundred thousand books over a two year period," according to a recent article in Harvard Magazine),[9] any critical approach, even the most radical, gets used up quickly by people for whom it amounts only to a means of getting, keeping, or improving a job. Think, for example, how routine the profound insights of deconstruction, Lacanian psychoanalysis, and ideological criticism have become, a situation predicted over twenty years ago by Roland Barthes:

> the new semiology—or the new mythology . . . it too has become in some sort mythical: any student can and does denounce the bourgeois or petit-bourgeois character of such and such a form (of

life, of thought, of consumption). In other words, a mythological doxa has been created: denunciation, demystification (or demythification), has itself become discourse, stock of phrases, catechistic declaration.[10]

As early as 1971, in other words, Barthes had intuited how redundant demystification had become, at least as an advanced theoretical practice. What else is there to do?

In talking about the story of "The Three Little Pigs," Jonathan Culler once suggested "that almost every *proper* question, such as 'What happened next?', will be critically less productive (less productive of critical discourse we find worth reading) than marginally improper questions, such as 'Why three little pigs?'"[11] Taking Culler at his word, this book's experimental sections amount to a collection of *improper* questions. Indeed, *The Avant-Garde Finds Andy Hardy* sets up a situation typical of contemporary film studies: it works with movies whose plots, characters, settings, and values seem *made* for the structuralist/semiotic/ideological/psychoanalytic/feminist approaches that have become the coin of the realm among those whom one French writer identified as "les enfants du paradigme."[12] This book's experiment, however, explicitly *forbids* such approaches. Instead, it requires the asking of "improper questions."

The importance of questions provides the basis of an anecdote from John Cage, whose method of lecturing (an important model for this book) I will describe later in this introduction. For the moment, the reader must take it on faith that this story will prove relevant to the project at hand:

A crowded bus on the point of leaving Manchester for Stockport was found by its conductress to have one too many standees. She therefore asked, "Who was the last person to get on the bus?" No one said a word. Declaring that the bus would not leave until the extra passenger was put off, she went and fetched the driver, who also asked, "All right, who was the last person to get on the bus?" Again there was a public silence. So the two went to find an inspector. He asked, "Who was the last person to get on the bus?" No one spoke. He then announced that he would fetch a policeman. While the conductress, driver, and inspector were away looking for a policeman, a little man came up to the bus stop and asked, "Is this the bus to Stockport?" Hearing that it was, he got on. A few minutes later the three returned accompanied by a policeman. He asked, "What seems to be the trouble? Who was the last person to get on the bus?" The little man said, "I was." The policeman said, "All right, get off." All the people on the bus burst into laughter. The conductress, thinking they were laughing at her, burst into tears and said she refused to make the trip to Stockport. The inspector then arranged for another conductress to take over. She, seeing the little man standing at the bus stop, said, "What are you doing there?" He said, "I'm waiting to go to Stockport." She said, "Well, this is the bus to Stockport. Are you getting on or not?"[13]

What kinds of "improper questions" should we ask, and where would such questions come from? I will start with this one: Why, if given the choice, would almost everyone, including film studies scholars, rather *see* a movie than read a critical article about it? Other questions follow: Why do certain movies become popular? Why do individual scenes in otherwise forgettable movies fascinate us? Why have two decades of rigorous critique done very little to undermine the glamour and seductiveness of the movies? Why is someone willing to spend $165,000 to own only *one* of the five pairs of slippers worn by Judy Garland in *The Wizard of Oz?*

Speaking at the University of Florida in the fall of 1988, anthropologist Michael Taussig reported that when he asked Colombian Indians to account for imperialism's success, they replied, "the others won because their stories were better than ours." In a very real sense, Hollywood's stories have been better than film criticism's. If we want to approach Hollywood's power without abandoning Habermas's "enlightenment project" (of critique and rational understanding), but want to achieve it by other means, we might begin by experimenting with the *forms* of criticism, which until now has worked almost entirely with one kind of rhetoric: that of scientific realism, with its premise of a transparent language. What are the alternatives? What if we still want the hermeneutic *effect* but feel we have exhausted hermeneutics as a tool?

Taussig has insisted that what is at stake with such questions is "the issue of *graphicness,*" a quality generally disdained by materialist critics who associate it with the enemies—commerce and mystification. Confronted by enormously popular, powerful, mysterious representations (the movies, for example), criticism should, in Taussig's words, attempt *"to penetrate the veil while retaining its hallucinatory quality,"* a process that "evokes and combines a twofold movement of interpretation in a combined action of reduction *and* revelation."[14] Where will we find the "improper questions" that might enable us to work in this way? The difficulty of that *proper* question derives from the historical condition diagnosed by Octavio Paz, who has observed that "the only Myth-Idea of the modern world" is Criticism: "From the 17th century onward," Paz writes, "our world has had no Ideas, in the sense in which Christianity had ideas during its time of apogee. What we have, especially from Kant on, is Criticism."[15]

Is there an alternative to criticism? Another source for "improper questions"? One place to look might be that branch of the humanities which, since the nineteenth century, has functioned as the equivalent of science's pure research: the avant-garde. If instead of thinking about the avant-garde as only hermetic self-expression, we began to imagine it as a field of experimental work waiting to be *used* (in the same way that pure science's exotica becomes another generation's technology), then we might begin to apply certain avant-garde devices for the sake of knowledge.[16]

. . .

That discussion—of film studies' impasse, of the avant-garde's potential—would amount to an alternative way to start this book, one that would concern itself less with the announced subject matter (the movies, and particularly the Andy Hardy series) than with the means that film scholars have developed for thinking and writing about them. We might imagine, however, another opening that would suggest the historical connections between this book's methodological source, the avant-garde, and its object of study, the cinema.

Here, then, would be yet another way to begin:

*Surprise is . . .*

For all its apparent strangeness, the suggestion that avant-garde "improprieties" might actually prove useful comes directly from the experimental arts' own historical justification for their emphasis on shock, provocation, and experiment. Anticipating communication theory's redefinition of "information," Apollinaire provided in 1917 the manifesto of the avant-garde's purposefulness:

> *Surprise is the greatest source of what is new.* It is by surprise, by the important position that has been given to surprise, that the new spirit distinguishes itself from all the literary and artistic movements which have preceded it.
>
> In this respect, it detaches itself from all of them and belongs only to our time.[17]

In effect, Apollinaire had intuited the founding problem of the communication science developed during World War II—how to strike the balance between a message whose high degree of redundancy made it easy to understand (even when received through a network weakened by military attacks and jammed by deliberate "noise") and one whose high proportion of entropy (redundancy's antonym) filled it with information. At the poles lay the traps to avoid: the purely redundant message (perfectly understandable, but useless) and the purely entropic one (perfectly informative, but illegible). You could transmit unchanged, for example, the four-line children's rhyme beginning "Roses are red" and assume that any two consecutive words would enable a listener to fill in the rest. As a consequence, however, such a message wouldn't be worth sending, since its ability to get through depends precisely on the receiver's *already knowing it.* With every change (for example, "Roses are red/*Rooftops* are blue"), the signal's "information" would increase, but so would the difficulty of its reception.

The avant-garde, Apollinaire proposed, was most needed during periods of redundancy, when, in effect, disciplines and institutions settle on unaltered messages. By claiming the avant-garde's provenance for the modern age, Apollinaire implied that with its powerful communications technologies (repetition machines), modern life would be haunted by the constant threat of boredom, now understood as the absence of information. The *ennui* detected by Baudelaire at the birth of the photographic era had become a defining condition. In this climate, as Roland Barthes saw, "the New is not a fashion, it is a value, the basis of all criticism."[18]

Writers and artists working in the avant-garde tradition (however oxymoronic that phrase may seem) have always tended to see crises as resulting less from disastrous innovation than from futile repetition. From this perspective, even Nazism appears as another recycling of worn-out attitudes about race, nation, and war, a catastrophe of redundancy. Inevitably, that situation prompted avant-gardists to demand experimentation, if for no other reason than to generate surprise, the source of "information." Thus, Walter Benjamin, writing during the Weimar Republic, would insist that "these are days when no one should rely unduly on his 'competence.' Strength lies in improvisation. All the decisive blows are struck left-handed."[19] And in another politically troubled context, Benjamin's friend Bertolt Brecht would similarly insist on experimentation: "The question of choice of artistic means can only be that of how we playwrights give a social stimulus to our audience (get them moving). To this end we should try out every conceivable artistic method which assists that end, whether it is old or new."[20]

From the start, in fact, avant-gardists have thought of themselves as practicing something like science. The science they have usually had in mind, moreover, has typically been some version of Auguste Comte's Positivism, with its faith in Baconian method as the surest route to progress. Appearing when Positivism had become the most influential philosophy of the age, Impressionism (the first avant-garde) established the dominant attitude: Monet, Seurat, and Degas regularly spoke of doing a kind of "research," and their critical champion Zola often cited Claude Bernard's call for a new attitude toward knowledge, one founded on the scientific method. Indeed, Zola's influential *The Experimental Novel* (1880) so thoroughly derived from Bernard's *Introduction to Experimental Medicine* (1865) that Zola admitted in his second paragraph, "All I have to do here is to adapt [Bernard] . . . it will be sufficient to replace the word 'doctor' by the word 'novelist.'"[21]

What the Impressionists increasingly found themselves researching was photography. To the extent that photography's invention amounts to a decisive break with traditional representation (especially with writing and painting), the avant-garde's attempts to understand it may seem less an attack on redundancy than an investigation of novelty. But as Friedrich Kittler has pointed out, the camera represents the first in a rapid succession of repetition machines (the typewriter, the phonograph, the cinema) whose capacity to randomly generate words, images, and sounds threw into question almost every traditional notion about human subjectivity and cultural value.[22] Flaubert had sensed the similar issues at stake with printing and mass-produced books: *Madame Bovary* portrays the clichés of pulp fiction as a fatal redundancy, preventing Emma from receiving information (about her situation, about her lovers); and the satiric *Bouvard and Pécuchet* associates clerical *copying* with the hopelessness of "The Dictionary of Received Ideas." But with its automatic capacity to reproduce the world, with its endlessly duplicatable negatives, photography dramatically accelerated what printing had begun.

If we think of the avant-garde as a kind of research into the consequences of new communications technologies, we can begin to make sense of something as apparently scandalous as Marcel Duchamp's readymades. By removing a pre-existing, found object (a urinal, a snow-shovel, a bicycle wheel) from one context and placing it in another (a museum, an artist's studio), Duchamp in effect produced an exact analogy of the photographic process, which *takes* (the operative verb in both cases) a picture, a bit of the world, and makes it available for relocation in an infinite number of other environments. Think, for example, of the famous news photograph of the Hindenberg disaster, reproduced (as a readymade) on the first Led Zeppelin album cover.

When we recall that André Breton defined automatic writing as the "true photography of thought," and that all three of Surrealism's examples of beauty (mimicry, "the expiration of movement," and the found object) were explicitly photographic, we have further evidence of the avant-garde-as-research.[23] Photography, in fact, initiates such a profound break with previous cultural assumptions that I will devote one chapter to its beginnings and another to Surrealism's simulations of it (and of its offspring, the cinema). For the moment, however, I only want to propose that for film studies, the avant-garde arts, with their long history of experimenting with technologies' effects, have use value beyond their simple capacity to surprise.

. . .

Another way of thinking about these questions would entail a different beginning for this book, one that would still concern the movies and the avant-garde, but that would look at things less in close-up (a studio's movies, a discipline's impasse) than in long-shot. Thus:

*Film studies is not . . .*

If on an autumn night, a reader opened this book, he or she might find it beginning with this sentence: "Film studies is not dead, but it does need reinventing." Here is one reason why. Summarizing a research tradition that Jacques Derrida calls "grammatology," a tradition that would include such scholars as Eric Havelock and Jack Goody, Walter Ong's *Orality and Literacy* makes three arguments enormously relevant to film studies. First, human history has seen only two revolutions in the means by which we store, retrieve, and communicate information: the first involved the shift from oral to alphabetic cultures; the second is the transition from alphabetic to "cinematic" or "electronic," which we are living through now. Indeed, the term "postmodernism" is the name for that period when awareness of this latter change first becomes widespread.[24]

Ong's second argument has even more consequence for film studies. In describing the transition from orality to literacy, Ong, of course, is talking about a culture's *dominant* means of storing and retrieving information: in an alphabetic culture, after all, people do not stop talking. But the presence of literacy transforms that talking, encouraging (among other things) a more complex diction, a higher percentage of abstractions, and a greater reliance on classificatory schemata—and the presence of literacy will have this effect *even on speakers who themselves remain illiterate*. By implication, therefore, the emergence of the "cinematic/electronic" mode has already begun to affect the speech and writing of everyone, even those who do not work directly with the new technologies, who are not filmmakers or computer programmers.

Furthermore, Ong's third argument proposes, different technologies of communication transform thinking itself. An oral culture, for example, relying entirely on human memory to store and retrieve its information, develops particular conceptual habits which appear strange to us, the inhabitants of a fully alphabetic society. Indeed, those habits often seem not to amount to thinking at all. As an example of oral logic, Ong describes a scene from A. R. Luria's famous study *Cognitive Development: Its Cultural and Social Foundation:* asked to identify the one dissimilar object in a group consisting of *hammer, saw, log,* and *hatchet,* illiterate subjects, accustomed more to concrete, situational thinking than to abstractions like "tool," insist upon the relatedness of all four. "They're all alike," one responded. "The saw will saw the log and the hatchet will chop it into small pieces. If one of these has to go, I'd throw out the hatchet. It doesn't do as good a job as a saw." When presented with the "correct" notion involving the concept of "tool," the same man stuck to his guns: "Yes, but even if we have tools, we still need wood—otherwise we can't build anything."[25]

While this answer would get you nowhere on an SAT test (an exam based almost entirely in the methods of literate culture), it does amount to a kind of thinking, however different from the conceptual process enabled by the alphabet. Although we take for granted our own notions of "thinking" and assume their permanence, we forget how much human consciousness was restructured by the invention of writing. *Orality and Literacy* outlines the most important effects of writing, including not only the larger consequences of "autonomous discourse" (writing's ability to function apart from both its author and any specific context), but also the particular effects of such typographic devices as lists and indexes (with their capacity to rearrange the world's objects into "unnatural" groupings, dictated by language alone).

If Ong and the research tradition he represents are right, if we are indeed in the midst of civilization's second communications shift toward what Ong calls "post-typography," then speaking, writing, and thinking itself will all feel the influence of cinematic/electronic technology. Academic writing, however, by adhering to modes of presentation and logic developed long before these technologies appeared, remains bound to conventions of representation challenged by photography, film, video, and computers, conventions long since abandoned by the experimental arts.

As I've suggested, one way to introduce this book would be largely negative, a desire for a different critical mode simply as an escape from the boredom afforded by a now-predictable discipline: as Barthes once wrote, in a similar pique of frustration with the very critical apparatus he had once sponsored:

> Every old language is immediately compromised, and every language becomes old once it is repeated. Now, encratic language (the language produced and spread under the protection of power) is statutorily a language of repetition; all official institutions of language [he includes "schools" among them] are repeating machines. . . . The opposition (the knife of value) is . . . *always and throughout* between the *exception and the rule*. For example, at certain moments it is possible to support the *exception* of the Mystics. Anything, rather than the rule.[26]

But however satisfying this reflexive iconoclasm may be, it does not seem quite enough—as, of course, Barthes himself thoroughly realized. Thus, although in this book the avant-garde arts could appear as nothing more than a provocation, a satisfying slap in the face of conventional film studies, they actually provide a means for bringing film criticism into some sort of relationship with the communications technologies revolutionizing everyday life. Indeed, far from being useless, the experimental arts amount to a "workshop for potential criticism."[27]

Which experimental arts in particular? While my purpose does not include attempting yet another definition of "the avant-garde," I can provide some justification for the figures I have chosen to work with: of all the major avant-gardes, the Surrealist tradition (to which Benjamin, Cage, Barthes, and Derrida belong) has attended most eagerly to this book's framing issue, the transition from alphabetic to electronic culture. This project, however, is open-ended: indeed, in the sense of André Breton's insistence on having books "left ajar," I want my readers to extend this experiment by using as models *other* avant-gardists untouched here.[28]

The model for the "potential criticism" that interests me—one that would both produce information (by remaining unpredictable) and respond to the new technologies (by becoming experimental)—was Walter Benjamin. In his most famous essay, "The Work of Art in the Age of Mechanical Reproduction," Benjamin designated photography as the crucial first step toward something other than alphabetic literacy. Photography, he argued, changed everything, forcing us to rethink art and writing and even thinking itself.[29] Two years before that essay, in 1934, Benjamin had already suggested that the modes of writing that we take for granted, and by implication the forms of thinking, were neither inevitable nor permanent:

> We have to rethink our conceptions of literary forms or genres, in view of the technical factors affecting our present situation, if we are to identify the forms of expression that channel the literary energies of the present. There were not always novels in the past, and there will not always have to be; not always tragedies, not always great epics; not always were the forms of commentary, translation, indeed, even so called plagiarism, playthings in the margins of literature; they had a place not only in the philosophical but also in the literary writings of Arabia and China. Rhetoric has not always been a minor form, but set its stamp in antiquity on large provinces of literature. All this to accustom you to the thought that we are in

the midst of a mighty recasting of literary forms, a melting down in which many of the opposites in which we have been used to think may lose their force.[30]

Benjamin was willing to act on this argument. The *Arcades Project*, his proposed study of nineteenth-century Paris, remains the great unbuilt prototype of a new, explicitly cinematic criticism, relying less on traditional exposition than on the forms basic to photography and film: collage and montage. The widespread recent interest in Benjamin's idea indicates that only now, more than fifty years after its proposal, has the academy begun to sense the need for a different way of writing.[31]

. . .

The issues that arise from these alternate beginnings have, in fact, determined the shape of this book, which concerns primarily the first technologies of Ong's "electronic culture": photography and film. Chapter 2 suggests that the nineteenth-century context in which photography emerged delayed the recognition of the camera's break with literacy. Chapters 3 and 4 take up Surrealism's intuition of that break and Breton's methods of simulating photographic and cinematic thinking. In Chapters 5 and 6, Roland Barthes's photographic fetishism becomes the means to a research strategy based on the fragment. Chapter 7 proposes Derrida's "signature experiment" as a "conductive logic" resembling the possibilities afforded by the cinema and the computer. Finally, Chapter 8 describes *Flaubert's Parrot* as a compendium of styles, linked by electronic thinking's fundamental modes, poetic patterning and anecdotal narration.

In some stretches, this book's titular hero, Andy Hardy, will have to yield the stage. With an experimental project of this sort, the burden of justification becomes especially great. In fact, although the book works in ways traditionally designated as "artistic," I know that while artists don't have to explain, teachers do. Indeed, the possibilities of this book's becoming useful depend on such explanations. Thus, although Andy Hardy must at first give way to the theoretical accountings which will re-present him, I have structured the book in such a way that experiments involving the Hardy movies bring him increasingly forward. I have also provided other examples so that these experiments might register with readers who do not know the Hardy films.[32]

But even with this revelation of my organizational scheme, I have still not exhausted the alternatives for beginning this book. I have tried to suggest my reasons for wanting a different kind of film criticism. In Walter Benjamin, we even have a model for it. But since Benjamin never produced his *Arcades Project,* having been refused Frankfurt School funding by Adorno (who came to regret that decision), how can we go about inventing this new kind of writing, desired but unseen? In a famous lecture about Proust, given at the Collège de France in 1978, Barthes spoke about his own search for a different writing whose very lack of definition qualified the quest for it as "an Adventure":

> There can be no "new life," it seems to me, except in the discovery of a new practice of writing. To change doctrine, theory, philosophy, method, belief, spectacular though this seems, is in fact quite banal: one does such things the way one breathes . . . intellectual conversions are the very pulsion of the intelligence, once it is attentive to the world's surprises; but the search, the discovery, the practice of a new form—this, I believe, is equivalent to that *Vita Nova* whose determinations I have described.[33]

And so, another way of beginning this book would acknowledge my own interest in writing differently about the movies. In classifying his works for his autobiography, Barthes distinguished "a labor of knowledge" (an encyclopedia article "on" something) from "a labor of writing," siding with the latter without ever quite defining it.[34] In the Collège de France Lecture delivered three years later, Barthes seemed closer to being able to say what he wanted: a hybrid form which, following Proust, would combine the novel (with its stories and details and weather) with the essay (with its questions and explanations and commentary). With this form, Barthes wrote,

> I put myself in the position of the subject who *makes* something, and no longer of the subject who speaks *about* something: I am not studying a product, I assume a production . . . I proceed to another type of knowledge (that of the Amateur), and it is in this that I am methodical.[35]

John Cage once described this project more simply, as an explanation for his own peculiar lecture style: "My intention has been, often, to say what I had to say in a way that would exemplify it; that would, conceivably, permit the listener to experience what I had to say rather than just hear about it."[36] Thus:

*What should this kind of book . . .*

If on an autumn night, I were to begin writing this book, I might start with a question: What should this kind of book resemble? Since my subjects include, in no particular order, the movies (which are fun), the avant-garde (which is experimental), and representation (which is every-thing), the best model for it might be something like the Marx Brothers' *A Night at the Opera* as described by Roland Barthes: "the steamer cabin [the stateroom scene], the torn contract, the final chaos of opera décors," scenes which Barthes called "emblems of textuality," and which prompted him both to praise "the preposterous" and to suggest how "the logical future" of criticism "would therefore be the gag."[37] Now there is a challenge. When she was a little girl, Gertrude Stein faced a similar problem with *her* first writing attempt, a play whose initial stage direction read, "Enter the courtiers, making witty remarks"—a line that stopped her cold, since she couldn't think of any witty remarks.[38] Thus, if I choose in this book to agree with Barthes about the value of the (apparently) preposterous, I will have to invent the equivalent of "witty remarks."

The reactions of my colleagues to this book's title suggest that I have already managed to come up with something preposterous. My fellow teachers snicker at the conjunction of the avant-garde and Andy Hardy— a response which, of course, has proved at least intermittently satisfying, since, as Barthes once argued, the pleasures of perversity should not be underestimated.[39] Even film scholars, however, tend to confuse the Andy Hardy series with either the "Hey! Let's put on a show!" Judy Garland–Mickey Rooney musicals *or* the Hardy Boys detective stories. That con-fusion has not deterred me from this project.

With my title having satisfied the preposterous requirement (and maybe the gag one, too), I have still had to imagine a mode of writing that would accommodate my interests in the movies, the avant-garde, and representation. Both theoretical reasons, which will become more explicit in subsequent chapters, and personal taste, which I can only point to here, have encouraged me to work occasionally in fragments, that form preferred by the founder of modern criticism, Nietzsche, and adopted by, among others, the Surrealists, Wittgenstein, Benjamin, Adorno, and Barthes. The fragment, which seems writing's equivalent of the photograph, responds perhaps to the shortening of our attention spans in this media age, with its glut of information. As a form, it permits a reader to drop in and out of relatively discrete sections without fear of losing some single, sustained train of thought. And it enables the writer to postpone until later, in Barthes's words, "what bores him," "to write *right away* what it pleases him to write."[40]

One kind of fragment has particularly interested me: the anecdote. This form, with its elliptical suggestiveness, has proved congenial to artists as different as Jorge Luis Borges, Joseph Cornell, and Jean-Luc Godard. And, beginning with Freud, even theoretical writings have frequently turned on the compressed narrative: think, for example, how Derrida's "My Chances/*Mes Chances*" uses the story of Freud's drive to the wrong address, or how *Roland Barthes*, virtually a book of anecdotes, manages to generate ideas from an incident as simple as a conversation about the weather.[41] With its roots in oral culture, the anecdote has resurfaced in what Ong has called "the secondary orality" of electronic civilization. Its appeal depends on attributes that Paul Auster attributes to another oral form, the fairy tale:

> These are bare-bone narratives, narratives largely devoid of details, yet enormous amounts of information are communicated in a very short space, with very few words. . . . The text is no more than a springboard for the imagination. "Once upon a time there was a girl who lived with her mother in a house at the edge of a large wood." You don't know what the girl looks like, you don't know what color the house is, you don't know if the mother is tall or short, fat or thin, you know next to nothing. But the mind won't allow these things to remain blank; it fills in the details itself, it creates images based on its own memories and experiences—which is why these stories resonate so deeply inside us. The listener becomes an active participant in the story.[42]

Auster's hypothesis is confirmed by one version of composition-by-fragment that relies heavily on the anecdote: John Cage's lecture style. In 1958, having contracted to speak in Brussels on the "New Aspect of Form in Instrumental and Electronic Music," Cage gave a talk that consisted exclusively of thirty unconnected anecdotes. Here is one:

> Staying in India and finding the sun unbearable, Mrs. Cooma-raswamy decided to shop for a parasol. She found two in the town

nearby. One was in the window of a store dealing in American goods. It was reasonably priced but unattractive. The other was in an Indian store. It was Indian-made, but outlandishly expensive. Mrs. Coomaraswamy went back home without buying anything. But the weather continued dry and hot, so that a few days later she went again into town determined to make a purchase. Passing by the American shop, she noticed their parasol was still in the window, still reasonably priced. Going into the Indian shop, she asked to see the one she had admired a few days before. While she was looking at it, the price was mentioned. This time it was absurdly low. Surprised, Mrs. Coomaraswamy said, "How can I trust you? One day your prices are up; the next day they're down. Perhaps your goods are equally undependable." "Madame," the storekeeper replied, "the people across the street are new in business. They are intent on profit. Their prices are stable. We, however, have been in business for generations. The best things we have we keep in the family, for we are reluctant to part with them. As for our prices, we change them continually. That's the only way we've found in business to keep ourselves interested."[43]

And here is another:

It was a Wednesday. I was in the sixth grade. I overheard Dad saying to Mother, "Get ready: we're going to New Zealand Saturday." I got ready. I read everything I could find in the school library about New Zealand. Saturday came. Nothing happened. The project was not even mentioned, that day or any succeeding day.[44]

This method amounts to Cage's solution to a particular problem—how to inform an audience about his announced subject, "Indeterminacy: New Aspect of Form in Instrumental and Electronic Music." In the traditional arrangement, the speaker would prepare something more conventional, an expository, informative, clear one-hour talk to be read to his assembled listeners. Such a talk would typically outline the field's recent developments, name its major figures, and speculate about its immediate prospects. The audience would leave satisfied with the transaction: it has spent time for information; the lecturer has delivered it. Whether the audience members will remember what they have heard is *another story*. Cage's experimental lecture, on the other hand, issuing from what Gregory Ulmer has called "a dramatic, rather than an epistemological, orientation to knowledge,"[45] will almost certainly baffle many who hear it. With its determined discontinuity, non-teleological structure, and obvious strangeness, however, it *represents* its subject matter—twentieth-century experimental music.

Here, then, is another story:

> When I was a boy, we lived in the country, twenty minutes outside of town, in a house on top of a hill, with a mile-long driveway that ran down the hill to the highway that led into town. Growing up, I remember my father always talking about a particular sports car that he had owned when he was younger, his first car in fact. Because he had once been involved in rallies and road racing, my father kept photograph albums of his former cars the way most people do of their children. But his favorite was his first, a red MG that he had wrecked a few months after his twentieth birthday (in a collision with a telephone pole) and which had been a total loss. Finally one day he saw an ad for such a car, went to look at it, and found to his amazement (for it was twenty years later) that the car advertised was not merely one *like* his old car, but *was* his old car. He bought it on the spot. I remember the day he brought it home, or rather when the tow truck brought it, since the car itself was still a wreck and wouldn't run. We had at that time a large house with an enormous cellar that ran the length of the house. The tow truck arrived, we opened the trap doors to the cellar, and lowered the car into it. For years after that day, my father spent most of his leisure time in the cellar, working on the car, taking it apart and putting it back together at least six times, straightening the frame (with weights hung from the ceiling), retooling the detailed aluminum work on the dashboard, working on the engine. Occasionally, we would go into town with him to make exotic purchases of a special kind of leather for the steering wheel. The car became my father's trademark; everyone knew him for it. Finally, after seven years, he declared that the car was ready. The tow truck came back, the trap doors opened, and the whole neighborhood stood around as the car came up the ramp my father had built for it. He looked around at the neighbor's children, smiled, and told them to hop in. The car was only a two-seater, and I got the privileged position in the front next to him, but six or seven other small kids piled into the rumble

seat in the back, and off we went down the mile-long driveway that ran down to the highway, with wheatfields and haystacks on either side. A minute into the drive, with all of us singing and yelling and having a wonderful time, I noticed that my father was sweating profusely. "Is there something wrong?" I asked. He turned, looked at me, and without saying a word, simply handed me the steering wheel which had come off in his hands. Just ahead, our driveway made a sharp turn to the right; straight ahead was a small cliff with a twenty-five-foot drop to a plowed field below. My father grabbed the steering column with both hands, and with all his strength managed to turn the car just enough to miss the drop and land us in the middle of a haystack just off the road to the right. When the car stopped, the kids cheered and said, "That was great! Can we do it again?"[46]

For the moment, I will leave it to the reader to decide what this story has to do with either Andy Hardy or the avant-garde, but here at the end of this introduction is one final anecdote from Cage:

What do images do? Do they illustrate? (It was a New Year's Eve party in the country and one of them had written a philosophical book and was searching for a picture that would illustrate a particular point but was having difficulty. Another was knitting, following the rules from a book she had in front of her. The rest were talking, trying to be helpful. The suggestion was made that the picture in the knitting book would illustrate the point. On examination it was found that everything on the page was relevant, including the number.)[47]

# Chapter Two

. . . . . . . . . . . . . .

## SNAPSHOTS:
## THE BEGINNINGS OF
## PHOTOGRAPHY

In the late twentieth century, the ubiquity of photography, especially as a document of certain events, has engendered a longing for both its earlier invention and its more extensive presence. We now wish that photography had always existed, and that it had been everywhere. What did certain things look like exactly?—the expression on Napoleon's face when Moscow first appeared in the distance? the hands of John Wilkes Booth, in hiding, waiting to assassinate Lincoln? the clothes worn by the Council of Trent? Einstein at the moment of completing the Theory of Relativity? More and more, to have not seen becomes equated with Walter Benjamin's definition of *catastrophe:* "to have missed the opportunity."[1]

Nothing encourages this desire for photographic evidence more than the cinema, which, as Jean-Luc Godard has pointed out, always provides, at the very least, a documentary record of a particular moment's objects and people: as Godard said about his own *Breathless,* "This film is really a documentary on Jean Seberg and Jean-Paul Belmondo."[2] Thus, if we want to know, for example, what Jean Harlow looked like less than a week after her husband Paul Bern was found dead in an apparent suicide, we have only to look at a scene from *Red Dust,* shot on her first day back on the set, but edited without the closeups which her haggard appearance made unusable.[3]

In fact, Hollywood's version of the cinema, what Noël Burch calls the Institutional Mode of Representation, dramatically stimulates the desire, and even the expectation, to observe everything.[4] By implicitly guaranteeing its audience the ideal vantage point for every narratively relevant event, by visually underlining (with, for example, closeups, rack focusing, and camera movements) every important detail or expression, Hollywood's "invisible style" accustoms us to expect photographic accompaniment for everything that might prove significant.

What about the origins of photography itself, its first moments of invention and use? What would they look like on film? What if, by the sheerest chance, we came across a roll of film containing a photographic record of just those things, but produced by a camera whose strange mechanism, an alternative to the lineage of our own, has been lost? Searching for a manual, we fall upon these remarks, which will serve as our instructions: "The past has left behind in literary texts images of itself that are comparable to the images which light imprints on a photosensitive plate. Only the future possesses developers active enough to bring these plates out perfectly."[5] Think, then, of each of the following sections as a snapshot of photography's beginnings, developed in terms of our current interests in texts, their ways of producing meaning, and their relation to what we still call "the real."

. . . . . . 1

In the course of his first random stroll through the boulevards and the rue de la Paix, Lucien, like all new-comers to Paris, took more stock of things than of persons. In Paris, it is first of all the general pattern

that commands attention. The luxury of the shops, the height of
the buildings, the busy to-and-fro of carriages, the ever-present contrast between extreme luxury and extreme indigence, all these things
are particularly striking. Abashed at the sight of this alien crowd,
the imaginative young man felt as if he himself was enormously
diminished.

   Honoré de Balzac, *Lost Illusions*, trans. Herbert J. Hunt

In the twenty-year period from 1830 to 1850, when the hero of Balzac's
*Lost Illusions* arrives in Paris, many of the features associated with "modern
life" begin to appear for the first time: the metropolis, the daily newspaper, mass transit, the department store, the democratization of culture.
In particular, between 1839 and 1842, three things happen: the word
*photography* begins to be used for the first time in English and German,[6]
the *physiologies* become the first best-selling mass-market paperback
books, and Poe invents the detective story. What connects these three
developments?

   Dana Brand has argued that modern urban life provoked a crisis of
"legibility."[7] As newcomers swarmed into the cities, abandoning their
native surroundings which time, size, and tradition had rendered effort-
lessly comprehensible, anonymity became a condition that almost everyone experienced at some point during the day—in a remote *quartier,*
visited for the first time on business; on an unknown street, turned down
by mistake; in a neighborhood encountered in the morning rather than
the afternoon. Inevitably, this dislocation encouraged crime: "It is almost
impossible," Benjamin quotes a Parisian undercover policeman observing, "to maintain good behaviour in a thickly populated area where an
individual is, so to speak, unknown to all others and thus does not have
to blush in front of anyone."[8] In December 1840, Edgar Allan Poe explicitly connected crime to the illegibility of the anonymous "man of the
crowd," who like "a certain German book . . . does not permit itself to be
read."[9] That man, for whom Poe's literate narrator can discover no
comforting classification, stands for "the type and the genius of deep
crime."[10]

   Thus, a proposition: what cannot be read threatens. The first sites of
this new anxiety were Paris and London, vast metropolises where people
could disappear without a trace, where (as in Balzac and Dickens, the
great chroniclers of the potential anonymity haunting all urban identities) credentials, antecedents, and even names became suspect. The first

clue connecting this experience to photography is geographical: photography was invented almost simultaneously in France (by Niepce and Daguerre) and in England (by Fox Talbot).

. . . . . . 2

The Count de Lanty was small, ugly, and pock-marked; dark as a
Spaniard, dull as a banker.
  Roland Barthes, *S/Z*, trans. Richard Miller

In *S/Z*, an analysis not only of Balzac's *Sarrasine* (the source of this description of the Count de Lanty) but of all popular narratives, Barthes repeatedly asks, how does Balzac know that Spaniards are dark, bankers dull? Barthes answers by proposing that the realistic novel works precisely to ensure that the source for such a sentence "cannot be discerned": "Who is speaking? Is it Sarrasine? the narrator? the author? Balzac-the-author? Balzac-the-man? romanticism? bourgeoisie? universal wisdom? The intersection of these origins creates the writing."[11] Barthes labels these formulaic expressions ("dark as a Spaniard," "dull as a banker") as "cultural codes" or "reference codes" and traces their origin not to reality itself, but to representations of it:

> The cultural codes, from which the Sarrisinean text has drawn so
> many references, will also be extinguished (or at least will emigrate
> to other texts; there is no lack of hosts). . . . In fact, these citations
> are extracted from a body of knowledge, from an anonymous Book
> whose best model is doubtless the School Manual. (*S/Z*, p. 205)

For Barthes, of course, the term "School Manual" functions as a metaphor for the imaginary collation of common sense, received ideas, and cultural stereotypes on which the Reference Code relies. In fact, however, something very like actual manuals, guides to the urban scene, did achieve enormous success in Paris between 1840 and 1842: the *physiologies*. The first mass-market, paperback, pocket-sized books, the *physiologies* proved enormously appealing to readers wanting an immediately legible account, however misleadingly simplified, of the cosmopolitan crowd. Roughly 120 different *physiologies* appeared during these three years, each offering what historian Richard Sieburth has called "pseudo-scientific portraits of social types": "the Englishman in Paris," "the drinker," "the creditor and the retailer," "the salesgirl," "the deputy," "the stevedore," and so on.[12] As books, the *physiologies* were brief, averaging around 120 pages, with 30 to 60 illustrations (p. 170). While the *physiologies* were not typically comic, their format obviously derived from the same ethos which had spawned the caricature, a form which, in fact, dominated the books' visual style.

Whatever usefulness the *physiologies* purported to have rested on a single, profound faith in the reliability of appearances. As Benjamin observed of these books, "They assured people that everyone was, unencumbered by any factual knowledge, able to make out the profession, the character, the background, and the life-style of passers-by."[13] Dana Brand points out that the plot of Poe's "The Man of the Crowd" turns on the narrator's frustrated desire to "read" the people who pass his coffeehouse window. Having identified (at least to his own satisfaction) noblemen, merchants, attorneys, tradesmen, stock-jobbers, clerks, pickpockets, gamblers, "Jew pedlars," professional street beggars, invalids, prostitutes, and "ragged artisans and exhausted laborers of every description," the narrator becomes fascinated by the illegible man to whom none of the readymade categories apply. Sieburth summarizes the *physiologies'* appeal:

> They served to reduce the crowd's massive alterity to proportions more familiar, to transform its radical anonymity into a lexicon of nameable stereotypes, thereby providing their readers with the comforting illusion that the faceless conglomerations of the modern city could after all be read—and hence mastered—as a legible system of differences. (p. 175)

This "legible system," as *S/Z* shows, is complicit with a culture's world view: in Barthes's words, "If we collect all such knowledge, all such vulgarisms, we create a monster, and this monster is ideology" (p. 97). But a recent *New York Times* article linking the persistence of stereotypes to their "usefulness" concludes that "the new explorations of the cognitive role of stereotypes find them to be a distortion of a process that helps people order their perceptions. The mind looks for ways to simplify the chaos around it. Lumping people into categories is one."[14]

. . . . . . 3

We didn't trust ourselves at first to look long at the first pictures  he [Daguerre] developed. We were abashed by the distinctness of these human images, and believed that the little tiny faces in the picture could see *us*, so powerfully was everyone affected by the unaccustomed clarity and the unaccustomed truth to nature of the first daguerrotypes.

> Dauthendey, quoted in Walter Benjamin, "A Small History of Photography," trans. Edmund Jephcott and Kingsley Shorter

If the *physiologies* offered to make urban life more comfortable by first making it more legible, photography must initially have seemed part of the same project. Soon after its discovery, the new technology became part of the proliferating systems of registration and surveillance described in Benjamin's *Charles Baudelaire: A Lyric Poet in the Age of High Capitalism.* Fingerprinting, physiological measurements, and photographs recorded identity, enabled its tracking, and circumscribed its possible escape routes into anonymity. After photography, the kind of situation described in *The Return of Martin Guerre,* where a man posing as a long-vanished husband fools an entire town, appeared decisively premodern.

Like the *physiologies,* photography had a pseudo-scientific basis, particularly in the late eighteenth and early nineteenth century rage for classification. But while the new technology seemed the ideal means of gathering the empirical data required by any system, almost immediately the first photographers noticed something going wrong. One historian cites Fox Talbot's surprise at what he found:

> And that was just the trouble: fascinating irrelevancy. "Sometimes inscriptions and dates are found upon buildings, or printed placards most irrelevant, are discovered upon their walls: sometimes a distant sundial is seen, and upon it—unconsciously recorded—the hour of the day at which the view was taken." To judge from his commentaries, Fox Talbot enjoyed such incidentals. At the same time, though, they were troublesome, for they meant that the instrument was only partially under control, recording disinterestedly in despite of its operator's intentions.[15]

The *physiologies* had subsumed all idiosyncrasies under the rule of the controlling term: "the banker," "the Spaniard." Indeed, their format seemed derived from La Fontaine's dictum, "Nothing more common than the name, nothing rarer than the thing."[16] Photographs, on the other hand, swarming with accidental details unnoticed at the time of shooting, continually evoked precisely what eluded classification—the distinguishing feature, the contingent detail. In doing so, they undercut the *physiologies'* basic project, which photography now revealed to be committed exclusively to language as a way of understanding and ordering the world. What resisted the narrator's efforts to read the man of the crowd?—"the absolute idiosyncrasy of [his] expression."[17]

By showing that every Spaniard was not dark, every banker not dull, photographs effectively criticized all classification systems and ensured that any such system attempted in photography (for example, August Sander's) would inevitably appear not as science but as art. In fact, although the longing for strictly objective, and therefore exact, representation had motivated photography's invention, photographs produced precisely the opposite effect—a mute ambiguity that invited subjective reverie. Quoting the semiotician Mukarovsky, Paul Willemen has proposed that "the signifying practices having recourse to images can thus be described . . . as 'designed to render things imprecise,' as a movement towards indeterminacy."[18] Thus, photography becomes yet another example of what Edward Tenner has called the "revenge effect" of all technology: a process designed for one purpose turns out not only to subvert that purpose but to achieve its opposite.[19]

. . . . . . 4

Beyond the obvious facts that he has at some time done manual
labour, that he takes snuff, that he is a Freemason, that he has been
in China, and that he has done a considerable amount of writing
lately, I can deduce nothing else.
    Sherlock Holmes, in Arthur Conan Doyle, "The Red-Headed League"

That the first detective story (Poe's "The Murders in the Rue Morgue") appeared in 1841, at the height of the *physiologies* craze, and that its author felt obliged to set his tale in Paris, a place he had never been, both suggest the existence of an underlying connection between the two forms. In fact, the detective story represents a transposition of the *physiologies*, an extrapolation from that earlier mode's purely descriptive purposes to narrative. Like the *physiologies*, the detective story offered to make the world, and particularly the urban scene, more legible. To do so, it relied incessantly on the very reference codes the *physiologies* had propagated. Thus, for Sherlock Holmes, physical evidence is always unproblematically indexical: "the writer" will inevitably display a shiny cuff and a worn elbow patch, "the laborer" a muscular hand, "the visitor to China" a particular Oriental tatoo.

Although the detective story arose almost simultaneously with the *physiologies,* it flowered only after their demise. In effect, it was not needed until later, when it functioned as an antidote to photography. "Between what matters and what seems to matter," *Trent's Last Case* begins, "how should the world we know judge wisely?"[20] By dramatically increasing the available amount of particularized information, photography not only undercut the *physiologies'* vulnerable, simplistic schema; it ensured that in every context where it intervened, distinguishing the significant from the insignificant would become treacherous. "The principal difficulty of your case," Holmes tells his client in "The Naval Treaty," "lay in the fact of there being too much evidence"[21]—precisely the problem, the proliferation of meaning, for which Susan Sontag blames photography.[22] Thus, the first Sherlock Holmes story, "A Scandal in Bohemia," inevitably revises Poe: the new threat, which the detective must find and destroy, is no longer a purloined letter, but an incriminating *photograph.*

And yet this story has another side, suggested, perhaps, by a coincidence of names and a convergence of ideas:

> Holmes #1: The "distinctness of the lesser details of a building or a landscape often gives us incidental truths which interest us more than the central object of the picture."
>
> Holmes #2: "If I take it up I must consider every detail. . . . Take time to consider. The smallest point may be the most essential."

Citing the first Holmes (Oliver Wendell), James Lastra proposes that photography replaced the "Albertian" hierarchy of well-made *pictures* with an "all-over" *image,* where marginal elements appear as detailed as the nominal subject. The second Holmes (Sherlock, speaking in "The Red Circle") suggests the detective story's ultimate *proximity* to photography. For, in fact, Doyle's hero depends upon a photographic way of seeing which, like rack focus, redirects the gaze from foreground to background, and, like a pan, from center to margin. In "Silver Blaze," the thrill of hearing Holmes insist on "the immense significance of the curried mutton" and "the curious incident of the dog in the night-time" derives from having one's attention shifted from the obvious (the gambler Fitzroy Simpson, the gypsies) to the marginal, which turns out, of course, not to be marginal at all. The Holmes stories, in other words, are the written equivalent of photographs, where apparently incidental details, like Barthes's third meanings, persistently replace the proffered *studium*. In the words of a mid-nineteenth-century writer, quoted by Lastra, "The most minute detail, which in an ordinary drawing, would merit no special attention, becomes on a photograph, worthy of careful study." Substitute *ordinary novel* for "ordinary drawing" and *in a detective story* for "on a photograph," and the connection becomes clear. Then a discovery: two days after writing these words, while visiting London's Sherlock Holmes museum, I discover a book, *The Unknown Conan Doyle: Essays on Photography,* which reveals Holmes's creator as one of late nineteenth-century England's most avid amateur photographers.[23]

To a certain extent, the detective story differed from its predecessor, replacing the *physiologies'* intolerance for the particular with an insistence on its value. "Singularity," Holmes instructs Watson, "is almost invariably a clue. The more featureless and commonplace a crime is, the more difficult it is to bring home." What neither the detective story nor the *physiologies* can admit, however, is chance, accident, randomness— precisely those properties of all signifying systems which, as Barthes's "Third Meaning" essay reveals, photography radically enhances.[24] Every photograph, even the starkly "impoverished"[25] ones favored by advertising and propaganda, can occasion a reading that fixates on contingent details whose precise meaning eludes, at least temporarily, all readily available symbolic systems. The survival of the *physiologies* and the detective story, on the other hand, depends on the *resistance* to the appeal of the accidental: if the blonde Spaniard has no place in the *physiologies,* the random crime proves fatal to the detective story—and, as Borges's "Death and the Compass" demonstrates, to the detective who wrongly insists on interpreting it. By repudiating the hermeneutic impulse in favor of the accidental, Borges's story marks the triumph of the photographic sensibility and, by implication, its most characteristic incarnation: the candid snapshot. Momentarily overcome, the anxiety to interpret, which had prompted both the *physiologies* and the detective story, returns in *Blow-Up,* where it is ironically evoked by exactly such snapshots which now reveal a crime. But while the movie cites the detective story form, it refuses to subordinate images to language, suggesting with its inconclusive ending that the need to explain must ultimately be abandoned.

. . . . . . 5

In the history of films, every great moment that shines is a silent one.

   King Vidor, quoted in Joseph Cotten, *Vanity Will Get You Somewhere: An Autobiography*

Without its [inner speech's] function of binding subject and text in
sociality [some system of shared meanings produced by shared
codes], no signification would be possible other than delirium.

   Paul Willemen, "Cinematic Discourse"

At the origins of photography, therefore, an intersection of related problems: the legibility of the surrounding world, the status of the detail, the
relationship between image and language. For the *physiologies* and the
detective story, rituals of the word's mastery over things, photography
represents the other which must be contained. In the twentieth century,
this contest finds a new site—the cinema.

   Filmmaking has, from the first, been shaped by the answers proposed
to a set of fundamental questions: How do we make sense of a film?
What happens when we encounter a movie segment for the first time?
How do we process cinematic information? During the experimental
phase of Soviet cinema, Boris Eikhenbaum suggested, in an especially
influential answer, that we accompany our film watching with an "inner
speech." In particular, inner speech makes the connection between separate shots. A useful example occurs in *Born Free*'s opening scene, which
cuts back and forth between a woman washing clothes in a river and a
stalking lion, apparently intent on an unseen prey. With the woman and
the lion never appearing together in any frame, the sequence culminates
in three shots: the lion springs, the woman turns and screams, and the
river rushes away, now littered with clothes and a spreading red stain.
The scene's meaning is clear: the lion has killed the woman. That
meaning, however, while an *effect* of the images, appears nowhere in
them. It occurs only in the mind of the viewer, whose inner speech responds to the movie's images and sounds with the linguistic formulation,
"lion kills woman."

   The notion of inner speech reaffirms, in Paul Willemen's words, "the
interdependence of the verbal and the visual in cinema."[26] Even the
nonverbal is grasped in relation to the verbal, which translates it into
our dominant meaning system, language. Significantly, the concept of
inner speech arises with silent film and in a genre (propaganda) where
unambiguous communication is the goal. In that context, what is most

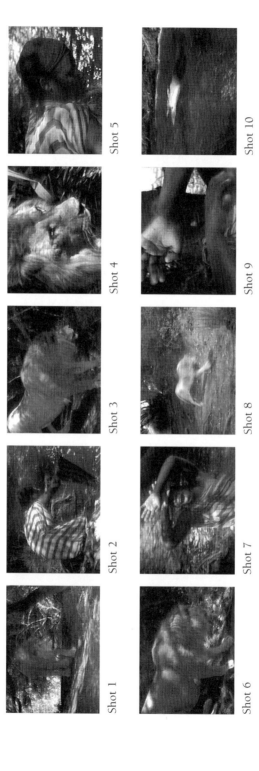

feared is images' capacity to produce not meaning, but what Willemen calls "delirium." Without a verbal soundtrack to anchor the images and constrain their potential drift, and with the continuity rules still inchoate, inner speech had to rely on other visual elements for the verbal formulations that would bind the unrolling pictures into a coherent statement.

Recognizing their images' potential for ambiguity and imprecision, silent-era filmmakers structured their shots around formulaic characters, sequences, and even verbal expressions. The silent cinema, in fact, represents the single most important revival of the *physiologies.* There we again encounter the *physiologies'* basic assumption that every character type has its own unvarying physical embodiment: villains look villainous (with moustaches and squinting eyes), heroines look virtuous (with petticoats and blonde hair), and business men look businesslike (with suits and starched shirt-fronts). Very early in the movies' evolution, filmmaking also gravitated to stock actions—the chase, the lovers' meeting, the deathbed vigil. In *S/Z,* Barthes designates such predictable sequences as part of the "proairetic code," that reservoir of generic actions such as "the stroll," "the murder," or "the rendezvous" (Barthes's examples) that trigger readymade inner speech; indeed, Barthes proposes that this "code of actions principally determines the readability of the text" (*S/Z,* p. 262). At its most extreme subservience to language, a silent film's image track would occasionally provide a *visual* translation of a stock phrase: *October's* juxtaposition of Provisional Dictator Kerensky with a mechanical peacock ("proud as a peacock") is only the most famous example of this device.

Sound moviemaking did not abandon these formulas; it simply relied on newly developed strategies for making them subtler. Most useful were Hollywood's continuity protocols, founded on the two principles of matching and centering, both designed to overcome film's fundamental discontinuity. While the matching rules ensured that editing would connect shots by means of certain cinematic grammar, centering guaranteed that all *mise-en-scène* elements (for example, lighting, framing, shot size) would visually underline narratively important events. To the extent that the continuity rules circumscribed the movies' images, regulated their meaning in terms of a single narrative, and vastly reduced their potential complexity, they became, like the detective story, *a means of policing photography*—and another example of language's control of the image.

While the notion of inner speech arises in film's infancy, Barthes's "third meaning" appears in its maturity. With its insistence on perverse readings that ignore, and indeed refuse, intended or contextually obvious significances, the third-meaning disposition clearly descends from Surrealist tactics designed to reassert the autonomy and ambiguity of images: think, for example, of Man Ray's habit of watching the screen through his fingers, spread to isolate certain parts of the image; of Breton's advocacy of eating and talking during showings as means for reorienting one's attention to the marginal incident or detail; of Breton's weekend moviegoing:

> When I was "at the cinema age" (it should be recognized that this age exists in life—and that it passes) I never began by consulting the amusement pages to find out what film might chance to be the best, nor did I find out the time the film was to begin. I agreed wholeheartedly with Jacques Vaché in appreciating nothing so much as dropping into the cinema when whatever was playing was playing, at any point in the show, and leaving at the first hint of boredom— of surfeit—to rush off to another cinema where we behaved in the same way. . . . I have never known anything more *magnetizing*; it goes without saying that more often than not we left our seats without even knowing the title of the film which was of no importance to us anyway. On a Sunday several hours sufficed to exhaust all that Nantes could offer us: the important thing is that one came out "charged" for a few days.[27]

Both Barthes's "third meaning" practice of reading movie stills and the Surrealist strategies of film watching amount to methods of *extraction, fragmentation*. In both, the individual segment, image, or detail is isolated from the narrative that would circumscribe it. "To a certain extent," Barthes proposes, the third meaning "cannot be grasped in the projected film, the film 'in movement,' '*au naturel*,' but only, as yet, in that major artifact which is the still."[28] Like the detective story, Hollywood filmmaking (still the international norm) "arrests the multiplication of meanings," as D. A. Miller argues, "by uniquely privileging one of them"[29]— that set designated "significant" by the unrolling story. In his autobiography, Barthes acknowledged his own "resistance to the cinema," attributing it to the "statutory impossibility of the fragment" in a continuous, "saturated" medium.[30]

Narrative, in fact, subordinates its images to the linguistic formulations they serve. "The sequence exists," Barthes writes of the action code, "when and because it can be given a name" (*S/Z*, p. 19). Thus, encountering a picture offering itself as "a still," we will immediately begin to imagine the missing story. Doing so typically involves a summoning of the received categories stored in inner speech, the "already-done," the "already-read" (*S/Z*, p. 19). If, for example, we were to come across this picture, to what plot would we imagine it belonging?

"A sad love story"? "A tale of vampires"? "A mystery"? To the extent that any of these constructions would immediately limit the image's possibilities, we can make this proposition: in late twentieth-century civilization, every image lies surrounded by invisible formulas whose inevitable activation reasserts our stubborn allegiance to language as the only means of making sense.

Artists have begun to play with this situation, implying the traps into which our preference for language leads us. Cindy Sherman's "Film Stills" have become the most famous case, a complex use of photography, disguise, and the word "still" to imply movies which do not in fact exist—and to snare the viewer into "explaining" the photographs in terms of the cinematic conventions (for example, *film noir,* Antonioniesque angst, Southern gothic) already available to inner speech. Equally suggestive is Chris Van Allsburg's children's book *The Mysteries of Harris Burdick,* a collection of fourteen captioned images, each purporting to be the single remaining illustration of stories never found.

What is at stake with this relationship between language and image? In the Introduction I cited Walter Ong's argument that different tech-

Chris Van Allsburg
A STRANGE DAY IN JULY
He threw with all his might, but the third
stone kept skipping back

Chris Van Allsburg
CAPTAIN TORY
He swung his lantern three times and slowly
the schooner appeared

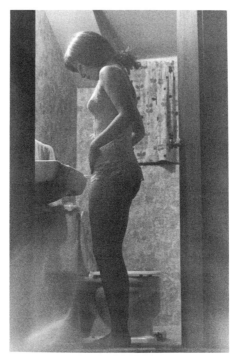

Cindy Sherman
*Untitled Film Stills #39*

nologies of communication occasion different ways of thinking. What are the consequences, characteristics, and modes of an age of photography, film, television, magnetic tape, and computers? How will what we call "thinking" change with this technology?

It will be up to us to decide. And here the matter of language and photography intervenes decisively. To the extent that such deciding will require invention, the persistence of formulas becomes inhibiting. The "already-read" categories of the *physiologies,* the detective story, and inner speech seek to define the new technology (photography, film) in terms of the old (language), and thereby restrict our capacity to admit the full implications of the revolution surrounding us. Roger Cardinal calls this way of dealing with images the "literate mode," derived from "habits of purposeful reading of texts," and assuming that "the artist has centred or signalled his image in accordance with the conventions of representation" so that "the viewer's gaze will be attuned to that focal message and will ignore its periphery." The alternative, "one which focuses less narrowly and instead roams over the frame, sensitive to its textures and surfaces," Cardinal associates with "non-literacy and with habits of looking which are akin to habits of touching."[31] This way of putting the matter seems absolutely consistent with the tradition we might call, following Susan Sontag, "against interpretation." Surrealism, Barthes's "third meaning" essay, and photography itself have all explicitly evoked eroticism as an analogue for a new practice of the image. If that practice involves, as *Blow-Up* suggests, a relaxation of the explanatory drive (our version of the will-to-power?), its motto might result from changing one word in the dictum thrown like a knife at the literary establishment almost thirty years ago, ironically by one who has become photography's enemy: in place of a hermeneutics we need an erotics, not of art, but of photography.[32]

*Chapter Three*

. . . . . . . . . . . . . . . .

# INVENTION FINDS A METHOD: SURREALIST RESEARCH AND GAMES

. . . . . . 1. Research as *Flânerie*

> At the point where surrealism has taken up the problem, its only guide has been Rimbaud's sibylline pronouncement: "I say that one must be a seer, one must make oneself a seer." As you know, this was Rimbaud's only means of reaching the *unknown*. Surrealism can flatter itself today that it has discovered and rendered practicable many other ways leading to the unknown.
>
> André Breton, "What Is Surrealism?"

In many important ways, the renewed interest in Surrealism owes itself to an evening in 1926 when a thirty-four-year-old German essayist, visiting his sister in Paris, began to read Louis Aragon's account, at once precise and enraptured, of his own wanderings—in an enclosed street near l'Opéra and in the strange Parisian park known as the Buttes-Chaumont. "I wanted to discover the face of the infinite," Aragon had written, "beneath the concrete forms which were escorting me, walking the length of the earth's avenues":

> At last each particle of space is meaningful, like a syllable of some dismantled word. Each atom suspends here, as a precipitate, a little of its human faith. Each breath of wind. And the silence is a mantle that is unfurling. See these great folds of stars. The divine brushes the illusory lightly with the tips of its slender fingers. Breathes out its delicate breath upon the window-pane of the abyss. Cables to anxious hearts its magic message: *Patience stop mystery in motion* and, betrayed, reveals itself to the glimmers of light. . . .

I was suddenly filled with the keen hope of coming within reach
of one of the locks guarding the universe: if only the bolt would
suddenly slip.[1]

Writing nine years later to his colleague Theodor Adorno, Walter Benjamin remembered this initial encounter with *Le Paysan de Paris:* "At
night in bed I could never read more than two or three pages at a time,
for my heartbeat became so strong that I was forced to lay the book
down."[2]

Benjamin's first response to Aragon's story was to imitate it: with his
friend Franz Hessel, who had accompanied him to Paris (and who
became the model for Jules in *Jules and Jim*),[3] Benjamin almost immediately conceived what has come to be known as the *Arcades Project,* an
analysis of streets precisely like Aragon's *Passage de l'Opéra.* Intended as
a materialist history of nineteenth-century Paris, portrayed as the birthplace of modern culture, Benjamin's narrative was planned from the
point of view of a *flâneur,* one of the idle yet attentive strollers who had
once drifted along the shop-lined, enclosed, gas-lit streets (now vanished) which became the prototypes of the modern shopping mall. When
a trip to Moscow in the winter of 1926 introduced him to the montage-based Soviet cinema of Eisenstein, Kuleshov, and Pudovkin, Benjamin
began to recognize Surrealism's common ground with film: the propensity for fragmentation and discontinuity, the reliance on recombination
and juxtaposition. From this perspective, André Breton's maxim (appropriated from Lautréamont), "Beautiful . . . as the chance encounter of a
sewing machine and an umbrella on an operating table," seemed like a
simple shot description, an example of "the montage of collisions" that
Eisenstein had championed as an editing strategy. The *Arcades,* Surrealism, the cinema—these events, Benjamin began to realize, were not
discrete; they were all part of what he would later call, in the now famous
phrase, "the Age of Mechanical Reproduction."

This age, Benjamin reasoned, was fundamentally different from its
predecessors, and its first grammar issued from photography. "The Work
of Art in the Age of Mechanical Reproduction" represents Benjamin's
preliminary analysis of that grammar's implications, first for art, but
more importantly for cognition itself. Even before that essay, however,
Benjamin had anticipated grammatology's insight: a new photographic
culture would spawn its own "writing" (redefined to include extra-al-

phabetic modes), and Surrealism and the movies were early examples. Benjamin's response was to re-imagine the *Arcades Project* as a kind of Surrealist film script, where meaning would result from the careful arrangement of found material: snapshots, advertisements, literary citations, maps. "Method of this work," Benjamin wrote to himself, "literary montage. I need say nothing. Only show."[4] Although prompted by particular technologies, the new way of "writing," Benjamin saw, was not medium-specific: even in an older form like the book, it could be simulated.

But this book would be different. First, it would depend, as one commentator observes, on "an epistemology of images, as opposed to concepts,"[5] and the juxtapositions would inevitably seem abrupt: "To write history therefore means to *quote* history," Benjamin warned himself in his notes. "But the concept of quotation implies that any given historical object must be ripped out of its context."[6] But if the objects in Lautréamont's slogan were fungible—a tape recorder, for example, could meet a steam shovel on an ironing board without any loss of effect—the objects in Benjamin's work were not. Photography's fundamental lesson had not escaped him: details counted. Indeed, they would provide the *Arcades Project*'s organization, whose goal was "to convince . . . without conceptualization."[7] "The eternal," Benjamin suggested, anticipating Barthes's "Third Meaning," "would be the ruffles on a dress rather than an idea."[8]

Looking for funding, Benjamin wrote to the Frankfurt School, proposing this new kind of book, a carefully arranged collage of found material from mid-nineteenth-century Paris. In a letter he would later regret, Adorno said no. He wrote that what his friend wanted to do "tends to turn into a wide-eyed presentation of mere facts":

> If one wished to put it very drastically, one could say that your study is located at the crossroads of magic and positivism. That spot is bewitched. Only theory could break the spell.[9]

As a phrase, "the crossroads of magic and positivism" precisely describes Surrealism. Benjamin, in fact, had intuited the connection between the nineteenth-century *flâneur* (Baudelaire's "dandy") and the twentieth-century Surrealist, urban wanderers, at once purposeful and aimless. But Benjamin had also sensed a crucial difference: for the dandy, *flânerie* had amounted to only a passive means of resisting a culture increasingly ruled by positivist notions of efficiency; for the Surrealist, it had become a means to revelation. Taking the next step, Benjamin proposed that the *flâneur*'s tactics—the preference for drifting, the openness to chance encounters, the attentiveness to details—might provide the basis for a modern epistemology, whose researcher would behave less like a philosopher than like a photographer or filmmaker. Accustomed himself to long days of idling through the archives of the Bibliothèque Nationale, Benjamin began to suggest that these tactics *already* lay at the heart of scholarship; one needed only to follow Surrealism's lead and formalize them.

In arriving at this position, Benjamin had been practicing a kind of implicit Surrealism, relying for his ideas on accidental meetings (*Le Paysan de Paris,* Russian cinema) which revealed coincidental connections. "In the fields with which we are concerned," he admitted, "knowledge comes only in flashes. The text is the thunder rolling long afterward."[10] In effect, he had translated Breton's *Nadja* into a manual for scholarship. Placed side by side, passages from the two writers reveal the connection:

I intend to mention, in the margin of the narrative I have yet to relate, only the most decisive episodes of my life *as I can conceive it apart from its organic plan,* and only insofar as it is at the mercy of chance—the merest as well as the greatest—temporarily escaping my control, admitting me to an almost forbidden world of sudden parallels, petrifying coincidences, and reflexes peculiar to each individual, of harmonies struck, as though on the piano, flashes of light that would make you see, really *see,* if only they were not so much quicker than all the rest. I am concerned with facts of quite unverifiable intrinsic value, but which, by their absolutely unexpected, violently fortuitous character, and the kind of associations of suspect ideas they provoke . . . I am concerned, I say, with facts which may belong to the order of pure observation, but which on each occasion present all the appearances of a signal, without our being able to say precisely which signal, and of what.

Breton, *Nadja*[11]

Comparison of others' attempts to setting off on a sea voyage in which the ships are drawn off course by the magnetic north pole. Discover *that* North Pole. What for others are deviations, for me are data by which to set my course.

Say something about the method of composition itself: how everything that comes to mind has at all costs to be incorporated into
the work one is doing at the time.

These notes, which deal with the Paris arcades, were begun under
the open sky—a cloudless blue which arced over the foliage—and
yet are covered with centuries of dust from millions of leaves;
through them blew the fresh breeze of diligence, the measured
breath of the researcher, the squalls of youthful zeal, and the idle
gusts of curiosity.

How this work was written: rung by rung, as chance offered a
narrow foothold.

Necessity of listening for every accidental quotation, every fleeting
mention of a book, over many years.

The dialectical image is like lightning. The past must be held like
an image flashing in the moment of recognition.   Benjamin, "N"[12]

As it evolved in Benjamin's mind, the *Arcades Project* became a mod-
ernized *flânerie,* combining the *disponibilité* (availability) of the dandy
with a materialism learned from Brecht. A prototype for a new way of
researching popular culture, it renewed the *flâneur's* original opposition
to positivism by taking on that philosophy's unexpected heir, what
Adorno called "the culture industry." Nevertheless, because film studies'
discovery of Benjamin coincided with the 1970s apogee of Marxism, his
connection to Surrealism did not become immediately apparent. Only
with later translations of *Arcades Project* fragments did film scholars
begin to realize that Surrealism had been more than just a passing phase
in art history.

Surrealism, in fact, is the twentieth century's most important avant-
garde. The movement invented in the early 1920s by André Breton, Paul
Eluard, Louis Aragon, and Benjamin Péret not only affected the subsequent direction of painting, literature, music, and theater; it also
shaped developments in Continental philosophy and the social sciences.
Indeed, almost every French intellectual born after 1900 has felt Surrealism's influence. The desire for a transformed everyday life, the faith in
chance, the reliance on automatism and collaboration, the delight in
provocation, the taste for a mechanized eroticism, the belief in procedures rooted in "the arbitrary" and accomplished in distraction—these

features of the movement have proved abidingly seductive. That they might also prove *useful* has not always been as obvious. But precedents for that way of taking Surrealism have existed all along: Jacques Lacan, for example, derived his psychoanalytic strategies less from medicine than from his Surrealist friends with whom, by his own account, he spent most of his leisure time.[13]

Surrealism's importance resulted from the premeditation behind it. Reacting against Dada's straightforward nihilism, Breton from the start conceived of the avant-garde arts as a partner in philosophy's fundamental project—the investigation of method. The Surrealists assumed that even creativity issues less from inspiration than from procedure, and despite the eccentricity of its "instructions" for such forms as automatic writing, the Soluble Fish, and headline poetry, the movement remained grounded in a Cartesian faith that rules enable discovery. This interest in impersonal, replicable protocols obviously descends from Baconian science, and the Surrealists promptly announced their devotion to "research," establishing their own journal (*La Révolution surréaliste*) and their own clinic (the *Bureau de recherches surréalistes*). Indeed, the most explicit expression of the avant-garde's commitment to science appears with the Surrealists, for whom the homonyms available in the words *expérience* (experience and experiment) and *recréation* (fun and re-creation) were crucial. Breton's *Manifesto of Surrealism* (1924) stated the position, which reflected both his own and Aragon's medical training: the *Manifesto* speaks repeatedly of knowledge, the failure of the old systems of reason and logic (which Breton thought had produced World War I), and the need to find new investigatory procedures:

> We are still living under the reign of logic, but the logical processes of our time apply only to the solution of problems of secondary interest. The absolute rationalism which remains in fashion allows for the consideration of only those facts narrowly relevant to our experience. . . . In the guise of civilization, under the pretext of progress, we have succeeded in dismissing from our minds anything that, rightly or wrongly, could be regarded as superstition or myth; and we have proscribed every way of seeking the truth which does not conform to convention.[14]

Citing Freud as a model for new ways of doing research, Breton warned against rejecting experimental methods that might prove useful, even if such methods at first seemed merely strange:

Perhaps the imagination is on the verge of recovering its rights. If the depths of our minds conceal strange forces capable of augmenting or conquering those on the surface, it is in our greatest interest to capture them; first to capture them and later to submit them, should the occasion arise, to the control of reason. [A key statement, indicating Surrealism's partial retention of the Enlightenment project.] The analysts themselves can only gain by this. But it is important to note that there is no fixed method *a priori* for the execution of this enterprise, that until the new order it can be considered the province of poets as well as scholars, and that its success does not depend on the more or less capricious routes which will be followed.[15]

The subtlety of this attitude toward science should not be missed. At first glance, Breton's enthusiasm may seem to betray his intellectual ancestor, the *flâneur*. Hadn't the dandy, after all, repudiated work, and by implication, the practical goals of modern science? Yes, but *flânerie* itself had been more complicated, existing as a kind of deadpan parody of the scientific method, a *reductio ad absurdum* of disinterested observation, practiced as an end in itself. Although Breton followed Baudelaire in disavowing work as the means to revelation,[16] he departed from the *flâneur* in seeing that science's mistake was not its goal but its methods, particularly its faith in procedures constrained by traditional logic. Surrealism's project, therefore, would become the invention of a new science, what its admired predecessor Alfred Jarry had called "pataphysics," a science of exceptions.

While Breton was arguing for new ways of working, alternatives to Criticism, he was also demonstrating *how* to invent them. His tactics, Gregory Ulmer suggests, show that creativity proceeds by emulation, and that, as a result, avant-garde manifestos "belong to the tradition of the discourse on method" and "tend to include a common set of elements." Those elements, Ulmer proposes, can be mnemonically summarized by the acronym CATTt, representing the following operations:

C = Contrast
A = Analogy
T = Theory
T = Target
t = tale (or form in which one will work).[17]

The *Surrealist Manifesto* confirms Ulmer's hypothesis. Breton's opening move involved Contrast, his opposition to literary realism and its conceptual bases, traditional reason and logic. For an Analogy, Breton, recalling his medical training, suggested that Surrealism take up the scientific model of experimentation and research. For a specific Theory, Breton borrowed Freudian psychoanalysis, aiming at an immediate Target of the arts, but ultimately at everyday life itself. Surrealism's "tale" would be the traditional arts and ad hoc provocations, both conceived of as conceptual interventions into politics and what Trollope once called "the way we live now."

Surrealism's influence results from its methodical attitude toward invention. "Forget about your genius, your talents, and the talents of everyone else," Breton advised, in the process of demonstrating that anyone could write "imaginative" poetry simply by following a set of impersonal rules.[18] That lesson, in turn, suggests how to invent an avant-garde criticism:

> **Contrast** this potential criticism with the conventional academic essay, formally conservative and devoted to critique.
>
> As an **Analogy**, propose the avant-garde arts as the research dimension of the humanities, the equivalent of pure science.
>
> For **Theory**, use Surrealism, with its emphasis on chance and collaboration.
>
> The **Target** becomes the academic institution, into which this new criticism will be introduced.
>
> And the **tale** will be a new form of critical writing.

This process of invention-by-extrapolation involves translation between disciplines: as John Cage once explained, "One way to write music: study Duchamp." Thus, Surrealism, an aesthetic/political movement, derived from Freudian psychoanalysis, but Freud found his offspring unrecognizable. That response suggests how high-handed and free the translation can become. Indeed, in a very real sense, the CATTt method resembles that aspect of photography objected to by Sontag, the "taking" which honors no original context:

> To photograph is to appropriate the thing photographed. . . . In a world ruled by photographic images, all borders ("framing") seem

arbitrary. Anything can be separated, made discontinuous from anything else: all that is necessary is to frame the subject differently.[19]

Brecht, on the other hand, proposed a more sanguine metaphor for this borrowing-for-other-purposes, the *Messingkauf,* the purchaser of brass:

> I can only compare myself with a man, say, who deals in scrap metal and goes up to a brass band to buy, not a trumpet, let's say, but simply brass. The trumpeter's trumpet is made of brass, but he'll hardly want to sell it as such, by its value as brass, as so many ounces of brass. All the same, that's how I ransack your theatre for events between people, such as you do more or less imitate even if your imitations are for a very different purpose than my satisfaction. To put it in a nutshell: I'm looking for a way of getting incidents between people imitated for certain purposes; I've heard that you supply such imitations; and now I hope to find out if they are actually the kind of imitations I can use.[20]

Just as the *Messingkauf*'s unembarrassed invention-by-appropriation thrives on infidelity to the theoretical source (Breton did not want to be a doctor), it can also work with something less than a profound knowledge of it (Breton had not read all of Freud). Thus, the *Messingkauf* method encourages experimentation: it frees a film scholar, for example, to use Surrealism without having to become a Surrealist. The Hollywood studios, after all, modeled *their* system on Henry Ford's, but they didn't make cars.

. . . . . . . 2. Games

a way of being serious without the worry of seeming so.
  Jean-Louis Bédouin, describing the "analogy card game,"
  in *Surrealist Games*

What is MGM?
A question, fugitive and lost.
  (an answer derived from the Exquisite Corpse)

Breton's interest in method linked Surrealism to the main traditions of European thought. His radical step was to associate method with games. In an initially offhand passage, Breton described this development's origin:

When conversations about current events and about proposals for amusing or scandalous interventions in the life of those days began to lose its vigor, we were in the habit of turning to *games*—written games at first, in which the elements of speech confronted each other in the most paradoxical way so that human communication, led astray from the start, caused the mind that registered it to run a maximum of adventures. From that instant, no preconceived unfavorable opinion—indeed, much to the contrary—was held toward childhood games, for which we felt the same earnestness, though perceptibly increased, as in times past.[21]

Eventually, two aspects of the Surrealist games proved most attractive: their automatic/collaborative nature, and their recreational (in both senses of that word) dimension.

Both of these features appear in the most famous Surrealist game, the Exquisite Corpse, which works from a fixed syntactical structure:

**What is a *(noun)*?**
    A *(noun)*, *(adjective)* and *(adjective)*.

The game requires four players, each of whom writes down (without consulting the others) her assigned part of speech (either noun or adjective). The result is a collaboratively produced metaphor: in Breton's words, "With the exquisite corpse we had at our disposal—at last—an infallible means of temporarily dismissing the critical mind and of fully freeing metaphorical activity."[22] Since the philosophy of science has shown that all knowledge systems rest on a few basic metaphors, and that a new paradigm always proposes a metaphoric shift, this game might have more profound consequences than at first appears.[23] At the least, it forces its players in directions that conventional research would not.

How? In the first *Surrealist Manifesto*, Breton had insisted that knowledge depends on "no method fixed *a priori*": new ways of working could be "the province of poets as well as scholars" and might at first appear "more or less capricious."[24] Even eccentric procedures (like games) could serve, after all, as a means of gathering material which, in Breton's own words, would "later" be submitted "to the control of reason."[25] The Surrealist research project, in other words, occurred in two stages, and games were only the first. From this perspective, many of Surrealism's strategies—especially the reliance on chance and automatism—seem less objectionable. Breton meant them less as ends in themselves than as alternative scanning devices, ways to notice what had previously gone unattended.

Here, then, is an assignment:

*Using the Exquisite Corpse game, generate with three other people 20–25 metaphors about a movie you wish to study. Pick the "best" five (that is, the most suggestive, stimulating, memorable). Use these five as topic sentences for paragraphs "about" the film in question. These paragraphs can be either analytical, speculative, anecdotal, conjectural, critical, or lyrical.*

Here are a few sample metaphors, produced by an undergraduate class, first on *The Maltese Falcon,* a more familiar movie than the Hardy series:

**What is a Spade?**
A virus, icy and perfect.
**What is the black bird?**
A Gregorian chant, lucid and economical.
**What is a romance?**
A dance craze, flashy and impressive.
**What is a sedative?**
A mechanic, loose and clean-as-a-whistle.
**What is a toughguy?**
A pinwheel, deep and bird-like.
**What is a *femme fatale?***
An alphabet, gregarious and small.
**What is a bribe?**
A script, erotic and gratuitous.
**What are the guns in Wilmer's pocket?**
A turning point, verbose and written.
**What is Captain Jacoby's dying thought?**
A clock, serene and disavowed.
**What is the bullet that killed Miles Archer?**
A dream, archaic and rejuvenating.
**What is the newspaper that wraps the Falcon?**
Redemption, gross and passionate.

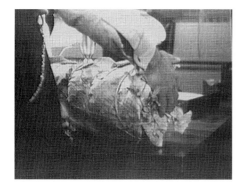

**What is the drugged drink?**

> A stamp, anomalous and geometric.

**What is the fire on the *La Paloma*?**

> A knife, masterful and aberrant.

**What is a client?**

> Soil, dark and promiscuous.

**What is Spade's desire?**

> An institution, collective and salvageable.

And a few examples from *Meet Me in St. Louis*, a movie designed to trade on the popularity of the Hardy films:

**What is a trolley?**

> A ballerina, still and massive.
>
> A painting, white and inky.

**What is the Halloween bonfire?**

> A window, hidden and electric.

**What is a long-distance phone call from New York?**

> A knife, flippant and moonstruck.

**What is Esther's (Judy Garland's) parasol?**

> A theology, measurable and courteous.

**What are snow people?**

> Marshmallows, self-indulgent and empty.

**What is Esther's perfume?**

> A reason, foreboding and whimsical.

**What is John Truett's Christmas present to Esther?**

> A riddle, clean and circular.

**What is Garland's glamour?**
   A furrow, languid and furious.
**What is the chandelier in the Smith house?**
   An engine, cockeyed and curious.

The knowledge-value of these metaphors derives from their capacity to suggest different lines of investigation. One student, for example, responds to the last metaphor in the list above:

**What is the chandelier in the Smith house?**
   An engine, cockeyed and curious.

The chandelier is the engine propelling the action in *Meet Me in St. Louis.* Love and lust, which motivate the characters, are checked and controlled by the anxious, proper chandelier. It appears omnipotent, overbearing as Esther and John stand beneath it, trying to put out its light. The characters are affected by the chandelier, however, only when they are in the house, and only when the chandelier is lit. Outside in the darkness, Esther and John can passionately fight and kiss, and Tootie can "kill" the Brokauffs and imagine a violent (sexual?) attack by John. Even the children around the bonfire's light behave with less inhibition. The engines, off-balanced and cockeyed, are responsible for the characters' misunderstandings, perhaps because they are not yet electric: the movie's emphasis on the Fair, a celebration of technological Progress, amounts to a longing for Edison's enlightenment, the American version of wisdom.[26]

As a research method, the Exquisite Corpse game is typically Surrealist, working by fragmentation (the isolated detail), automatism (players producing elements only on the basis of their grammatical value), and recombination (the juxtaposition with unexpected adjectives). As a procedure, the game mimics photography, perhaps intentionally: as I have mentioned, Breton once described automatic writing, a similar game, as "a true photography of thought."[27] In fact, however, the Exquisite Corpse more closely resembles another activity, one also relying on collaboration, fragmentation, recombination, and (to a surprising degree), automatism, an activity whose invention occurred simultaneously with the origin of Breton's game. That other activity is the studio system of filmmaking.

The theory, history, and practice of Hollywood cinema have turned on a single issue: control. The studio heads modeled their operations on Henry Ford's factory, with its geographical concentration, division of labor, standardized parts, and hierarchical management. For Marcus Lowe, Nicholas Schenck, L. B. Mayer, and Irving Thalberg at MGM, this arrangement had the advantage of reining in, or eliminating, filmmaking's unpredictable elements (an extravagant director like Von Stroheim, a capricious environment like the Italian location for *Ben Hur*). With production largely confined to MGM's own sets, with scriptwriters and directors reporting to line producers, and with Thalberg overseeing the entire operation, making movies would become, or so it appeared, *rationalized*. In the 1950s and 1960s, the *auteur* theory would offer an alternative view of this situation, suggesting that the greatest directors had managed to slip those restraints in order to impose their own recognizable signatures on the films they made. I will take up this argument in more detail in Chapter 7, but for the moment I want to point out that *auteurism* merely relocated the site of control from producer to director: the theory still presumed a predictable, rationalized process.

Under Thalberg, however, MGM's filmmaking (and by implication, that of the other studios) had less in common with Ford's assembly lines than with Surrealism's Exquisite Corpse. With its system organized around stars and genres, with its commitment to hire and retain the best technicians (cameramen, set designers, light and sound experts), MGM could define its production process as a syntax, like the Exquisite Corpse's question-and-answer, in which could occur an infinite number of variations. In fact, Breton's game amounts to a diagram of MGM's procedure:

**What is** *(name of a star)*?
A *(character)*, *(adjective)* and *(adjective)*.
Hence *Grand Hotel:*

**What is** *Garbo?*

A *ballerina, fading* and *desperate.*
Or *Flesh and the Devil:*

**What is** *Garbo?*

A *temptress, faithless* and *destructive.*

In fact, however, the process was more subtle. Who, for example, is in control of this shot, taken from *Grand Hotel?*

Edmund Goulding, the movie's director, never a candidate for *auteurist* canonization? Garbo? Barrymore? William Daniels, the cameraman? Cedric Gibbons, the art director? Adrian, the costumer? As Thalberg and Mayer knew, changing any *one* of these elements would result in a dramatically different shot. A *Grand Hotel* with Warner's Joan Blondell or Dick Powell? Garbo directed by Howard Hawks?

As a game, the Exquisite Corpse rewards players with rich vocabularies: "interesting" nouns and adjectives produce the most appealing metaphors, even if they seem accomplished by utter accident. Compiling a literate team stacks the deck, increasing the chances of turning out striking phrases. In Hollywood, Mayer and Thalberg quickly intuited something similar: having Garbo, Barrymore, Gable, and Harlow amounted to having the best "nouns," the ones capable of entering into the most likely combinations when inflected by the studio's "adjectives," the most reliable directors and scriptwriters, the most innovative cameramen, set designers, and costumers. Thus, the shot from *Grand Hotel* amounts, at the least, to this Exquisite Corpse:

**What is *Garbo?***

A *ballerina* (the role created by the writers), *photographed by William Daniels* and *paired with John Barrymore, dressed by Adrian, on a set designed by Cedric Gibbons.*

Having established this syntax, and collected MGM's stars and technicians, Thalberg could relinquish control of his movies' details, certain that the results would fall within a range of acceptable possibilities. Studio filmmaking, therefore, issued from a delicate balance of accident and design, and no experience more perfectly simulates that process than playing the Exquisite Corpse.

. . .

Here, then, are a few sample Exquisite Corpse metaphors about two of the most readily available Hardy movies, *Love Finds Andy Hardy* and *Andy Hardy Meets Debutante,* both with Judy Garland (I have provided an occasional summary of the resulting paragraphs):

**What is Polly Benedict?**

A typewriter, vivacious and repetitive.

A chart, purchased and substantial.

A Carriage, ethical and seductive.

(Suggesting Polly's simultaneous old-fashionedness and sexuality.)

**What is 1930s sexism?**

A song, infantile and quiet.

(Which accompanies the movies as background music.)

**What is an Andy Hardy movie?**

A disease, monochromatic and happy.

(The Hardy films as symptomatic of both the Depression and sexual repression: "monochromatic" means both "simplistic" and "black-and-white film.")

**What is a debutante?**

A gadget, promiscuous and amiable.

A *mise-en-scène,* fluent and careless.

A landscape, ignorant and elusive.

(The deb, Daphne Fowler, as a screen for projection.)

*Love Finds Andy Hardy*                    *Andy Hardy Meets Debutante*

**What is Betsy's formal dress?**

    A mist, damp and geometric.

    (The still-dewy Garland; the typical triangular love plot of
        Andy/Polly/X made quadrilateral: Andy/Polly/Cynthia/Betsy.)

**What is a carriage ride through Central Park at dawn?**

    Dogma, stately and devastating.

    A mystery, fallacious and hungry.

    A yearbook, inaccessible and obligatory.

    A crutch, quiet and gallant.

    A birthday, impure and hostile.

    Airwaves, ended and historic.

    A park, bleak and inappropriate.

**What is Polly's kiss?**

    A gesture, sweet and minute.

    A hyperbole, responsible and opaque.

    A coincidence, elliptical and restless.

    (The elliptical kiss = the geometry of dating, incomplete, defective,
        falling short of the perfect circle, the wedding ring; dating as the
        ellipse, the shape of the lips.)[28]

**What are Emily's Christmas packages [*Love Finds Andy Hardy*]?**

    Roads, silent and braided.

**What is a man-to-man talk?**

    A demarcation, distant and bare.

**What is a telegram?**

    A stairwell, whimsical and lone.

    (The crucial role of telegrams, the telephone, the radio, and
        newspapers in the Hardy series: communication-as-disaster, both
        funny and desperate.)

**What is poverty?**

> An echo, silent and persistent.
>
> (The Depression background just outside the series' frame.)

**What is courtship?**

> A monologue, exhilarating and foreign.

**What are coincidences [such as, for example, Betsy's knowing the debutante]?**

> A church, transparent and blank.
>
> A deception, stimulating and quiet.

**What is a clue?**

> A physics, strange and complete.

**What are Judge Hardy's eyebrows?**

> A crash, luminous and ferocious.

> (They are objects designed especially for parental supervision—not the supervision of domination or of constant prohibition, but the supervision of observance, amusement, and guidance. Yet, never to be crossed, they are deep, dark lines, with definite angles exploding when confronted by failure or baseness. To live in the shadow of these brows is to become particularly aware of the usury exacted by freedom. For the son, the brows are footsteps, passkeys, a secret handshake. For the daughter, the mother, the aunt, they are unsprung traps, the last gas for 200 miles, the growl of the vacuum, the comfort of satin.)[29]

These metaphors, and the assignment I made of them, may seem merely whimsical. To that objection, I can only make two responses. First, this method is still in its infancy; we may not yet know how to use it most effectively. Second, the Surrealist games began as devices enabling their players to approximate another research situation, one with its own strange, but strict, rules, one that from the outside appears as a kind of game: the psychoanalytic session. Here are Freud's instructions to a patient "beginning the treatment":

What you tell me must differ in one respect from an ordinary conversation. Ordinarily you rightly try to keep a connecting thread running through your remarks and you exclude any intrusive ideas that may occur to you and any side-issues, so as not to wander too far from the point. But in this case you must proceed differently. You will notice that as you relate things various thoughts will occur to you which you would like to put aside on the ground of certain criticisms and objections. You will be tempted to say to yourself that this or that is irrelevant here, or is quite unimportant, or nonsensical, so that there is no need to say it. You must never give in to these criticisms, but must say it in spite of them—indeed you must say it precisely *because* you feel an aversion to doing so. Later on you will find out and learn to understand the reason for this injunction, which is really the only one you have to follow. So say whatever goes through your mind. Act as though, for instance, you were a traveller sitting next to the window of a railway carriage and describing to someone inside the carriage the changing views which you see outside. Finally, never forget that you have promised to be absolutely honest, and never leave anything out because, for some reason or other, it is unpleasant to tell it.[30]

Although these instructions seem simple enough, they are, as Freud soon discovered, extraordinarily difficult to follow—as are the corresponding "rules" for the analyst.[31] Indeed, this game, *like any other,* rewards practice: the more you play it, the easier it becomes. But at the beginning, it is a game so difficult to play that the Surrealists invented *other* games as a way of learning it—games such as automatic writing and the Exquisite Corpse.

Another Surrealist game with which film students might experiment is the "irrational enlargement of a film scene," a descendant of an earlier game called "interrogation of the object."[32] This game involves from three to ten players and, when applied to the movies, requires the principal to ask such questions as these:

On *The Maltese Falcon* (with selected answers):

**Why didn't Miles Archer's wife love him?**
His gambling debts.
His bug eyes.

His flirting with other women.

His impotence.

**Is Spade having an affair with his secretary, Effie?**

Only in leap years.

No, she is his stepsister.

**How does Spade always know when Brigid is lying?**

She flares her nostrils when she lies.

He has a sixth sense, given to him at birth by gypsies.

By the flickering of the lights next door.

**What is Gutman's *exact* weight?**

300½ pounds.

335.

225 (he's shorter than he looks).

Exactly the weight of a filing cabinet, filled with out-of-date maps, in
    Spade's office.

**Where is the *real* Maltese Falcon?**

In the bathroom (behind the toilet) of a rich Viennese merchant.

On a plane bound for Australia.

In a cardboard box in Frankfurt.

Hidden behind a first edition of Poe's "The Purloined Letter."

**What used to be on the empty lot where Spade goes on the bum steer?**

Spade and Archer's main competitors, until a bomb put them out of
    business.

**What did Gutman's "agents" do to Kemidov to "persuade" him to give up
the Falcon?**

They stole his toupée.

They made love to him passionately.

They shook his hand and offered him a meal that included
hash-brown potatoes, his favorite.

They threatened him with a reading of *Troilus and Cressida.*

**What was the *next* object stored in the Baggage Claim *after* the Falcon?**

A prescription.

A picture-puzzle of an apartment building facing the Eiffel Tower.

A leopard-skin lampshade.

**Who was the artist who created the *fake* Falcon?**

Hieronymus Bosch.

Marcel Duchamp.

**Why was the Falcon stored in Box no. 746?**

Box no. 745, Spade's first choice, was full.

746 = the number of jewels supposedly encrusted on the bird's body.

746 = the last three digits of John Huston's social security number.

746 = Spade's birthday (July 4, 1906) [oddly, Bogart's exact birth date
is uncertain, but despite his modernity, he appears to have been
born in the nineteenth century, in 1899].

**What happened to the letter posted immediately *after* Spade's letter?**

It went to Effie's uncle in Texas.

A mail worker thought it contained money; he opened it and threw it
away in disappointment.

I have it at home, framed on my wall.

What else did Wilmer set on fire besides the *La Paloma*?
>   The house where he was born.
>   The real Falcon.
>   Spade's desire.

On *Meet Me in St. Louis:*

What happened to Grandma?
>   She died a horrible death involving machinery.

How is Mr. and Mrs. Smith's bedroom decorated?

From where did the Truetts move?
>   From Jay Gatsby's house.

At what age will Tootie die?
>   She will live a long life, preoccupied by death.
>   At age five because she falls off a ride at the Fair.

What four fatal diseases do Tootie's dolls have?

Where in the house was the orchestra hiding?

What does John Truett read in bed at night?
>   Victorian novels.
>   "Irrational Enlargement of a Film Scene."

Who lives at 5134 Kensington Avenue?

When Tootie cuts her lip, the doctor asks, "What is it this time, Tootie?"
   What was it the last time?

What else is in Grandpa's chest besides his tuxedo?
>   His favorite hat.
>   Grandma's blood-stained wedding gown.
>   Marbles and Surrealist games.

What did Grandpa do for a living before he retired?

What is Alonzo's major at Princeton?

What song would the characters sing if they *didn't* live in St. Louis?

What would have happened if the Brokauffs' handsome son (who dances
   superbly) appeared on Esther's dance card?

What does Tootie become when she grows up?
>   A mortician.

What does John Truett do after the first party?
>   He goes home and practices turning on and off all the lights in his
>   own house.

**What happened to Tootie to cause her fascination with death?**
> She once saw a dead body on the streetcar tracks in her quiet
> suburban neighborhood.

**What was the case that Mr. Smith lost?**

**Why doesn't Esther's singing wake her parents?**
> The house has thick walls.
> They take sleeping pills.
> It does, but they don't want to interrupt.

**Would anyone famous have died if the trolley *had* gone off the tracks?**
> No one famous, but Elvis's grandfather was on the trolley.

Five examples "about" *Madame Bovary:*

**What should happen when Emma is in the attic contemplating suicide?**
> She turns into a lamp.
> A sudden fire traps her in the attic, and she burns to death.
> The Ghost of Christmas Past tells her to shape up.
> Knives float over her head in the shape of a pentangle.

**What happens to Berthe [Madame Bovary's only child] in later life?**
> She becomes a nun.
> She writes a book called *Madame Bovary,* filled with clichés.

**What do bees symbolize in *Madame Bovary?***
> The spread of disillusionment with reality.
> The need to work steadily and to attend to one's own life.
> The inadequate support for adultery.

**What happens to Emma's dog, and why does he run off?**
> He realizes the hopelessness of the situation and chooses to leave
> with a circus.

**What happens to the priest and the pharmacist when they fall asleep while sitting up with Emma's corpse?**
> Each dreams he is the other.

And here are a few samples involving *Love Finds Andy Hardy:*

**What is the name of the road that Andy and Betsy [Garland] take to drive home from the Christmas Eve dance?**
> Magnolia Lane.
> A road that winds back on itself and becomes the same road.

Whom does Mrs. Hardy meet on the airplane coming back from Canada?

How does the boy who answers the ham radio call *get* to the Forest farm?

When Polly Benedict first left home, how did she travel?

What physical traits did Polly inherit from her mother [who, in the entire series, is seen in only one shot (in *Private Secretary's* graduation sequence), although her voice is occasionally heard calling to Polly from an adjacent room]?

> Blonde hair, blue eyes.
>
> Straight teeth.
>
> High cheekbones.
>
> None, she's adopted—that's why we never see the mother.

What does Polly's bedroom look like?

What names did the Hardys consider before settling on Andy?

Whom does Polly eventually marry?

> She never marries.
>
> The Central Park hansom driver [from *Andy Hardy Meets Debutante*].

Where is Carvel?

> In Idaho [as the original play specified].
>
> In the Midwest [as stereotype would suggest].
>
> Under Niagara Falls.
>
> In Saskatchewan, off Highway 476 near Bolinda.

When would a gun be useful in the Hardy movies?

> Polly could shoot off the hood ornament given to Andy for his car by Betsy.
>
> A rifle could be hung over the fireplace.

What is in the package that Andy gives to Betsy for Christmas?

*Love Finds Andy Hardy*

Who owned Andy's jalopy before he did, and how did it get into the
  shape it is now?
Who lived in the Hardy house before the Hardys?
    A failed gymnast.
    Thomas Edison, who used Carvel as a retreat where he could work in
      peace.
What is inside the trunk in Judge Hardy's study?
What did Marian do before *her* senior prom?
What is the predominant color of the Hardy kitchen?
Where is the nearest railroad track in relation to the Hardy house?
What was Aunt Millie's favorite subject at school?
What did Betsy regret having left at home in New York when she came to
  Carvel to visit her grandmother for Christmas?
To whose love does the title *Love Finds Andy Hardy* refer?

What can we say about this game other than that it often yields funny
answers? Several things:

1. These questions confirm how elliptical, how *witty* (in Freud's sense
of condensation) cinematic realism is. We think that after nearly two
hours with the Smith family, or fifteen movies with the Hardys, we must
know everything about them and their house and their neighborhood.
But, of course, we know nothing, since the movies, like all realisms,
work metonymically, giving us the part from which we can imagine the
whole. When she worked as an adviser to the film crew making the
movie of her book *The Return of Martin Guerre,* historian Natalie Davis
tried to ensure authenticity by cramming the *mise-en-scène* with medie-
val details. The director explained, however, that they were unnecessary,
since Hollywood worked on "the camel principle": if you want to suggest
Egypt, you simply put a camel in the corner of the frame, and the
audience does the rest. The Irrational Enlargement questions suggest
specifically how that elliptical, metonymic process works by pointing to
the places in the story where it struggles, where the viewer, however
unconsciously, wants to know more.

2. The questions asked in the Irrational Enlargement game are often
the kind expressly forbidden by New Criticism, whose paradigmatic
example of an Improper Question was "What did Hamlet study in
Wittenberg before the play begins?" New Criticism forbade such questions because the text, on which everything depended, could neither

verify nor disprove any answer to them. Such questions, however, are precisely the kind which occur to us as a film unwinds, but which we suppress because the narrative shows them to be irrelevant. Their appeal represents a moment of delayed recognition on the viewer's part: he hears spoken, made explicit, something he wondered about without even realizing it, which he censored as inconsequential to the movie—exactly as Freud's patients censored fleeting thoughts for *their* apparent irrelevance or indiscretion, and could then retrieve them only with a game: the psychoanalytic session with its rules. At first baffled by his patients' inability to talk openly about their problems, Freud ultimately found that the twin mechanisms of resistance and repression were essential to the diagnostic process: they, in fact, pointed directly to the determining areas of a patient's experience, those leading to his symptoms.[33] Freud's "game" enabled him to listen to his patients in a different way. Although the comparison of the cinema to dreams is as old as Lumière and Méliès, film studies has developed almost nothing comparable to Freud's radical form of attention, one, in his own words, "without any purpose in view," one willing "to be taken by surprise," one "with an open mind, free from any presuppositions."[34] At its best, the Irrational Enlargement game approximates this disinterested listening. It simulates the *flâneur's* attention, which Walter Benjamin, in opposing it to "concentration" and "contemplation," once called "distraction," the most fundamental characteristic of the new way of thinking occasioned by film and photography:

> The tasks which face the human apparatus of perception at the turning points of history [here, the advent of photography] cannot be solved by optical means, that is, by contemplation alone. They are mastered gradually by habit, under the guidance of tactile appropriation.
>
>   The distracted person, too, can form habits. More, the ability to master certain tasks in a state of distraction proves that their solution has become a matter of habit. . . . Reception in a state of distraction, which is increasing noticeably in all fields of art and is symptomatic of profound changes in apperception, finds in the film its true means of exercise.[35]

As a tool, the Irrational Enlargement game has the advantage of indirection. Unlike conventional critique, it works from the premise that even ordinary movies (like the Hardy pictures) remain, at some impor-

tant level, mysterious, opaque: a door opens, the wind moves the leaves in an unimportant tree in the background, a woman straightens the sleeve of a new dress. "The worst films I've ever seen," Man Ray observed, "the ones that send me to sleep, contain ten or fifteen marvelous minutes. The best films I've ever seen only contain ten or fifteen valid minutes."[36] In *Love Finds Andy Hardy,* a scene appears, at once typical and strange: wanting to send a consoling message to Emily, tending to her critically ill mother in a Canadian farm without a telephone, the Judge resorts to a ham radio operated by his son's younger friend. In a room (basement? attic?) whose chiaroscuro (Goya? de la Tour?) invokes the fatalism generally repressed by MGM's normally high-key lighting, the three figures arrange themselves around the crucial objects: a light, a clock, the radio. Hours pass. Finally, a voice answers, and Andy's friend sends: "This is W8XZR. Listen, Brigham [the Canadian town], get this right. Emergency. Will you take down a message and then get it to the Forest farm near Brigham? No telephone. Sickness, maybe death, in the place, so . . ., so don't disturb anybody. Take this message."

The grandmother will survive, the mother will return, but in the meantime, the scene has managed to reenchant the most ordinary objects of everyday life in the 1930s: the telephone (defamiliarization-by-absence) and the radio (redefined as a two-way system, thereby fulfilling Brecht's call for the completion of the communication loop). In the midst of the series' studious normality, the surrealism of this scene derives from its discovery of the potential dislocations in normal lives. Benjamin: "Any serious exploration of occult, surrealist, phantasmagoric gifts and phenomena presupposes a dialectical intertwinement to which a romantic turn of mind is impervious. For histrionic or fanatical stress on the mysterious side of the mysterious takes us no further; we penetrate the mystery only to the degree that we recognize it in the everyday world."[37]

Aragon made his own case:

All our emotion exists for those dear old American adventure films that speak of daily life and manage to raise to a dramatic level a banknote on which our attention is riveted, a table with a revolver on it, a bottle that on occasion becomes a weapon, a handkerchief that reveals a crime, a typewriter that's the horizon of a desk, the terrible unfolding telegraphic tape with magic ciphers that enrich or ruin bankers. . . .

> Poets without being artists, children sometimes fix their attention on an object to a point where the concentration makes it grow larger, grow so much it completely occupies their visual field, assumes a mysterious aspect and loses all relation to its purpose. . . . Likewise on the screen objects that were a few moments ago sticks of furniture or books of cloakroom tickets are transformed to the point where they take on menacing or enigmatic meanings.[38]

The Irrational Enlargement game attends to this aspect of the cinema. As a means to knowledge about the movies, it satisfies Michael Taussig's demand that cultural criticism "penetrate the veil while retaining its hallucinatory quality." Like Freud's way of listening, the game locates a film's hot spots, those scenes (for example, the Central Park hansom ride in *Andy Hardy Meets Debutante,* the ham radio sequence) where the emotional effect seems greater than the narrative weight. What makes the ham radio scene evocative? The low ceiling? The stark lighting? The urgent exchange of operators' codes replacing ordinary names? Freud proposed that in a dream, "intensity" results from condensation, the work that enables a single dream element to represent, by means of common features, multiple events and objects.[39] Like other such moments (for example, *Meet Me in St. Louis*'s Halloween sequence), the ham radio scene is, in Freud's words, a *"nodal point."*[40] At that site, multiple pathways converge: the solitariness of childhood, the remoteness of rural December nights, Edison and the heroism of invention, the Hardy Boys' adventures *(The Short Wave Mystery),* historical emergencies (the *Titanic* calling for rescue), police bulletins and *Dick Tracy,* Walter Winchell on-the-air. All of these paths (and innumerable others) are simultaneously available to a viewer struggling to make sense of what she sees. The speed of that sense-making renders it invisible; the Irrational Enlargement game alerts us to its having occurred.

. . .

These games are still at a primitive stage of use. Nevertheless, they seem to promise a complement to semiotic critique. As one further demonstration of a Surrealist game's possibilities, here is a modified Irrational Enlargement, this one invented by Christopher Dove, an undergraduate at the University of Florida.

In the 1924 *Manifesto of Surrealism,* having described how "To Write False Novels" (with the procedures leading to "The Soluble Fish"), Breton adds this provocation: "Of course, by an analogous method, and provided you ignore what you are reviewing, you can successfully devote yourself to false literary criticism."[41] Responding to Breton's challenge, this game begins with the selection of a film about which the critic should know as little as possible. His associate then watches the movie and selects three narratively important shots. Using randomly generated counter times, the associate then chooses three *other* shots, none significant to the film's plot. After scrambling these six, he presents them one at a time to the critic, who must not know where in the movie the still occurs, what precedes or follows it, or what accompanies it on the soundtrack. After seeing each shot, the critic immediately replies to the questions below, the responses to which form a speculative narrative to be compared to the actual film.

1. What is the characters' relationship?
2. What is happening?
3. What, other than a human being, is the most important object in the frame? Why?
4. What will the next shot be?
5. The critic invents questions in advance about a randomly selected object: for example, Who is wearing a hat? What significance will the hat have?
6. Who is saying what to whom? What does this dialogue have to do with the story?
7. When does this scene occur in the film?

This game should encourage a sensitivity both to meanings communicated stereotypically and to those produced (or received) unconsciously, the result of details in the *mise-en-scène.* (In effect, the game encourages the critic to adopt Breton's youthful movie-watching habits,[42] or to imitate the *Nouvelle Vague* directors' willingness to view foreign-language films without subtitles.)

Dove plays his own game with six shots from Renoir's *La Règle du Jeu,* a film he had never seen. Here are his responses to three of the shots:

**1. What is the characters' relationship?**

They are romantically involved in an illicit relationship. He (Claude) would like to be married, but she (Rena) merely leads him on. He is weak and morally muddled, she stronger and less morally anxious.

**2. What is happening?**

Paris 1952: Claude and Rena stand on a racetrack balcony watching a race, having bet on a horse recommended by a gentleman eager for Rena's affections. Behind them stands George: he has nothing bet on this race, but will lose a large amount over the course of the day's wagering.

**3. What is the most important object in the frame? Why?**

The telescope. Claude sees that their horse is limping. The tip was wrong. Later that afternoon, the telescope, bought for this occasion, will be left behind in a taxi.

**4. What will the next shot be?**

The horse (Perspicacity) limping towards the finish line (through an iris filter, simulating the view through a telescope). His jockey will be frantically gesturing to offscreen handlers.

**5. Who is wearing a hat? What significance will it have?**

Both characters wear hats, his bought for inconspicuousness, hers for sophistication. Neither hat will reappear after this scene.

**6. Who is saying what to whom? What does this dialogue have to do with the story?**

"Say," Rena nudges Claude, "you seem to have found something interesting." He tells her about the limping horse.

**7. Where does this shot occur in the film?**

In the exact middle.

1. **What is the characters' relationship?**

   Karl (the policeman) holds Rena after she has been shot.

2. **What is happening?**

   Rena has followed Raoul into the woods near Bordeaux to confront him about his other lover, Lorette. Claude and Karl follow her there after staking out her hotel. Seeing Raoul aiming at him, Claude grabs the gun. Raoul shoots Rena by mistake, and Karl picks up her dead body.

3. **What is the most important object?**

   Rena's coat, which she stole in order to better blend into the darkness. Camouflaged so thoroughly, she is accidentally shot.

4. **What will the next shot be?**

   A closeup of Claude and Raoul reacting to Rena's death. Behind them is the moon.

5. **Who is wearing a hat?**

   Karl, but his hat will soon fall off as he carries Rena's body. He will replace it with one costing 112 francs. Rena is wearing a hood, which made her more invisible and vulnerable to accident.

6. **Who is saying what to whom?**

   There is a deathly silence.

7. **When does this shot occur in the film?**

   It is the last scene.

1. **What is the characters' relationship?**

    Claude (on the right) attacks a man (Robert) who is sleeping with Rena.

2. **What is happening?**

    After Raoul's racing tip, Claude becomes jealous. Never having met Raoul, he mistakenly tracks Robert to an elegant club, where he attacks him. Robert will not press charges because, by coincidence, he is also having an affair with Rena and does not want Claude to know.

3. **What is the most important object?**

    Robert's tuxedo, which caused Claude to mistake him for Raoul, who is eating in another restaurant across Paris.

4. **What will the next shot be?**

    A closeup of Robert, explaining that Claude has the wrong man.

5. **Who is wearing a hat?**

    Neither man. Robert's top hat has been knocked off.

6. **Who is saying what to whom?**

    Neither man is speaking.

7. **Where does this scene occur in the film?**

    About 35 minutes into it.

Astonishingly, with no knowledge of *La Règle du Jeu* other than these stills, Dove deciphered

1. that the movie turns on infidelity, real or imagined;
2. that Rena (actually Christine) is the main character;
3. that the telescope is important;
4. that the gamekeeper (actually Schumacher) deserves a Germanic name (Karl);

5. that a hood and cape cause a fatal mistaken identity;
6. that an accidental shooting concludes the film.

This version of Irrational Enlargement of a Film Scene suggests that film works even more economically than we had imagined, conveying an enormous amount of information in only three shots. Dream logic, indeed.

*Chapter Four*

·  ·  ·  ·  ·  ·  ·  ·  ·  ·  ·  ·  ·  ·  ·

## NADJA AND SIMULATION

These are the days when no one should rely unduly on his
"competence." Strength lies in improvisation. All the decisive
blows are struck left-handed.

    Walter Benjamin, "One-Way Street"

The most famous Surrealist literary work is, not surprisingly, a curious,
unclassifiable book. Often labeled "a novel," *Nadja* in fact purports to
tell the true story of Breton's accidental encounter with a young woman
and the ten days they spent together in Paris in October 1926. Like
Aragon's *Le Paysan de Paris, Nadja* rejects the traditional novel's conventions while demanding new ways of writing more responsive to modern
life. The *Manifesto of Surrealism* had announced this move by beginning
with an attack on the realistic novel's thinly disguised characters and
tedious descriptions. "Keep reminding yourself," Breton had warned in
the instructions for automatic writing, his proposed alternative, "that
literature is one of the saddest roads that leads to everything."[1]

One way of understanding *Nadja* is to see it as a deliberate experiment
with the form of the novel. Citing Claude Bernard's notion that "*To
experiment is to do violence to the object*," Daniel S. Milo has proposed
that all such experimenting involves at least one of the following procedures: "*adding* to X an element Y which is foreign to it; *removing* from
X an element X1 that usually helps constitute it; and *changing the scale*:
to observe and analyze X on a scale against which it isn't usually measured."[2] From this perspective, *Nadja* appears to *add* to the novel photographs (replacing descriptions), philosophical meditation ("Who am I?"
the book begins), actual names, a poetic coda, and an amateur aesthetic
comparable to "home movies." Indeed, while locating this aesthetic in

Roberto Rossellini's films, Jacques Rivette also provides an uncannily exact description of *Nadja:*

> Now he is no longer filming [writing] just his ideas . . . but the most everyday details of his life; this life, however, is "exemplary" in the fullest sense that Goethe implied: that everything in it is instructive, including the errors; and the account of a busy afternoon in Mrs. Rossellini's [Nadja's, Breton's] life is no more frivolous in this context than the long description Eckermann gives us of that beautiful day, on 1 May 1825, when he and Goethe practiced archery together. So there, then, you have this country, this city; but a privileged country, an exceptional city, retaining intact innocence and faith, living squarely in the eternal; a *providential city.*[3]

*From* the novel, on the other hand, *Nadja* removes almost all descriptions (replaced by photographs), character motivation, and plot. In this new context of experimental science, Breton's book thus appears less as a novel than as the new hybrid which Rivette called "the essay":

> For over fifty years now the essay has been the very language of modern art; it is freedom, concern, exploration, spontaneity; it has gradually . . . buried the novel beneath it; since Manet and Degas it has reigned over painting. . . . [It is] almost everything they prayed for: metaphysical essay, confession, log-book, intimate journal.[4]

For Breton, all experimentation came down to one thing—automatism. In his own proposed dictionary entry, he had already designated it as Surrealism's defining activity:

> SURREALISM, n. Psychic automatism in its pure state, by which one proposes to express—verbally, by means of the written word, or in any other manner—the actual functioning of thought. Dictated by thought, in the absence of any control exercised by reason, exempt from any aesthetic or moral concern.[5]

Breton, of course, had begun with trances and automatic writing, simulations of technology's recently developed "random generators":[6] the camera, the phonograph, and the typewriter. "We do not have any talent," he had claimed, in the scandalous line, insisting that the Surrealists had only made themselves "into simple receptacles of so many echoes, modest *recording instruments.*"[7] In effect, Breton had anticipated

Christopher Isherwood's famous opening, "I am a camera." By the time he wrote *Nadja*, however, he had refined the experiment. Always willing to allow revision of matter acquired by automatic procedures, Breton had begun to see automatism less as an end in itself than as a means of gathering raw material—the startling image disclosing unexpected information, the accidental meeting that transformed an October afternoon. *Nadja* shows what Breton meant by his *Manifesto* acknowledgment that such material could later, "should the occasion arise," be submitted "to the control of reason." He waited, after all, nine months before writing about Nadja, and by then, he had come to see her as a metaphor revealing connections he had not anticipated.

Breton's account relies on two devices disdained by the realistic novel: anecdote and coincidence. "Consider this anecdote," Breton writes, at the very beginning of his book:

> Hugo, toward the end of his life, took the same ride with Juliette Drouet every day, always interrupting his wordless meditation when their carriage passed an estate with two gates, one large, one small; pointing to the large gate, Hugo, for perhaps the thousandth time, would say: "Bridle gate, Madame," to which Juliette, pointing to the small gate, would reply: "Pedestrian gate, Monsieur" . . . we have reason to believe that this marvelous, poignant ritual was repeated daily for years on end; yet how could the best possible study of Hugo's work give us a comparable awareness, the astonishing sense of what he was, of what he is? . . . I should be privileged indeed to possess, in the case of each of the men I admire, a personal document of corresponding value.[8]

For all of its apparent eccentricity, this critical method has a pedigree. It belongs, in fact, to an intellectual tradition whose origins coincide with the spread of photography and the snapshot, the anecdote made visible and compressed to pocket-size. Nietzsche, the prophet of the age of random generation,[9] had reached the same conclusion:

> The only thing of interest in a refuted system is the personal element. It alone is what is forever irrefutable. It is possible to present the image of a man in three anecdotes; I shall try to emphasize three anecdotes in each system and abandon the rest.[10]

In the next generation, Freud would suggest that a patient's "screen memories," anecdotal recollections marked by both vivid persistence and apparent irrelevance, hold the key to treatment: the Wolf Man remembers a carriage driving off with his father, mother, and sister on an ordinary summer day, and Freud detects his patient's unconscious in miniature. This emphasis on the marginal as the way into a problem, the faith in the curious detail, the reliance on the anecdote as a privileged clue—these habits converge at the beginning of the twentieth century in what Carlo Ginzburg has called "the conjectural paradigm."[11] In this practice, a fragment's opacity assures its worth. "It is important," Sherlock Holmes explains when presented with the problem of Lord Baskerville's missing boot, "because it is inexplicable."[12]

"I am concerned," Breton announces early in *Nadja*, "with facts which . . . present all the appearances of a signal, without our being able to say precisely which signal, and of what" (p. 19). But Breton also recognized that in the *quartiers* of Paris, even the most idle autumn afternoons offered more "facts" than he could ever use. He also needed a principle of selection, a scanning procedure capable of marking, from the swarm of information around him, the incidents worth minding. In *Nadja*, that principle is *coincidence*, the curious overlap of details that makes apparently discrete domains seem to "match." "I intend to mention," Breton announces, in the famous passage I have already cited in Chapter 3,

> only the most decisive episodes of my life *as I can conceive it apart from its organic plan,* and only insofar as it is at the mercy of chance, temporarily escaping my control, admitting me to an almost forbidden world of sudden parallels, petrifying coincidences, and reflexes peculiar to each individual, of harmonies struck as though on the piano. (p. 19)

Significantly, the adventure begins with an accident, one of those incidents of metropolitan life so important to Baudelaire and Benjamin:

> Last October fourth, toward the end of one of those idle, gloomy afternoons I know so well how to spend, I happened to be in the Rue Lafayette: after stopping a few minutes at the stall outside the *Humanité* bookstore and buying Trotsky's latest work, I wandered aimlessly in the direction of the Opéra. The offices and workshops were beginning to empty out from top to bottom of the buildings, doors were closing, people on the sidewalk were shaking hands, and already there were more people in the street now. I unconsciously watched their faces, their clothes, their way of walking. . . . I had

just crossed an intersection whose name I don't know, in front of a church. Suddenly, perhaps ten feet away, I saw a young, poorly dressed woman walking toward me; she had noticed me too. (pp. 63–64)

From that point on, Breton will attend to moments charged by coincidental alignment. "For a change," he takes the *right* sidewalk of a street, and runs into Nadja who had intended to miss their rendezvous. She has spent the day reading about chance meetings. In the streets one evening, Nadja points to a darkened apartment building and, indicating a window, announces that "In a minute it will light up. It will be red": "The minute passes. The window lights up. There are, as a matter of fact, red curtains" (p. 83). Seeing a fountain, Nadja compares it to their thoughts, rising and falling back, only to hear Breton exclaim that he has used this exact image in an unfinished work which she could not have seen. Wandering aimlessly from the Place Dauphine, Breton and Nadja suddenly realize that they have stopped at a bar called Le Dauphin, the animal (dolphin) most often associated with Breton in a Surrealist game (p. 89). Nadja responds to Breton's kissing her teeth by comparing their embrace to a communion "where her teeth 'substituted for the host'"; Breton awakens the next morning to a letter from Aragon, who includes a reproduced detail from Uccello's painting *The Profanation of the Host*. When Nadja reads letters from her former lover, Breton recognizes the lover's name as also that of a judge who has just condemned a woman for murdering *her* lover; on the back of Nadja's envelopes, Breton notices "a pair of scales" (pp. 97–98).

In *Nadja*, Breton simply records such anecdotes without trying to explain them. When Nadja herself expresses disappointment that Breton's earlier account of similar events contained no commentary, he replies, "I know nothing about it . . . in such matters the right to bear witness seems to me all that is granted" (p. 78). Salvador Dali, however, was willing to extend Breton's procedures by using anecdotes and coincidental associations for what he called "the paranoiac-critical method." In *The Tragic Myth of Millet's Angelus*, Dali showed how paranoia-criticism could produce knowledge about a single painting. His starting point— Millet's *Angelus* as opaque anecdote:

In June, 1932, the image of the *Angelus* of Millet suddenly appeared in my mind without any recent recollection or conscious association to offer an immediate explanation. . . . It left me with a profound impression, I was most upset by it, because, although in my vision of the aforementioned image everything "corresponded" exactly to the reproductions that I knew of the picture, it nevertheless "appeared to me" absolutely modified and charged with such a latent intentionality that the *Angelus* of Millet suddenly became for me the most troubling of pictorial works, the most enigmatic, the most dense, the richest in unconscious thoughts that had ever existed.[13]

Jean François Millet
*The Angelus*

As Naomi Schor describes, Dali's method begins with paranoia's assumption that everything is meaningful. Following the lines of association triggered by Millet, Dali discovers that of all the painting's details, it is its setting *at dusk* that most haunts him. With dusk, Dali associates atavism, death, and a violent sexuality, this last notion prompted by the submissive posture of the picture's female figure, reminding Dali of the praying mantis. Like Breton, Dali relies on the chance encounter. Driving through a small town at dusk, he "sees in a shop window a set of coffee cups and a coffee pot, all bearing on their sides miniaturized reproductions of *The Angelus*."[14] Since Dali has always regarded the pouring of coffee from pot to cup as an image of "brutal copulation," his accidental discovery clinches his interpretation of *The Angelus:* the painting, he concludes, represents a displaced version of a violent, possibly fatal, sexual act. Quoting James Thrall Soby, Schor points out that as outrageous as this reading appears, "It has been supported in more recent years by the rediscovery of some exceptionally vicious drawings of sexual subjects by the presumably angelic painter of *The Angelus*."[15] And an X-ray of Millet's painting, taken at Dali's suggestion, long after he had written his analysis, revealed at the bottom of the picture, painted over, a child's coffin.[16]

. . .

*Nadja* is not a novel. To retell his adventures with the strange woman he had met one afternoon in the Rue Lafayette, Breton had invented a different kind of writing. The traditional novel's sustained, conclusive narrative was fractured into anecdotes, whose sequence would be determined by chance and coincidence, reconceived by Breton less as embarrassments to his story than as "magnetic fields," sources of energy and potential revelation.

By extending this mode, Dali demonstrated that it could produce useful knowledge about texts; it could, in other words, become critical. "Dali has endowed surrealism with an instrument of primary importance," Breton wrote, praising the paranoiac-critical method. It "has immediately shown itself capable of being applied with equal success to painting, poetry, the cinema; to the construction of typical surrealist objects, to fashions, to sculpture and even, if necessary, to all manner of exegesis."[17]

As I will suggest in Chapter 7, the paranoiac-critical method, although apparently abandoned, has in fact been regularly practiced (in modified form) by contemporary theory's most important figure, Jacques Derrida. *Nadja* itself, however, suggests a way of working more radical than even Dali's extravagant hermeneutics. Adopting the Surrealists' own term, we can name this way of working *simulation*.

Breton's own interest in simulation was explicit. Automatic writing was designed to approximate psychoanalytic free association, and when automatic writing itself proved too difficult, he invented other games for practicing the abandonment of conscious control necessary to both. By 1930, Breton was publishing simulations of madness: mental deficiency, acute mania, general paralysis, interpretive delirium, and dementia praecox.[18] This approach had obvious advantages. Compared to traditional reason, with its requirement of objectivity and its preference for abstraction, simulation offered a way of understanding something from the inside. To mime the *experience* of free association or of paranoia would produce, Breton proposed, an immediate sense of those mental states unavailable to distanced analysis.

Breton thought of simulation as another kind of automatism. He recognized, however, that it would be no easier to practice than any other mental activity requiring the suspension of old habits. Freud, after all, had warned that patients resisted free association, and that only the specifically designed psychoanalytic situation enabled the loosening of accustomed self-censorship. For Breton, the solution lay not only in his Surrealist games and exercises, but even more in the strict rules he produced for them. These instructions asked the player to forgo (at least initially) conceptualization in favor of yielding to the generative power of a particular operation. "What is a ———?" asked the Exquisite Corpse, and the rigorous grammar exacted a noun and two adjectives in reply. The games and exercises thus issued from a hypothesis: because such activities embody knowledge, simply using them will teach us something about what they know. "Yield the initiative to words," Mallarmé had advised, in the motto for this way of working which assumes that activity precedes conceptualization.

As a tactic, simulation appealed enormously to Walter Benjamin. As discussed in the previous chapter, the *Arcades Project* was intended to mime the experience of *flânerie*, an idle, attentive drift through the everyday details of mid-nineteenth-century Parisian life: a prostitute's glance, a snatch of song blown down an unfamiliar street, a store window filled with exotic fabric. In the liberal arts, simulation still seems a radical idea. In physical education, medicine, and the natural sciences, however, it has always been the norm. What if those disciplines approached their subjects the way philosophy does? A semester course on tennis might then involve weeks of learning about the game's history, more weeks of readings distinguishing it from other racket sports, long discussions about "Tennis" as a concept, proliferating theories about strokes. Instead, of course, physical education teachers have their students *play* tennis, assuming that, as with language, understanding results from use.

*Nadja* represents Breton's attempt to simulate what Benjamin once called "the dialectics of intoxication,"[19] the experience of "the soul in limbo," adrift like the *flâneur,* but with revelation in mind. Indeed, if Surrealism is the art of *the encounter* and of *getting lost,*[20] then *Nadja,* with its interrupted sequences, its unexplained departures and arrivals, its intervening reveries, is a simulation of Surrealism itself. The anecdotes' compression, their lack of resolution, leave them infinitely available, like a door left ajar, or the image of a woman, glimpsed at a crossroads from a passing train (love at last sight). Their abruptness conveys the feeling, as Breton put it, of an "arrival in a strange place . . . accompanied by the direct sensation that something momentous, something essential depends upon them" (*Nadja,* p. 20). In this narrative world, where atmosphere replaces conclusions and logic, the reader experiences Breton's sense that anything can become an "obscure clue" which signals "it (?) will happen here" (p. 32).

For Breton, the coincidences which intruded so unexpectedly into his days with Nadja suggest "an almost forbidden world of sudden parallels" (p. 19). As a model for critical practice, they identify unnoticed points of overlap between domains. Indeed, Breton's book suggests an alternative rhetoric, a way out of the traditional prison of sequential exposition and logical argument. One name for that rhetoric is "the poetic," the logic of computer hypertext and cyberspace. As Marcos Novak has observed, with poetic logic, "every image [is] an index," and "meanings overlap, but in doing so call forth associations inaccessible to prose."[21]

Another name for that rhetoric is *the cinema.* In the movies, every detail—a man's torn overcoat, an ashtray on a bedside table, a white curtain fluttering in a half-opened window—represents, as does every hypermedia object, a node of information, capable of being opened into endlessly connecting lexicons. A single shot of Betsy Booth (from *Andy Hardy Meets Debutante*) asks a viewer to activate, just for a start, everything he knows about Judy Garland, and fur coats, and white-tie balls, and lipstick, and cold winter air, and hair styles, and young love, and dawns in a strange city. These details are themselves anecdotes, available for linking with others in an editing system whose principal device has always involved *matching.* With its structure based on anecdotes and coincidence, *Nadja,* therefore, amounts to a simulation of what Walter Ong would call "cinematic thinking."

What is "cinematic thinking"? If Ong is right that "alphabetic thinking" is now giving way to "cinematic/electronic thinking," this question has enormous consequences. But it is also preposterously difficult. Only a few people have even begun to think about it, and if I were to ask students to write expository essays defining "cinematic thinking," I would not be likely to get very much. But if *Nadja* amounts to a simulation of such thinking, I can provide students with the *experience* of at least one kind of cinematic logic by simply asking them to imitate Breton.

The instructions for such an exercise might develop out of three propositions: (1) Film's basic structure involves the opposition between shot and sequence. (Godard: "The only great problem with cinema seems to me more and more with each film when and why to start a shot and when and why to end it.")[22] (2) The shot results from photography (Godard: "Photography is truth, and the cinema is truth twenty-four times a second"), and thus it will inevitably offer the kind of accidental details (Barthes's "Third Meaning") which intrigued Fox Talbot. (3) From film's beginnings, the sequence (the result of editing) has represented what Noël Burch calls the "struggle against the accidental." But that struggle involves using the shot's accidental details for "matching":

In the peace and quiet of the cutting room, the editor has always been the first to reflect on the extraordinary variety of material that the world of chance, once captured on film, provides him and the creative power of his scissors. Even in the case of the most meticulously "staged" films, the editor will soon notice that minor accidents completely beyond the control of the director, who was not able even to see them during the shooting, have given him an opportunity to create a very strong articulation between shots. . . .

The accidental in fact provides far more subtle and more complex cutting possibilities than any filmmaker can foresee. . . . In the scene in *October* where the buxom bourgeois women in their rustling laces poke out the young sailor's eyes with the tips of their umbrellas, Eisenstein brings the camera right up to the action and follows it very closely, aware that, in addition to the intrinsic beauty of the shots thus obtained, this kaleidoscopic flurry of dancing silhouettes, whirling cloth, and dripping blood will result in a cascade of images, visible in all their detail only in the developed film, for the cameraman himself will not even have seen them as he views the action through his small eye-piece (a feather boa visible on the screen for a few fractions of a second, a flare frame only a few inches long), aware that these "accidents" will later afford him the possibility of cutting to another shot in a visually interesting way at almost any frame.[23]

Here, then, would be one possible set of instructions (derived both from *Nadja* and from Gregory Ulmer's "mystory"),[24] for simulating "cinematic thinking":

> *Produce an essay that triangulates among three different domains: (1) a theoretical position (expressed in one or more essays); (2) a public, historical event; and (3) a set of autobiographical circumstances. Try to discover points of intersection that connect the personal (autobiography), the popular (the public/historical), and the expert (the theoretical position). Your "matches" may involve apparently accidental details (a feather boa, a flare frame) which can serve as bridges between domains.*

To demonstrate the simulation I am proposing, I will have to tell a few stories. I promise, however, that they will all be true.

*My first story.* In the spring of 1992, I received an invitation to a conference at Miami University in Ohio. The conference looked promising: first, its subject was Walter Benjamin. Second, the conference required that papers be submitted early enough to allow for their advance distribution to participants. Speakers, the invitation went on, freed from the obligation to read their work, would lead discussion about it, entertaining questions from an audience of prepared listeners. This plan seemed designed to guarantee the conference some measure of unpredictability, that element of chance which, as Derrida has argued, "conditions the very structure of an event":

> Would an event that can be anticipated and therefore apprehended or comprehended, or one without an element of absolute encounter, actually be an event in the full sense of the word? There are those who lean toward the assumption that an event worthy of this name cannot be foretold. We are not supposed to see it coming.[25]

Acting dutifully, I sent off multiple copies of the essay on photography and the detective story which appears as Chapter 2 of this book. Like the other papers, I presumed, it would reach the participants weeks before the meeting, a schedule that would presumably ensure the conference's status as "an event," a set of circumstances whose outcome I could not predict, could not see coming.

When the conference began on a Friday afternoon in April, I detected almost immediately the betrayal of the planners' intentions. Participants either had not sent their papers in advance, and thus had to read them to a captive audience, or worse, *had* sent them in advance but still chose to read them to listeners who had supposedly already done their homework. This situation confirmed what all academics know: that the conference as a form, so easily parodied by journalists (as in the annual, predictably scathing, local newspaper accounts of MLA meetings), repeatedly dramatizes precisely those problems exacerbated by higher education's crisis: the flood of specialized knowledge, the remoteness of research. By allowing papers to be read, the conference, like the classical concert (which requires musicians to perform a written score), excludes the possibility of an event, since what, exactly, in that situation can be "unexpected"? Thus, a proposition: by severely restricting the possibilities for chance (defined not as "opportunity" but as "noise"), the academic conference reveals the tendency of all traditional disciplines to regard their knowledge as, in Barthes's word, catechisms.

At Miami University, however, early on a Saturday afternoon, the conference's second day, an event suddenly occurred. Craig Saper from the University of Pennsylvania gave a presentation whose collage of words, music, slides, and videotape drew less on the conventions of the conference paper than on performance art. Speaking about invention and technology, Saper repeatedly offered images of Thomas Edison and Elvis, figures embodying American myths of creativity. Concluding, he asked us to imagine what would have happened if Walter Benjamin had *not* died in 1940 at the Spanish border. What if, like Kafka's Karl, Saper asked, he had come to Amerika and found a job at the Chicago World's Fair, which mounted yet another celebration of Edison and his phonograph? In the 1950s, Saper continued, Benjamin began to write about Elvis and eventually took up lodgings, if only for a brief time and for research purposes, in Graceland itself.

With its high degree of unpredictability, Saper's talk constituted an event. Not surprisingly, it fell on deaf ears. The scheduled respondent chose not to reply at all, a decision which apparently set the tone. As a result, no discussion occurred, and the conference simply moved on to the next set of papers. As I sat thinking about what had taken place, I realized that I found myself in a difficult position. Having taken the conference organizers at their word, I had not planned to read my paper during my scheduled slot, the last of the three days. But I had also not prepared an *additional* talk, since I had assumed that my time would be given over to discussion. Now, however, I realized that I would need something more to say, and the stimulation of Saper's unpredictability encouraged me to make the conference into an event, at least for me. Thus, during the readings of the next papers, I began to write what follows, which I finished only later that night, after excusing myself from the conference party, and delivered the next day, Easter Sunday morning.

. . .

I would like to make a context for what I have written (Chapter 2 of this book), and perhaps also for Craig Saper's talk about Edison, invention, Elvis, and Benjamin. The form of his presentation issues out of a pedagogical method of simulation and experiment suggested by Walter Benjamin.

I might define that method by saying that it has as its goal *the staging of knowledge*. This enterprise takes as its motto Godard's famous proposition:

> Cinema, Truffaut said, is spectacle—Méliès—and research—Lumière. If I analyse myself today, I see that I have always wanted, basically, to do research in the form of a spectacle. The documentary side is: a man in a particular situation. The spectacle comes when one makes this man a gangster or a secret agent.[26]

By scandalously proposing that the key to the nineteenth century lay in the Arcades' spectacle of consumerism, with its *flâneurs* and shop windows and gas-lit evenings, and by further outlining a historical method that must at first have seemed both the extreme of scholarly research ("everything that comes to mind has at all costs to be incorporated into the work") and its abnegation ("I need say nothing. Only show"), Benjamin anticipated Godard's concerns. Indeed, the idea for the *Arcades Project* finds its fruition in a film like Godard's *Two or Three Things I Know about Her*, where staging knowledge provides one solution to what Benjamin called "a central problem of historical materialism":

"Must the Marxist understanding of history necessarily come at the cost of graphicness?"

In *The Pleasure of the Text,* Roland Barthes took a similar tack, observing that philosophical knowledge becomes more receivable, more *pleasurable,* when grounded in those details of everyday life he named "the novelistic":

> Why do some people, including myself, enjoy in certain novels, biographies, and historical works the representation of the "daily life" of an epoch, of a character? Why this curiosity about petty details: schedules, habits, meals, lodging, clothing, etc.? . . .
>
> Thus, impossible to imagine a more tenuous, a more insignificant notation than that of "today's weather" (or yesterday's); and yet, the other day, reading, trying to read Amiel, irritation that the well-meaning editor (another person foreclosing pleasure) had seen fit to omit from this Journal the everyday details, what the weather was like on the shores of Lake Geneva, and retain only insipid moral musing: yet it is this weather that has not aged, not Amiel's philosophy.[27]

Only two years later, in his autobiography, Barthes recognized that this matter of staging went beyond the simple tactics of presentation; it is itself a mode of cognition, a way of conducting research:

> The Lacanian subject (for instance) never makes him think of Tokyo; but Tokyo makes him think of the Lacanian subject. This procedure is a constant one; he rarely starts from the idea in order to invent an image for it subsequently; he starts from a sensuous object, and then hopes to meet in his work with the possibility of finding an *abstraction* for it, levied on the intellectual culture of the moment: philosophy then is no more than a reservoir of particular images, of ideal fictions (he borrows objects, not reasonings). Mallarmé speaks of "gestures of the idea": he finds the gesture first (expression of the body), then the idea (expression of the culture, of the intertext).[28]

In 1925, looking for a way to formulate the rhetorical complement to this epistemology, Benjamin wrote that "To convince is to conquer without conceptualization,"[29] an epigram suggesting knowledge's dependence on something other than abstractions—on, for example, the weather near Lake Geneva, or the moment in the July Revolution when "it turned out that the clocks in towers were being fired on simultaneously and independently from several places in Paris."[30] "In the fields with which we are concerned," Benjamin observed, "knowledge comes only in flashes. The text is the thunder rolling long afterward."[31]

In teaching lower-division classes, I have become increasingly aware that ideas, works, and issues which are difficult to discuss and understand abstractly can be approached through simulation exercises resulting from concrete instructions. Extrapolating from Benjamin's epigram, we might say: to teach is to communicate without initial conceptualizations.

For example, in a course on the avant-garde, I avoid the obvious question "What is the avant-garde?"—a problem that has prompted a huge number of books and articles, none of which has managed to settle the matter. If I want my students to have some sense of avant-garde activity, asking them to think about "the avant-garde" as an abstract aesthetic category seems less effective than giving them instructions about how one might *invent* an avant-garde practice. I can show them, for example, that individual avant-gardes develop by extrapolating from models found in other disciplines: that one obvious case, Surrealism, an aesthetic/political movement, derives from Freudian psychoanalysis, a medical treatment. I can then set the following task:

> *For the sake of this assignment, assume that the avant-garde attitude, which since Impressionism has appeared in painting, music, literature, theater, film, and dance, has begun to enter the realm of* **criticism.** *Using either Surrealism or the French New Wave as your model, invent a new form of literary or film criticism and apply it to either a single film or a work of literature.*

The instructions are important. After we had read *Roland Barthes*, I recently asked a graduate class an apparently simple question: If you were using this book in a freshman class, and if you wanted the students to produce a paper modeled on it, what five **concrete** instructions would you give? Because the graduate students were intelligent, ambitious, and well versed in contemporary theory, they immediately proposed such instructions as (1) "Write in such a way that you call into question the notion of the autonomous subject, uninflected by the discourses in which it is imbricated." Or, (2) "Suggest how your own sense of self

hovers between the Imaginary stage of gratifying, but regressive, iden-
tifications, and the Symbolic stage of anxious, yet empowering differences."

Of course, for a freshman (or almost anyone), such instructions would
be utterly useless. Indeed, if you could understand and use them, you
would *be* Roland Barthes, and the work you would produce would not
be an *extrapolation* from his autobiography, but *Roland Barthes* itself. My
instructions may at first seem simply banal:

1. *Write in fragments, none longer than a page.*
2. *Give each fragment a title, based on some key word, and arrange
   them in alphabetical order.*
3. *In addition to writing, use photographs, drawings, and other images.*
4. *For the autobiographical element, use anecdotes about yourself, but
   pick ones that concern the less obvious facets of your life.*
5. *Use the anecdotes to suggest how your life has connected with the
   knowledge associated with any of your vocations or avocations.*

Let us imagine that using *Nadja* as our model, we want to produce a
simulation of "cinematic thinking." What would such an exercise look like?

. . .

I am interested in the Walter Benjamin who was interested in the movies
and in Surrealism; who read Aragon's *Le Paysan de Paris* and couldn't
sleep; who found Aragon saying that the world seemed to house a series
of doors which, if opened, would reveal the secrets of the universe, if
only you could discover the key; who read *Nadja*, where Breton proposed
that the key might involve the coincidences of everyday life that he
called "objective chance," where an object or word from one person's
life found its rhyme in another very different place in your own, where
you randomly walked across Paris from the Place Dauphine to a bar that
turned out to be called Le Dauphin, where the lesson was that "life needs
to be deciphered like a cryptogram. Secret staircases, frames from which
paintings quickly slip aside and vanish . . . buttons which must be
indirectly pressed to make an entire room move sideways or vertically,
or immediately change all its furnishings" (*Nadja*, p. 112). I am interested in the Walter Benjamin who insisted that, as opposed to information and explanation, stories contained something useful; in the Walter
Benjamin whose philosophical thinking, like Roland Barthes's, emerged

from a mixture of chance and the autobiographical, of the novelistic detail of such things as "the first glance through the rain-blurred windows of a new apartment."[32] Thus, I would frame my argument about photography with two stories that have something to do with some of these themes, and with chance, Edison, Elvis, the movies, and even Walter Benjamin.

But before I could tell those stories, I had to mention that something had happened to me the day before, at exactly 5:23 P.M., an *event* that encouraged me to take the step of what could seem an eccentric, oblique strategy. What was that event?

*My second story.* Having two young daughters, who announced their resentment at my attending a conference during Easter (known in our house as a *presents* holiday, as opposed to a scorned *food* holiday like Thanksgiving, in which they have no interest), and reminded that I had also missed Halloween (for another conference), I went for a walk to redeem myself, to buy them presents. Returning to Bachelor Hall (the conference site) from downtown Oxford, Ohio, I took the hypotenuse, cutting through the old campus. Nearing Bachelor, I passed an odd building, the significance of whose name (Upham Hall) we can perhaps defer for another time. This building's oddness came from its appendage, a greenhouse (which attracted my attention because a greenhouse proves a crucial place in my favorite movie, *La Règle du Jeu*) which grew out of the building's south side like a vine. But what I noticed at 5:23 P.M. were the words, traced in the dirt of the greenhouse's windows: SURREALIST BALL 9:00 (the exact time of the Easter morning session at which I was to speak).

Since this is exactly the kind of event so important to Breton in *Nadja* and to Aragon in *Le Paysan de Paris*, I decided to go ahead with this next story, which has something (everything?) to do with my interest in the movies, my interest in Walter Benjamin, and my being at an academic conference in Oxford, Ohio, on a cold Easter Sunday.

*My third story.* For the past few years, I have lived a sort of double life, working on the one hand as a professor at the University of Florida, teaching classes, doing research, reading books; and on the other, as a member of a rock band (The Vulgar Boatmen), writing songs, putting out records, playing an occasional show. In thinking about this second activity, I realize that it results from the influence on me of a place where

I grew up, Memphis, most well known, of course, for having been the home of Elvis. But, in fact, *both* of my roles (film professor and rock musician) trace back, through a series of links, to someone else from Memphis, a childhood friend named Dudley Weaver. It was this person who first taught me the guitar; with him I played records and copied parts and started bands. We were the same age and knew each other from infancy. We went to different colleges and then to different graduate schools. But while I was finishing law school at the University of Virginia, I used to visit Dudley at Harvard Business School, and these visits so attracted me to Harvard that I, too, went to Harvard Business School, and there I discovered the movies and changed careers. To be specific, one movie changed my career: one night, while lying in bed in my Harvard dorm, I saw Orson Welles come on Johnny Carson and be asked to name "the two greatest movies of all time." "*The Rules of the Game,*" Welles replied, "and *The Rules of the Game.*" I had never heard of *The Rules of the Game,* but it happened to be playing at the Brattle Theater that week, and I saw it.

While I was in graduate school in 1975 and 1976, Dudley returned from New York (where he had been trading sugar) to Memphis, where he began to work in his family's cotton business, reopened by his father who had emerged from retirement. With Dudley as the family's trader on the floor of the Memphis Cotton Exchange, and with his father making the decisions about buying and selling, the family made, over a matter of several months, more than ten million dollars. But in 1976, two things happened almost simultaneously. First, without telling anyone, Dudley began to disregard his father's trading orders and to act for the family on his own decisions, arrived at in the heat of the action, and thus presumably more responsive to the market's increasingly volatile fluctuations. He made even more money for his family. But then, the second event: a violent and rapid collapse of cotton prices. Failing to heed his father's caution, his orders to cease trading, Dudley, in less than two afternoons, lost not only everything the family had made, but several million more.

At the end of the second afternoon, Dudley went home to his apartment, packed a single suitcase, and caught a flight to Dallas. There, he went to see his Harvard roommate, suggesting to him that they "take a trip." When the roommate said that he couldn't get away from work,

Dudley took a plane to Atlanta and disappeared. No one I know has seen him since. The FBI and private detectives, called in to investigate, could find no traces of him after his leaving Dallas. He had vanished.

Walter Benjamin, of course, was interested in precisely this kind of story, connecting such disappearances to the rise of the urban metropolises, especially London and Paris, described by their chroniclers, particularly Dickens and Balzac, as places where people could disappear, where credentials were easily forged, antecedents unsure, and all identities suspect—where anyone can turn out to be anyone else, where anyone can disappear without a trace. By concentrating on the moment of the Arcades, Benjamin, in effect, dates this effect of the vast metropolises. People began to disappear with increasing frequency in the 1830s, exactly when photography was invented, with its promise of exact recordings of identity and the repudiation of anonymity.

*My fourth story.* My last story is about the cinema and comes from Christopher Rawlence's book *The Missing Reel.*[33] In the spring of 1976, looking for a place to live in North Leeds, British filmmaker Rawlence came across a 100-year-old red-brick, terraced building in both disrepair and a declining neighborhood. He wanted to buy the house, but learned that the Leeds City Council, in a move of Haussmannization, had plans to demolish it. When he balked at the purchase, the seller insisted, "They can't knock it down because the inventor of the movies once lived here." When Rawlence scoffed, the seller opened the door and pointed down the long hall, extending from the front to the dining room beyond, saying, "He built the house this way, with this 60-foot hall for his film shows."

Digging through old records at the local library, Rawlence discovered that the man who had lived in this house was a Frenchman named Augustin Le Prince (a nice rock and roll name, but not "the King"). In 1885, when he was 44 years old and living with his family in New York, which he had seen dramatically illuminated by Edison the year before, Le Prince began his first moving picture experiments. In 1887, having applied for a U.S. patent for the production of animated pictures, but fearing spies and industrial piracy of his ideas, he removed himself to Leeds where he could work in isolation, away from the man he most feared would steal from him—Edison.

Work on the camera went smoothly, and Le Prince was apparently able to take moving pictures as early as 1887. But projecting them was another story, since satisfying persistence of vision's minimum of 16 frames per second required several technical breakthroughs. The most important of these involved a mechanical means for advancing and arresting the film intermittently, because film must be at rest (however briefly) at the exact moment of exposure or projection (a perfect image of Benjamin's understanding of the confounding of the temporal and spatial). By June 1890, Le Prince had solved the problem, successfully demonstrating one of his projections to the Secretary of the Paris Opera.

In September 1890, Le Prince took a vacation to visit his brother in Dijon. On Tuesday, the 16th of September, 1890, he left Dijon for Paris. His brother Albert took him to the station, but he missed the morning train. After an early lunch, they drove back to the station for the 2:42 P.M. train to Paris. This time, to be on the safe side, they arrived early. At 2:39 P.M., the train drew into the station. Le Prince climbed on, carrying a single black valise that contained documents related to his invention. He leaned out of the window to wave goodbye to his brother. The train began to move, and Albert waved back.

In Paris, Le Prince's friends were waiting for him at the station, watching the train arrive in a cloud of smoke and steam, disgorging passengers, precisely as in the Lumière brothers' film, shown that December night in 1895 when motion pictures were projected for the first time.

Le Prince was not on the train, nor was his valise. Extensive, protracted searches all along the route from Dijon to Paris discovered no traces of either. Le Prince had vanished. His disappearance has never been solved. A few months later, Edison applied for three patents for his moving picture apparatus. Le Prince's widow insisted that Edison had stolen her husband's invention, and indeed, there was evidence that Le Prince's workshop in Leeds had been ransacked. Attempting to see Le Prince credited for his work, his widow went to court, wrote her memoirs, and spoke to anyone who would listen about the wrong that had been done to her husband, the true inventor of the movies. And when she realized that he would not be found and that she would need to leave New York for someplace less expensive, she moved to the city where she spent the rest of her life working on the case, and where her children and grandchildren and now great-grandchildren continue to live after she died in 1926. And that city, of course, was Memphis.

*Chapter Five*

· · · · · · · · · · · · · · · · · · ·

ROLAND BARTHES:

FETISHISM AS

RESEARCH STRATEGY


Knowledge must be made to appear where it is not expected.

   Roland Barthes, "Outcomes of the Text"

In a book proposing the avant-garde arts as a model for different ways of writing and thinking about the movies, what place does Roland Barthes have? Barthes, after all, explicitly acknowledged his own "resistance to the cinema",[1] and his reputation rests on critical analyses of common sense (*Mythologies*), clothes (*The Fashion System*), narrative (*S/Z*), and photography (*Camera Lucida* and the essays collected in both *Image Music Text* and *The Responsibility of Forms*). Elected in 1977 to the Collège de France, he assumed the Chair of Literary Semiology. In his autobiography, however, published only two years earlier, Barthes had listed "fidelity" as one of his "Dislikes." His electors, therefore, should not have been surprised when he almost immediately announced feelings that promised a betrayal of semiotics—his weariness with criticism and his desire for "writing":

> And then a time comes . . . when what you have done, worked, written, appears doomed to repetition: What! Until my death, to be writing articles, giving courses, lectures, on "subjects" which alone will vary, and so little! (It's that "on" which bothers me.) This feeling is a cruel one; for it confronts me with the foreclosing of anything New or even of any Adventure (that which "advenes"—which befalls me); I see my future, until death, as a series: when I've finished this text, this lecture, I'll have nothing else to do but start again with another . . . Can this be all?[2]

Barthes used his 1978 lecture "on" Proust to speculate about the "new life" that would issue from "a new practice of writing." But this theme had occurred to him long before. As early as 1963, he had challenged the assumed difference between criticism and "creative" writing,[3] and beginning with *The Empire of Signs* (1970) he had worked to replace straightforward analysis ("a labor of knowledge") with the more pleasurable practice he called "a labor of writing."[4] Increasingly, Barthes tended to dismiss his earlier "scientific" achievements. By 1978, he could declare his intentions: "I expect to break with the uniformly intellectual nature of my previous writings (even if a number of fictive elements taint their rigor)."[5]

Although Barthes seemed to associate this new writing practice with the traditional novel (a form he never took up), he had, in fact, already broken with conventional criticism. He had located a model in a *"third form,* neither Essay nor Novel," which he traced back to Proust, who had stood "at the intersection of two paths, two genres, torn between two 'ways' he does not yet know could converge." Barthes described this hybrid:

> Metaphor sustains any discourse which asks: "What is it? What does it mean?"—the real question of any Essay. Metonymy, on the contrary, asks another question: "What can follow what I say? What can be engendered by the episode I am telling?"; this is the Novel's question. . . . Proust is a divided subject . . . he knows that each incident in life can give rise either to a commentary (an interpretation) or to an affabulation which produces or imagines the narrative *before* and *after*: to interpret is to take the Critical path, to argue theory . . . to think incidents and impressions, to describe their development, is on the contrary to weave a narrative, however loosely, however gradually.[6]

This *third form* would not abandon criticism's knowledge effect. But it would adopt what Barthes called "the novelesque," a method of writing that would draw on fiction's resources: stories, images, details about the weather. This practice, Barthes wrote, "subject[s] the objects of knowledge and discussion—as in any art—no longer to an instance of truth, but to a consideration of *effects*."[7]

Barthes's explicit calls for a new kind of writing occurred only near the end of his life. But he had begun experimenting much earlier. In retrospect, the decisive year appears to be 1970, when he published *Empire of Signs, S/Z,* and "The Third Meaning." Later, in his autobiography and interviews, Barthes would admit that of all his early work, the only book that fully satisfied him was *Empire of Signs,* a study of Japan, which he had visited without being able to speak, read, or understand Japanese. The opening paragraph of *Empire of Signs* gives some idea of what Barthes meant by the "fictive elements" in his writing:

> If I want to imagine a fictive nation, I can give it an invented name, treat it declaratively as a novelistic object, create a new Garabagne, so as to compromise no real country by my fantasy (though it is then that fantasy itself I compromise by the signs of literature). I can also—though in no way claiming to represent or to analyze reality itself (these being the major gestures of Western discourse)— isolate somewhere in the world (*faraway*) a certain number of features (a term implied in linguistics), and out of these features deliberately form a system. It is this system which I shall call: Japan.[8]

The tone of this passage is important. With its curious mixture of scholarly allusions (to "literature," "linguistics," "discourse," "system") and aesthetic invocations (to the imagination, novels, and "fantasy"), the paragraph seems en route to the "third way" of writing that Barthes found in Proust. Perhaps *Empire of Signs* pleased Barthes because there he had begun his change of course, and he had done so openly. In fact, however, this shift appears just as decisively (if more subtly) in *S/Z,* a much more important book.

On the surface, *S/Z* seems the *summa* of semiotics, the ultimate ideological/structuralist analysis of a literary text. Barthes, after all, was undertaking a microscopic, line-by-line reading of a single Balzac novella (*Sarrasine*) in order to demonstrate the coded operations upon which narrative realism depends. Almost certainly, the project began as another "labor of knowledge," a successor to *The Fashion System:* having proposed his five codes (Hermeneutic, Proairetic, Symbolic, Semic, and Referential), Barthes would merely have to show how they functioned throughout Balzac's story. In fact, however, with *S/Z,* Barthes had invented his own surrealist game, one whose "rules" (the five codes must be used, *Sarrasine* must be exhaustively examined) *automatically* generated unpredictable results.

In writing *S/Z*, Barthes could not have avoided experiencing the avant-garde's basic lesson: by "yielding the initiative" (in Mallarmé's phrase) to *a form,* particularly to an *unusual* one, a writer will find himself led in surprising directions. Committed to a close reading, Barthes must have initially resigned himself to considerable repetition: "in this passage, we see how the Hermeneutic code delays the revelation of the Lanty secret"; "here again we see the Reference code's ability to insist upon the text's *natural* authority"; and so forth. In fact, however, the escape from this tedium lay precisely in the arrangement dictated by what Barthes called, using a cinematic term, a *"slow motion"* reading: the fragmentation of *Sarrasine.* Confronted by a novella fractured into discrete units (the "starred text" of "lexias," the arbitrary blocks of reading), Barthes recognized that passages unstuck from the larger narrative prompted speculation, different readings, play. Thus, although Barthes's patient analyses of *Sarrasine's* coding quickly became predictable, the mini-essays ("divagations") appended to certain sections contained the flamboyantly inventive material marking his experiments with a new kind of critical writing.

*S/Z* represents the transition from structuralism to poststructuralism. The book's analytical purpose, its quasi-scientific faith in semiotics and ideological critique, its demystification of literary realism all issue from the heady moment of Continental criticism, with its roots in Lévi-Strauss, Saussure, Marx, Althusser, and Brecht. But the divagations' unembarrassed playfulness, their awareness of *Sarrasine's* limitless possibilities, constrained only by the imagination and subjectivity of the individual reader, recall the willful strangeness of the Saussure who claimed to have found concealed anagrams in classical Latin poetry. Take, for example, section XLVII, carefully placed at the exact center of the book's 93 units:

XLVII. *S/Z*
*SarraSine:* customary French onomastics would lead us to expect *SarraZine:* on its way to the subject's patronymic, the *Z* has encountered some pitfall. *Z* is the letter of mutilation: phonetically, *Z* stings like a chastising lash, an avenging insect; graphically, cast slantwise by the hand across the blank regularity of the page, amid the curves of the alphabet, like an oblique and illicit blade, it cuts, slashes, or, as we say in French, *zebras;* from a Balzacian viewpoint, this *Z*

(which appears in Balzac's name) is the letter of deviation (see the story *Z. Marcas*); finally, here *Z* is the first letter of La Zambinella, the initial of castration, so that by this orthographical error committed in the middle of his name, in the center of his body, Sarrasine receives the Zambinellan *Z* in its true sense—the wound of deficiency. Further, *S* and *Z* are in a relation of graphological inversion: the same letter seen from the other side of the mirror: Sarrasine contemplates in La Zambinella his own castration. Hence the slash (/) confronting the *S* of SarraSine and the *Z* of Zambinella has a panic function: it is the slash of censure, the surface of the mirror, the wall of hallucination, the verge of antithesis, the abstraction of limit, the obliquity of the signifier, the index of the paradigm, hence of meaning. (*S/Z*, pp. 106–107)

Barthes's precise location of this passage suggests its importance to him. If we take this section as *S/Z*'s most fully realized example of Barthes's new writing practice, and further, if we want to think about its implications for a different film criticism, several points present themselves:

1. The almost complete absence of commentary on this striking paragraph, so obviously significant to Barthes's own conception of *S/Z*, indicates how ill prepared most academics are to deal with departures from the conventional essay. As I argued in the Introduction, poststructuralist criticism, especially as practiced by Barthes and Derrida, has increasingly engaged in experimentation, with form assuming a role as decisive as in poetry and fiction. Rosalind Krauss has observed that "it is not surprising that the medium of a poststructuralist literature should be the critical text wrought into a paraliterary form. And what is clear is that Barthes and Derrida are the *writers,* not the critics, that students now read."[9] Nevertheless, the formal properties of texts like *S/Z* continue to be ignored by most critics, who cite only their substance, as if that substance had been conveyed in the transparent language of the traditional essay.

2. *S/Z* turns on Barthes's discovery, prompted by his fragmentation of *Sarrasine,* that even the page-turning narratives and received ideologies of popular fiction cannot prevent a reader from producing, at any point, meanings never contemplated by the author. Barthes referred to this idea of "polysemy" as "textuality," and he advocated using it to replace the old notion of the literary "work," presumed to contain a stable body of meanings waiting for discovery. In "The Theory of the Text," an ency-

clopedia article published three years after *S/Z,* Barthes proposed that
"the exact development of this theory, the blossoming which justifies it,
is not this or that recipe for analysis, it is *writing itself. Let the commentary
be itself a text:* that is, in brief, what the theory of the text demands."[10]
This manifesto connects Barthes to the avant-garde tradition of invention-by-extrapolation: indeed, he appears as a Brechtian *Messingkauf,*
eager to "use" a text for his own purposes. Those purposes' extravagance
(the "S/Z" passage is an example) also suggests Barthes's links to dandyism, a practice intimately connected not only with fashion and everyday
life, but also with the historical avant-garde, whose nineteenth-century
Parisian origins lay in Baudelaire's revolt against bourgeois custom (described in his essay "The Dandy") and his embrace of "the painting of
modern life." Not surprisingly, Barthes's autobiography would explicitly
evoke dandyism as a contemporary possibility;[11] only three years after
*S/Z,* he had already assumed the definitive dandy position: "Anything,
rather than the rule."[12]

3. I have suggested earlier that the avant-garde's revolt against con-
vention finds its rationale in the discovery (by communication theory)
that "information" is a function of surprise. Barthes's late work, with its
repudiation of traditional analysis, demonstrates how to achieve a hermeneutic *effect* without hermeneutics. Even at his most experimental (as
in the "S/Z" passage), Barthes *produces knowledge:* we learn something
about *Sarrasine* from his paragraph about that novella's names and their
spellings. Because, however, he generates that "information" in unconventional ways, it is easy to dismiss: in a positivist culture, after all, what
counts as "knowledge" often depends less on content than on method;
even the most banal conventional analysis, in other words, may seem
more "true" than a striking idea derived from "illegitimate" means. And
Barthes's means are, indeed, unconventional. In "The Theory of the
Text," he offers a compressed instruction-manual:

> This practice . . . presupposes that one has passed the descriptive
> or communicative level of language, and that one is ready to pro-
> duce its generative energy. It thus implies that one accepts a certain
> number of procedures: generalized recourse to anagrammatical dis-
> tortions of the enunciation ("word-plays"), polysemy, dialogue-
> writing, or inversely "l'écriture blanche," which thwarts and de-
> ceives connotations; "irrational" (implausible) variations of person

and tense; the continuous subversion of the relation between writing and reading, between the sender and the receiver of the text. It is thus a practice which is strongly transgressive in relation to the main categories which found our current sociality: perception, intellection, the sign, grammar, and even science.[13]

Barthes was to experiment with every element on this list. If for the moment, however, we simply apply the tactic used in *S/Z*'s "Section XLVII," we might produce something like this paragraph about *Casablanca:*

> **K/V:** Somewhere between pre-occupied Paris and semi-occupied Casablanca, Richard Blaine becomes "Rick," a transformation marked, as is typical of American nicknaming, by both abridgment and percussion: the soft "h" replaced by the aggressive "k," which appears twice in Rick's first on-screen moment (he signs his bold "OK, Rick" to authorize a gambling advance). In Casablanca, only two people avoid this "k," Sam and Ilsa, both of whom persist with the original, longer form, "Richard." While *Casablanca* at first appears to resolve by repudiating "Rick" for the previous, more gentle "Richard," the ending, in fact, insists on the harder "k," required by the exigencies of war with its Krauts and K-rations; with Ilsa sent away, and Sam apparently forgotten, the hero leaves with Captain Renault, who uses only the more cynical diminutive. We learn, of course, that Richard's "k" (a wounding sound, identical to the cutting "c") has resulted from Ilsa's discovery of Victor's being alive. This "V," neither as harsh as the "K," nor as whispered as the "H" left behind, stands obviously for Churchill's Victory Salute. More important, it diagrams the intersection of two lines (Richard/Rick and Victor) in Ilsa, in Casablanca. Ultimately, this "V" must be inverted, turned upside-down (as the War has done to the world) and the lines allowed to diverge again ($\Lambda$). Inverted, the V appears (1) as the sign for "Up" (the escape-by-plane) and (2) as an incomplete "N" (the rejection of the "M" in "blame," Rick's first response to Ilsa, for the "N" in "Blaine," the rescuing agent). This truncated "N," initially the mirror of Rick's post-Ilsa self, a fragment of the freedom-fighter he once has been, will ultimately be made whole. For in acknowledging the impossibility of returning to "Richard," Rick recovers himself by joining forces with Victor, a merger represented graphically by the "V" which now appears, turned on its side

and pointing like an arrow to the "N's" missing line, in the last letter of Richard Blaine's new name, Ric**K**.

4. The *épatant* style of Barthes's "S/Z" passage confirms that the avant-garde attitude, which since Impressionism has appeared in painting, music, literature, architecture, theater, ballet, and film, has begun to enter the realm of criticism itself. In retrospect, this development seems inevitable. Given the avant-garde's urgent need to contract the gap between the appearance of innovative work and its ultimate acceptance, it had to depend on theory as its advocate. Bohemianism, after all, was from the start what the Goncourt brothers called "a freemasonry of publicity."[14] Sooner or later, having invented the script for this project, the supporting player would have to take center stage. We have reached that moment now.

Experimental contemporary theory has taken shape around one avant-garde in particular: Surrealism. While Walter Benjamin openly acknowledged his own debts to Aragon and Breton,[15] Barthes hardly mentioned them. After 1970, however, he was clearly practicing a kind of surrealist criticism, one whose principal method involved the earlier movement's preferred tactic: *fragmentation*. In all the major works of his last period, Barthes abandoned the sustained arguments of his "labors of knowledge" for Nietzschean fragments, whose meaning depended on their assemblage within some larger conceptual scheme (in *S/Z*, the issue of "narrative"; in *Pleasure of the Text*, the place of the reader; in *Roland Barthes*, the dispositions of the "self"; in *Lover's Discourse*, the discourse of romance). With these texts, Barthes effectively took up Benjamin's great unachieved project: he was producing his own *Arcades Project*.

The Surrealists had explicitly championed fragmentation as a means to knowledge, especially regarding the cinema. As I described in Chapter 2, such maneuvers as Breton's moviegoing habits (which depended on ignorance of both the film's title and its showing times) and Man Ray's trick of isolating details by watching the screen through barely parted fingers were intended to release individual images from the narratives that constrained them. Under normal conditions, for example, you would never notice a wrinkled map, spread casually across a writing table, when the story was telling you to look at the gun in the heroine's pocket. But, the Surrealists had asked, what if *the map* contained the potential for revelation, and the movie made you miss it? Or, as Walter Benjamin asked, "What form do you suppose a life would take that was determined at a decisive moment precisely by the street song last on everyone's lips?"[16]

By the late 1920s, Benjamin had already assimilated the surrealist lesson. "To someone looking through piles of old letters," he wrote, describing how that lesson applied to research, "a stamp that has long been out of circulation on a torn envelope often says more than a reading of dozens of pages."[17] Like the purloined letter, however, such a stamp, even in plain sight, was easy to overlook. Freud had recognized the problem, proposing as its solution the "evenly hovering attention" which would enable analysts to listen differently. Extending Freud's method, the Surrealists had, in effect, offered training in how to notice something like Benjamin's stamp. For such training, the cinema inevitably became a crucial site, for with the movies' power both to illuminate everyday details and to make them disappear, film was at once the miracle cure and the old problem. On the one hand, by extracting its people and objects from the world at large, the cinema made them more visible than ever before. Aragon described the mechanism and its effect:

> To endow with a poetic value that which does not yet possess it, to wilfully restrict the field of vision so as to intensify expression: these are two properties that help make cinematic *décor* the adequate setting of modern beauty.[18]

On the other hand, by subjecting every detail to what Noël Burch has called "linearization"—in other words, by making every aspect of the image subservient to the narrative—the movies radically discouraged the kind of attention that notices a forgotten stamp instead of an obvious letter. In Barthes's words:

> *Le plein du cinéma*—Saturation of the cinema
>    Resistance to the cinema: the signifier itself is always, by nature, continuous here, whatever the rhetoric of frames and shots; without remission, a continuum of images; the film . . . *follows,* like a garrulous ribbon: statutory impossibility of the fragment, of the haiku.[19]

Barthes had liked Japan because his almost total ignorance of Japanese had produced a surprising effect: a magical defamiliarization of everyday objects. Cut off from the linguistic systems which simultaneously explained and diminished, Barthes had been, in his words, "delivered from any fulfilled meaning,"[20] and the things of the world surrounding him—streets, packages, food—lay stranded, glittering, available. The trick was to reproduce this sensation within his own culture. His solution was the fragment, described at times as a mere taste,[21] but quickly developed into a means to knowledge.

The 1970 essay "The Third Meaning" represents the first stage of this strategy: if the movies' relentless unrolling prevents your noticing anything except the narratively underlined details, the only response is to stop the film. In "The Third Meaning" Barthes did just that, working not with Eisenstein's films, but with individual frames extracted from them. In suppressing the movies' continuity, he had, in effect, managed to simulate the experience of traveling in a foreign country without knowing the language. More exactly, he was reinventing Breton's experiment of entering an unidentified film *in medias res* and leaving when its point became too clear. Perusing images liberated from their plot, Barthes discovered his attention drawn to details (a scarf, an eyebrow's curve) whose significance he could not attribute to information or symbolism. This "third meaning" (or "obtuse meaning"), Barthes wrote, "is a signifier without a signified," "is outside (articulated) language," "is discontinuous, indifferent to the story and to the obvious meaning." Indeed, "it outplays meaning—subverts not the content but the whole practice of meaning."[22]

What Barthes had located was the point where, to use Walter Ong's formulation, alphabetic culture gives way to the photographic. As an essay, "The Third Meaning" was Barthes's third attempt to develop a semiotics of the photographic image. The first two, "The Photographic Message" and "The Rhetoric of the Image," had hinted at the radical ambiguity of photographs, but had emphasized the connotative procedures and verbal captions that controlled them. If those first two essays had used a "labor of knowledge" approach to explain photography in terms of language, "The Third Meaning" cheerfully abandoned that project, taking the first step into uncharted territory. Barthes made his proposition explicit:

> It is at the level of the third meaning, and at that level alone, that the "filmic" finally emerges. The filmic is that in the film which cannot be described, the representation which cannot be represented. The filmic begins only where language and metalanguage

end. Everything that can be *said* about *Ivan* or *Potemkin* can be said of a written text . . . except this, the obtuse meaning.[23]

In Eisenstein, Barthes had picked an example that strengthened his own case. For if Eisenstein's photographic images, among the most organized and symbolic of any filmmaker's, could provide "third meanings," then *anyone's* would. For as Barthes admitted, "Eisenstein's 'art' is not polysemous: it chooses the meaning, imposes it, hammers it home . . . Eisensteinian meaning devastates ambiguity."[24]

Like camp, however, the "third meaning" is ultimately less a property of objects than a way of looking at them. In both cases, a reading disposition results from a dislocation: *Reefer Madness,* for example, "becomes" camp when its justifying context recedes; third meanings "appear" when *Ivan the Terrible* vanishes. At stake here is the issue of the Fragment-versus-the-Sequence, around which so much of the twentieth-century's avant-garde has turned. The issue is particularly crucial for the movies. In *On Photography,* Susan Sontag argues that "strictly speaking, one never understands anything from a photograph. . . . Only that which narrates can make us understand."[25] At the origins of the cinema, as I suggested in Chapter 2, lies exactly this fear of a photograph's mute ambiguity. Unless individual shots could be made to signify in predictable ways, they would induce in their viewers only delirium. While movement within a single shot could suggest a narrative (or at least the beginnings of one), the main solution was the *sequence,* a succession of images arranged in a grammar that would indicate (and fix) their meaning. So troubling was the isolated image that almost all attention focused on securing this grammar (known as "continuity"), which, once achieved, would presumably take care of everything else.[26]

Continuity grammar had serendipitous effects. Recall the scene from *Born Free* mentioned in Chapter 2: a montage of a lion attacking a woman. Continuity sequences portraying such familiar actions, even if incompletely, proved able to prompt a viewer's "inner speech" to fill in the blanks. In the spectator's imagination, the event appeared whole and the images cured of their insufficiency. The problem of the individual shot was solved.

In *S/Z,* however, Barthes showed that such sequences are inevitably formulaic, the realm of the already-read. Indeed, a novel's discrete actions make sense only when the reader can gather them under available

names like "kidnapping," "rendezvous," or "lion killing a native woman."
Thus, editing in narrative films generally turns on the relatively simple
question, How much do we need to show of a given action for an
audience to make sense of it? Or, conversely, as Godard so often asked,
beginning with his first feature, *Breathless,* how much can we leave out?[27]

These questions, however, are not simply formal: Barthes argued in
*S/Z* that narrative realism has a profoundly conservative effect precisely
to the extent that it depends on stock sequences whose familiarity
discourages reading's free play. Barthes called this dependence "proairetism," a neologism drawn from the Greek word connoting the ability to
predict an action's outcome. Proairetism encourages skimming: a reader
anticipating a narrative's developments is like a spy getting a message he
already knows—neither is likely to dwell on his document's language.
Breton had intuited the same problem with the movies: if you wanted
to really *see* the cinema's images, you had to catch them off-guard,
unprotected by their stories. Hence his irregular filmgoing habits, conceived as a means of evading the popular cinema's predictability. And his
discovery: despite continuity cinema's suppression of its own means (in
Hollywood cinematographer Allen Daviau's exact formulation, "While
an image could be beautiful, it wasn't to be so beautiful as to draw
attention to itself"), the Surrealists found that when you avoided their
plots, even the worst films "contain ten or fifteen marvelous minutes."[28]

With prose fiction, the image-sequence opposition appears as lan-
guage-sequence. But as Barthes saw, the effect of *not* entering in the
middle is identical:

> Basically, by its very structure (clearly revealed in the utter simplic-
> ity of the sequence), proairetism comparatively depreciates lan-
> guage ("action," it is said, speaks louder than "words") . . . proaire-
> tism, when reduced to its essential terms, like so many knives (the
> knives of asyndeton), itself becomes an instrument of castration.[29]

The association of conservative politics with conventional sequences
helps account for the avant-garde's preoccupation with *interruption.*
Duchamp's readymades, Surrealism's found objects and filmmaking
methods, Brecht's tableaux and alienation effects, Benjamin's *Arcades
Project,* Godard's jump-cuts, Barthes's "third meaning"—each of these
practices involves a strategy of fragmentation designed to defeat a given
continuity's ideological effect.[30]

Barthes referred to his own practice by several terms. In "The Third Meaning," he acknowledged that what he was doing with Eisenstein's stills was a "scandal." Three years later, renaming this reading disposition "pleasure," he claimed for it a political effect:

> Pleasure, however, is not an *element* of the text, it is not a naïve residue; it does not depend on a logic of understanding and on sensation; it is a drift, something both revolutionary and asocial, and it cannot be taken over by any collectivity, any mentality, any ideolect.[31]

After another four years, Barthes identified this working procedure as a form of "perversity," insisting that "the pleasure potential of a perversion . . . is always underestimated." "Henceforth," he wrote in his autobiography, "it is a goddess, a figure that can be invoked, a means of intercession."[32] He recognized, moreover, that his taste for the fragment (the rhetorical means of interruption) derived from one perversion in particular: *fetishism*.

For an intellectual like Barthes, this embrace of fetishism represented a decisive break with the Enlightenment tradition underlying conventional criticism. In its history, after all, fetishism has appeared most prominently as knowledge's opposite, as a means of false consciousness and disavowal. Marx, for example, had argued that the "fetishism of commodities" encourages us to ignore the exploitative social relations that such objects simultaneously embody and conceal. The commodity is a "hieroglyph," all right, but not one meant to be read. It substitutes the lure of things for a curiosity about their production. Similarly, Freud had posited fetishism as the result of an investigation's *arrest*. Fearing the sight of the mother's genitals, misunderstood as "castrated," the male infant stops at another place (a foot, an ankle, a skirt's hem), investing this replacement with libidinal energy, but denying the sexual difference his gaze has discovered.

Despite these accounts, Barthes sensed the swivel character of fetishism, its origins in passion (to possess, to know), shunted into safer routes. What if that passion could be activated for the purposes of knowledge? That experiment, Barthes saw, would begin by blocking access to those safe routes, which he defined as a culture's sanctioned narratives. Balzac's *Sarrasine,* for example, offered a story, but that story was everywhere implicated in the most conventional of world views. *Ivan the Terrible* was no different: however leftist Eisenstein's explicit politics may have been, his "readerly" films, by discouraging "plural" readings, merely reproduced traditional narrative's "intimidation."[33]

For Barthes, blocking access to these narrative routes consistently involved interruption. At first, this tactic appeared in his work primarily as means only to a solipsistic eroticism: thus, he rhapsodized that a "third meaning" detail (a signifier without a signified) "maintains a state of perpetual erethism, desire not finding issue in that spasm of this signified which normally brings the subject voluptuously back into the peace of nominations."[34] But that same essay recognized in such details "the epitome of a counter-narrative" which emerges only when Eisenstein's is suppressed.[35] *S/Z* developed this idea, using the lexia's fracturing effect to prompt multiple readings.[36] Having seen what this way of working could do, Barthes then applied it to his own writing, designing his autobiography as a series of fragments, whose alphabetical arrangement would short-circuit any continuity:

> The alphabetical order erases everything, banishes every origin. Perhaps in places, certain fragments seem to follow one another by some affinity; but the important thing is that these little networks not be connected, that they not slide into an enormous network which would be the structure of the book, its meaning. It is in order to halt, to deflect, to divide this descent of discourse toward a destiny of the subject, that at certain moments the alphabet calls you to order (to disorder) and says: *Cut! Resume the story in another way.*[37]

Barthes's choice of a cinematic metaphor (*"Cut!"*) indicates how readily fetishism is associated with the movies. Recall that Aragon, in the remark I cited earlier, proposed that film's remarkable capacity to endow everyday objects with "modern beauty" arises from its need "to wilfully restrict the field of vision," a precise definition of the fetishist's gaze.[38] Even more significantly, the development of classical narrative cinema finds its exact parallel in the etymology of the word *fetish*.

As William Pietz has shown, the problem of fetishism first arose in a specific historical context: the trading conducted by Portuguese merchants along the coast of West Africa in the sixteenth and seventeenth centuries.[39] Renaissance businessmen, the Portuguese were looking for straightforward economic transactions. Almost immediately, they were frustrated, particularly by what Pietz evocatively calls "the mystery of value." For the Africans, material objects could embody—"simultane-ously and sequentially—religious, commercial, aesthetic and sexual" worth, and the balance among these categories seemed, at least to the Europeans, a matter of "caprice." Especially troubling was the Africans' unpredictable estimate of not only their own objects, but also those of the European traders, which the merchants themselves regarded as "trifles."[40]

Like the Portuguese traders, commercial filmmakers began naively by proposing an uncomplicated deal: a story in exchange for the price of a ticket. Almost immediately, however, they were surprised by their view-ers' fascination with individual players. For a brief moment, the industry resisted this unintended consequence of the movies, this admiration for actors which seemed an "overestimation of value," a fetishism. Preserv-ing the players' anonymity, after all, had minimized their power and kept them cheap. Inevitably, however, Hollywood came to see this fetishism as a means of making money, and the star system deliberately set out to encourage it. In fact, although continuity cinema's insistence on story often reduced the immediate attraction of its components ("while an image could be beautiful, it wasn't to be so beautiful as to draw attention to itself"), inadvertently the movies glamorized everything: faces, clothes, furniture, trains, landscapes. A dining car's white, starched linen (*North by Northwest)*, a woman's voice (Margaret Sullavan's in *Three Comrades*), a cigarette lighter *(The Maltese Falcon)*—even the most ordinary objects could become, as Sam Spade put it, in a rare literary allusion, "the stuff that dreams are made of."[41]

With both the West Africans and movie audiences, this "fetishizing" of goods appeared to result from what Freud would later call, in another cinematic term, "projection," the process whereby a subjective value is assigned to an external thing. Thus, for Michel Leiris, fetishism resem-bles "crisis moments":

> There are moments which one can call the *crises* which alone are important in a life. These are moments when the outside seems abruptly to respond to the sum of what we throw forth from within, when the exterior world opens to encounter our heart and estab-lishes a sudden communication with it.[42]

Leiris described such moments as "in appearance futile and stripped of symbolic value and, if one wishes, *gratuitous*": in other words, they resembled Barthes's description of "third meanings." From this perspective, fetishism appears as a means of interrupting the "rational" trade relations which determine so much of everyday life. When Barthes realized that these relations also structure our dealings with popular fiction, he saw that fetishism could become an effective critical strategy. What the novel (and by implication, Hollywood cinema) offers, Barthes proposed in *S/Z*, is a contract: a story in exchange for money. There are, of course, conditions: in return for the fiction's promise to abide by the rules (all hermeneutic enigmas will be resolved, all cultural codes honored), the reader agrees to "consume" the plot by moving from beginning to end.

One tactic immediately offers itself as a means of resisting this system:

> rereading, an operation contrary to the commercial and ideological habits of our society, which would have us "throw away" the story once it has been consumed ("devoured"), so that we can then move on to another story, buy another book, and which is tolerated only in certain marginal categories of readers (children, old people, and professors), rereading is here suggested at the outset, for it alone saves the text from repetition (those who fail to reread are obliged to read the same story everywhere). (*S/Z*, pp. 15–16)

Rereading encourages fetishism. Freed from a plot's tantalizations, the rereader, like the viewer looking only at a movie's stills, inevitably interrupts the story he already knows, taking time to inspect details, follow leads, imagine other outcomes. Doing so enables him to enter a text at places not yet marked. Fetishism, in other words, can amount to a research strategy, and Barthes's late work is its model.[43]

That strategy's justification might derive from Carlo Ginzburg's essay "Clues," with its proposition that the nineteenth century's last decades witnessed the emergence of an epistemological paradigm grounded in apparently incidental details. Ginzburg locates this "conjectural" approach in the work of three men, each trained as a medical doctor: art historian Giovanni Morelli, psychoanalyst Sigmund Freud, and detective story writer Arthur Conan Doyle. Confronted by paintings of uncertain attribution, Morelli discovered that an artist's "signature" appears most readily in a composition's most trivial elements: although a forger could imitate conspicuous characteristics, "earlobes, fingernails, shapes of fingers and toes" betrayed him. Morelli's connection to Freud and Sherlock

Holmes is obvious: as Edgar Wind puts it, "To some of Morelli's critics it has seemed odd that personality should be found where personal effort is weakest. But on this point modern psychology would certainly support Morelli: our inadvertent little gestures reveal our character far more authentically than any formal posture we may carefully prepare."[44] A patient's slips-of-the-tongue, a crime's marginalia—these were the symptoms where an investigation should begin.

By emphasizing isolated details (recall Holmes's insistence, in "Silver Blaze," on "the immense significance of the curried mutton"), Morelli, Freud, and Doyle had, in effect, founded their epistemology on the logic of fetishism. Indeed, this "conjectural" way of working, Ginzburg suggests, amounts to the twentieth century's great challenge to Galilean science. As our understanding of this approach grows, practices committed to interruption and fragmentation begin to seem less willful: Cubist collages, Surrealist film-watching habits, Duchamp's readymades, Pop Art's cartoons and soup cans, Joseph Cornell's flea-market boxes, Benjamin's *Arcades Project,* Barthes's "Third Meaning"—these activities, from intellectual history's perspective, now appear as methods of research, legitimized by the established models (medical diagnosis, criminal detection) which they resemble.

Barthes appears to have recognized this affiliation. He readily acknowledged that his "third meaning" practice, however preliminarily solipsistic, "compels an interrogative reading," but one in which the investigation "bears precisely on the signifier not on the signified, on reading not on intellection: it is a 'poetical' grasp."[45] *S/Z* represents Barthes's own development of this method, which derives "counter-narratives" from textual fragments. In suggesting that cinematic details or literary fragments might function as *provocateurs* for other texts, Barthes had reinvented Max Ernst's surrealist *frottage,* a method of generating pictures from rubbings of striking (but apparently trivial) patterns.[46] Before demonstrating this approach's potential for film studies, I would like to compare it with two analogous ways of working, found in Robert Darnton's *The Great Cat Massacre* and Sophie Calle's *Suite vénitienne.*

In his now-famous essay "Workers Revolt: The Great Cat Massacre of the Rue Saint-Séverin," historian Robert Darnton analyzes a grotesque incident which occurred in an eighteenth-century Parisian printing shop.[47] The business's owner employed two apprentices, whom he treated miserably: "They slept in a filthy, freezing room, rose before dawn, ran errands all day while dodging insults from the journeymen and abuse from the master, and received nothing but slops to eat" (p. 75). Indeed, even the house cat, beloved by the master's wife, had better food. As the apprentices' sufferings increased, they began to direct their resentment toward the neighborhood cats whose nightly howlings disturbed their sleep. Forced to start the day before dawn, the chronically exhausted apprentices toiled as the master and his wife slept late.

They began their revenge. One of the apprentices, with an exceptional talent for mimicry, stationed himself on the roof above the master's bedroom and howled "so horribly that the bourgeois and his wife did not sleep a wink" (p. 76). Several nights of this treatment convinced the master to order the apprentices to get rid of the cats. They did so:

> Gleefully Jerome and Léveillé set to work, aided by the journeymen. Armed with broom handles, bars of the press, and other tools of their trade, they went after every cat they could find, beginning with *la grise* [the mistress's favorite]. Léveillé smashed its spine with an iron bar and Jerome finished it off. Then they stashed it in a gutter while the journeymen drove the other cats across the rooftops, bludgeoning every one within reach and trapping those who tried to escape in strategically placed sacks. They dumped sackloads of half-dead cats in the courtyard. Then the entire workshop gathered round and staged a mock trial, complete with guards, a confessor, and a public executioner. After pronouncing the animals guilty and administering last rites, they strung them up on an improvised gallows. (pp. 76–77)

Twenty-five years later, when Jerome told this story in his memoirs, he described it as the funniest thing he ever saw.

Darnton's approach to this strange anecdote closely resembles dream interpretation. Like Freud, Darnton begins by suspecting that this event can and must be read for its repressed meaning—it is a *symptom*, determined by censorship. Prevented from making their anger explicit, the workers act by means of disguise, which, as in dreams, results from condensation and displacement. An array of concerns (the workers' situation, sexual attitudes, labor struggles) are compressed into the single symbol of *cats*, an all-purpose sign also achieving the requisite displacement from forbidden themes. Thus, the cat incident becomes a sort of *intended* dream over which the workers have some control, although almost certainly they would not have been able to articulate their symbolic manipulations.

Described in this way, Darnton's account of the great cat massacre seems relatively uncomplicated cultural history. His introductory remarks, however, suggest his method's proximity to the kind of "photographic thinking" described by Barthes's "The Third Meaning":

> There is no better way, I believe, than to wander through the archives [the *flâneur* strategy again]. One can hardly read a letter from the Old Regime without coming up against surprises. . . . What was proverbial wisdom to our ancestors is completely opaque to us. Open any eighteenth-century book of proverbs, and you will find entries such as: "He who is snotty, let him blow his nose." When we cannot get a proverb, or a joke, or a ritual, or a poem, we know we are on to something. By picking at the document where it is most opaque, we may be able to unravel an alien system of meaning. The thread might even lead into a strange and wonderful world view. (pp. 4–5)

An archive resembles a collection of stills, the remains of films that have disappeared. Thus, the researcher finds himself in the position of Harris Burdick's editor (see Chapter 2): he must rediscover for these fragments the stories that once contained them.[48] In most cases, a specialist like Darnton has no trouble imagining an isolated anecdote's larger context. But his ability to do so becomes precisely the signal to begin elsewhere: in Darnton's formulation, "the best points of entry in an attempt to penetrate an alien culture can be those where it seems to be most opaque" (p. 78). Jerome's account of the great cat massacre is such a point: Darnton cannot understand how the apprentice could find it funny.

The similarity of Darnton's way of working to Barthes's is striking. Both "interrogative readings" start from a "stubborn" detail, one resisting available meanings. Darnton calls such details "opaque"; for Barthes, they are "obtuse." As a historian, Darnton, of course, works to enlighten, to recover the circumstances that would restore his opaque anecdote to transparency. Barthes's project is less certain. If "The Third Meaning" amounts to a celebration of "obtuseness," *S/Z* implies that Barthes had discovered in fragments the potential for a kind of knowledge based as much on invention as on recovery.

The presence of "third meanings" reminds us of photography's (and by implication, the cinema's) fundamental property—*automatism.* Derrida and Ong have pointed out that Plato used the *Phaedrus* to criticize writing as "artificial memory." That characterization issued from Plato's own anxious, prescient intuition of all technology's fundamental automatism, its potential to continue producing (either goods or meanings) long after the control exacted by human consciousness has been relinquished. For Plato, the ghost in the machine was language, which survived not only its author, but also every context of its enunciation. In the twentieth century that fear has persisted, finding representation in the movies' fatal robots *(Blade Runner),* Frankensteinian monsters, devouring assembly lines *(Modern Times),* and computers-run-amok *(2001).*

What is automatic about writing? Its ability to mean even in the absence of its author, and even more important, its ability to mean in ways its author never comprehended (think of the anagrams Saussure detected in Latin poetry). Photography and film, as I described in Chapter 2, further these effects. Barthes's "third meanings," *Blow-Up's* inadvertently discovered murder—these texts amount to allegories about photography's inevitable involvement in chance details that imply significance, in accidents that become clues. Barthes's essay and Antonioni's movie are parables of cinematic thinking which we only need decipher.

Sophie Calle's *Suite vénitienne* is another such parable.[49] Calle, a conceptual artist and photographer, begins abruptly:

> *For months I followed strangers on the street. For the pleasure of following them, not because they particularly interested me. I photographed them without their knowledge, took note of their movements, then finally lost sight of them and forgot them.*
>
> *At the end of January 1980, on the streets of Paris, I followed a man whom I lost sight of a few minutes later in the crowd. That very evening, quite by chance, he was introduced to me at an opening. During the course of our conversation, he told me he was planning an imminent trip to Venice.*

With only that cursory explanation, Calle begins her book, a record of her own efforts to follow and photograph "Henri B.," a man whom she does not know, whose reasons for traveling to Venice remain concealed from her, whose daily itinerary eludes prediction. Thus Calle's project, by its own definition, must admit the accidental into its calculations, just as photography and filmmaking must acknowledge the ineradicable presence of third meanings.

Calle uses Henri B.'s unpredictable wanderings to draw a map of Venice never contemplated by conventional tourism. In a pure detective story, Henri B. might become a discovered stencil which, when placed over a document, reveals the secret message hidden there. In *Suite vénitienne,* however, meanings are not found, but rather *produced,* achieved by the automatism of the machine that Calle has set in motion. She decides only one thing: she will follow Henri B. wherever he goes in Venice. The rest is in the hands of the machine, which functions like a camera, left to film on its own.

Calle "reads" Venice through Henri B., reporting her discoveries in snapshots and through forms borrowed from popular literary genres: the detective story, the travel guide, and the diary. Her experiment simulates a photo shoot, undertaken without preconceptions about what will appear in developing.[50] Henri B. is her equivalent of Darnton's opaque point of entry, of Barthes's obtuse detail: by using him, by tolerating surprise, she generates a kind of "information" about Venice unobtainable by straightforward means.

·  ·  ·

We have arrived at this proposition: if Barthes's "Third Meaning" essay represents our most profound thinking about the cinema's radical break with alphabetic culture, then it should provide the ideal basis for a new kind of film criticism. The form of that criticism might issue from a combination of Darnton's historicism and Calle's cartography. Here are the instructions for this "Third Meaning Criticism" and two samples of it, taken from student essays:

> In "The Third Meaning," Roland Barthes describes a kind of attention prompted by stills and photographs. This attention resists a film's meanings, but, as Barthes points out, "it compels an interrogative reading."
>
> Assume that Barthes's essay offers a model for a new kind of research derived from photographic logic. Select a single detail from a movie. The detail you choose should resemble those discussed in "The Third Meaning": it should not be obviously symbolic, and the purpose to which you put it should not be the filmmaker's obvious intention. Follow

*this detail wherever it leads and report your findings. Your goal is to propose a new way of understanding the movie you discuss.*

## 1. David Kidd on Fritz Lang's M

If I were to start from the detail which arrests my attention, the *bowler* hats found almost everywhere in M except on the head of the killer, I would first be tempted to regard this costuming as a means of suggesting the underlying resemblance of Schranker (the underworld boss) and Lohmann (the police inspector). But that motivation, too symbolic, doesn't satisfy me. It is the obvious answer, the one offered by Lestrade to Holmes, always wrong.

Let's begin instead with René Magritte's painting *The Menaced Assassin*, a work immediately proposing a series of questions. Is the murderer the hatless man standing beside the phonograph? Or is he the detective who has arrived too late to prevent the crime? Who are the bowler-hatted men, lurking with clubs just outside the door? With no answers forth-

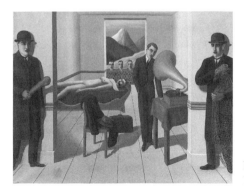

René Magritte
*The Menaced Assassin*

coming, we can conclude only that Magritte's painting represents *Mystery* itself. If Magritte associates this Mystery with bowlers, the hat on the chair seems the most significant. To whom does it belong? An analogy: the menacing figures in bowler hats (Schranker and Lohmann) versus the bareheaded man at the record player (the murderer). (Perhaps he is playing Grieg's "The Hall of the Mountain King.") The three identical men at the window reproduce Lang's treatment of crowds: all rules of differentiation have broken down. In two other paintings, *The Month of the Wine Harvest* and *Golconde,* Magritte extends this repetition to hats: all the identical figures wear bowlers—in Poe's terms, it is "the hat of the crowd." In this sinister world, the *physiologies* no longer obtain: surrounded by sameness, one can no longer distinguish doctor from lawyer, good from evil. Anyone could be the murderer.

If I were to start again, from a still less predictable place, I would call attention to *bowler*'s other meaning, nowhere explicitly evoked by the film. *The Encyclopedia Britannica* reveals that while bowling has existed in almost every culture, bowling *at pins* originated in Germany, specifically as a religious rite: placed at one end of a runway, the pins represented the *Heide* (the "heathen"); knocking them down purged the community of evil and sin.

René Magritte
*The Month of the Wine Harvest*

René Magritte
*Golconde*

In *M*, Schranker's men chase Peter Lorre down *the alleys* of the city where he (one of the *Heide*) must *hide*. *M* portrays a city cleansing itself of its greatest sin. The entire society, both outlaw and official, combines to topple Lorre, thereby driving from its midst one of what the movie's original title called *The Murderers among Us*.

**2. Darryl Palmer on Ernie Gehr's *Eureka*** [an experimental movie that uses optical printing to prolong a single-take, three-minute film, shot from a moving trolley, of San Francisco's Market Street *circa* 1904—in effect, a film version of *S/Z*'s "slow-motion reading" of a found text].

Obtuse meanings often appear as vague, but persistent, visual memories. What we remember of an image is frequently a marginal detail which for some reason has for us a certain undefinable significance. Such details become afterimages which survive as pure signifiers, available to make associations and produce meanings along any number of unpredictable, but signifying, chains. Let me demonstrate this proposition by describing a particularly haunting afterimage from Ernie Gehr's *Eureka*:

a pair of very long, very thin legs walking across a street crowded with trolleys, automobiles, horses, and pedestrians. Off to the side stands a globular-looking policeman with large round buttons on his uniform. This image comes to mind whenever I think of the film. What interests me is that while this afterimage corresponds to no single frame of the movie, it nevertheless contains *exactly* the details I find significant in it.

I can use this detail of a pedestrian's legs to generate the following points about *Eureka:*

1. The extreme slow motion obtained by optical printing enables a viewer to distinguish the motions of each pedestrian as he or she crosses the street. Suddenly gestures matter: they signify an individual personality, and I become aware that the film is a record of the actions of real people, every one of whom is now dead. I am reminded that the Russian word for a film showing, *céanc,* not only sounds like the word *séance,* but also may be etymologically linked to it. Thus, viewers attending a showing of *Eureka* (or any other film, for that matter) are participating in a séance, a communion with the dead.

2. The spidery legs, the indistinct body remind me of Ignatz Mouse, while the policeman recalls Offissa Bull Pup, both characters from *Krazy Kat,* a comic strip whose landscapes constantly change behind the action: a mesa appearing in one frame becomes a cloud or tree in a succeeding one. In *Eureka,* a similar disorientation: along the fixed path of the trolley, the automobiles, bicycles, horsecarts, trolleys, pedestrians are remembered as interchangeable. In both cases, I can establish the boundaries of the frame (a street in *Eureka,* a desert in *Krazy Kat*), but within that space, the landscape is in constant flux.

3. A personal favorite of William Randolph Hearst, *Krazy Kat* began appearing in Hearst Syndicate newspapers around 1910. While the strip was never a popular success, Hearst, taking a personal interest, enlarged it in 1913 to a full-page Sunday feature. Certain potentially ominous parallels exist between this ordered format change and Citizen Kane's promotion of Susan Alexander. Interestingly, in both "Kane" and "Krazy Kat," a "k" has been substituted for the more correct or familiar "c." Further, *Citizen Kane*'s opening, in which the letter "K" on Xanadu's gate figures prominently, involves a series of tracking shots moving in on the lighted window of Kane's bedroom. In terms of camera movement, *Eureka* (again the appearance of the percussive "k") consists of one long tracking shot into the trolley station, where the bright light of the clock

provides a possible goal—one resembling the light in Kane's bedroom window, whose extinction signals his death. In *Eureka,* the clock face disappears as the trolley enters the station's dark archway: light gives way to darkness as the movie reaches the *terminal,* the *end of the line,* the film's death.

4. In my notes, I notice that I accidently refer to my shadowy pedestrian as "Legs Diamond," thereby triggering another set of associations:

—Kane's diamond stickpin, in the shape of the letter "K."

—Diamonds, a precious stone, are mined like the gold at the origin of both Kane's fortune and California's settlement (Eureka was a mining town).

—The discovery of gold provided the 18*k* "carrot" for Manifest Destiny, a persistent movement in one direction imitated by *Eureka's* sustained, unvarying tracking shot.

—We now associate Manifest Destiny with the genocide committed against the Native Americans who sought to impede it. I discover that Eureka, California, was the site of several Indian uprisings between 1853 and 1865.

## Chapter Six

· · · · · · · · · · · · · · · · · ·

## THE ALPHABET

One might call "poetic" (without value judgment) any discourse in which the word leads the idea.

Roland Barthes, in *Roland Barthes*

Because an argument proposing fetishism as a research strategy inevitably requires justification, I devoted most of Chapter 5 to a history of that idea's development, providing by way of "proof" only two brief demonstrations of "third meaning film criticism." This chapter reverses that allocation. With Barthes's autobiography, I assume that examples of a critical practice derived from it will prove more useful than extensive theoretical exposition. *Roland Barthes,* after all, amounts to the apotheosis of its author's embrace of fragmentation and the most explicit acknowledgment of his fetishism.

Barthes's autobiography consists of a series of alphabetized fragments, including at least one for every letter. These fragments are, by turns,

*epigrammatic:*  "*the subject is merely an effect of language*" (p. 79)
"it is a labor of knowledge, not of writing" (p. 74)
"I write maxims . . . *in order to reassure myself*" (p. 179)

*metaphorical:*  "words are shifted, systems communicate, modernity is tried (the way one tries all the push buttons on a radio one doesn't know how to work)" (p. 74)

*anecdotal:*  "The Lacanian subject (for instance) never makes him think of Tokyo; but Tokyo makes him think of the Lacanian subject . . . he rarely starts from the idea in order to invent an image for it subsequently; he starts from a sensuous object, and then hopes to meet in his work with the possibility of finding an *abstraction* for it" (p. 99)

*playful:*   the list of "Projected books" (pp. 149–150)
            the exam questions set as an "Academic exercise" (p. 158)

*lyrical:*   "Different discourse: this August 6, the countryside, the
            morning of a splendid day: sun, warmth, flowers, silence,
            calm, radiance. Nothing stirs, neither desire nor aggression;
            only the task is there, the work before me . . ." (p. 179)

*analytical:*   "Frequently he starts from the stereotype. . . . And it is
            because he does not want that stereotype (by some aesthetic
            or individualist reflex) that he looks for something else. . . .
            The risk is that since the stereotype shifts historically,
            politically, it must be followed wherever it goes: what is to
            be done if the stereotype *goes left?*" (p. 162)

Surprisingly, Barthes developed his book's method to overcome a
writer's block, caused in particular by his confessed inability to "get into
my writing the *enchantment* (pure image) of a seduction" (p. 86). The
advantages of the serial form, with its discrete units compelled by the
alphabet's order, became immediately apparent: it enabled him to write
what "he wants to write *right away,* what it pleases him to write"
(p. 174). Above all, he could avoid the "enormous falling off" which he
had come to associate with "the treatise." In its place, the alphabet's
"euphoria":

> Temptation of the alphabet: to adopt the succession of letters in
> order to link fragments is to fall back on what constitutes the glory
> of language (and what constitutes Saussure's despair): an unmoti-
> vated order . . . which is not arbitrary (since everyone knows it,
> recognizes it, and agrees on it). The alphabet is euphoric: no more
> anguish of "schema," no more rhetoric of "development," no more
> twisted logic, no more dissertations! (p. 147)

Barthes openly admitted that he had found this way of working in
Nietzsche, whose aphoristic books, so perfectly adapted to what Gilles
Deleuze has called "nomad thought," seem structured by a single mode,
the *digression.* As Nietzsche described *The Dawn:*

> A book such as this is not for reading straight through or reading
> aloud but for dipping into, especially when walking on a journey;
> you must be able to stick your head into it and out of it again and
> again and discover nothing familiar round you. (sec. 454)

By casting his thoughts in these alphabetized fragments, Barthes found himself able to achieve an oscillation between anecdote and analysis. In this situation, the slightest pressure applied to even the most everyday incident could generate surprising results:

> *Le temps qu'il fait*—What the weather is doing
> This morning the woman in the bakery said: *It's still lovely, but the heat's lasting too long!* (people around here always feel that it's too lovely, too hot). I add: *And the light is so beautiful!* But the woman does not answer, and once again I notice that short-circuit in language of which the most trivial conversations are the sure occasion; I realize that *seeing the light* relates to a class sensibility; or rather, since there are "picturesque" lights which are certainly enjoyed by the woman in the bakery, what is socially marked is the "vague" view, the view without contours, without object. . . . In short, nothing more cultural than the atmosphere, nothing more ideological than what the weather is doing. (pp. 175–176)

This approach seems ideally suited for film studies. Indeed, it anticipates the notion of cyberspace, which assumes that we are always operating "within information." In the world of Hollywood filmmaking in particular, the strict management of signification makes every object an index, capable of opening at a touch into stores of knowledge. A hat, a street address, the shape of a restaurant's menu—such things make up the fabric of popular movies, and their meaning depends on our knowledge both of what they are and of what they are not. Why does Bogart drink champagne in *Casablanca?* Because everything known about champagne makes it, and not beer, the ideal signifier of cosmopolitan elegance.

Barthes had detected a similar connotative density in prose fiction, where the single cue *the Elysée-Bourbon* could metonymically indicate not only a neighborhood (the Faubourg Saint-Honoré), but also the kind of wealth to be found there (*nouveau* and suspect).[1] Among filmmakers, Godard has best intuited cyberspace's proposition that "every node in a hypermedium is . . . a space of potential information"[2]—think of *Two or Three Things I Know about Her,* where his camera's near-exclusive attention to an ordinary object (a cup of coffee) releases a lyrical meditation about subjectivity's place in the modern world.

Computer software has made this process literal: in hypermedia, touching the screen (at a word, an image, even a marginal detail) activates the information stored there. Despite these developments, however, film criticism has been slow to adopt this method, which, like poetic thinking, regards every object as a potential metaphor. What follows are two experiments with Barthes's alphabetized version of this way of thinking. The first amounts to my response to a journal assignment: *Write an essay about contemporary theory's relationship to concrete poetry, the movement which insisted that a poem's typography should assume an importance equal to its other elements.* After a two-week crash course of reading had left me overwhelmed by information, I decided to try Barthes's serial method. The result, which has primarily to do with the advantages of yielding the initiative to a given form, might appeal to the general reader less interested in the particulars of film studies. The second experiment is about Andy Hardy.

. . . . . . 1. The ABCs of Visual Theory

A    *THE AGATE RULE.*

Constraints Encourage Invention I. The most influential nineteenth-century American newspapers forbade typographical embellishments, requiring all advertising to be set in neat rows of microscopic agate type. James Gordon Bennett, publisher of *The New York Herald,* insisted that this rule forced merchants to concentrate on what was being said rather than how. In fact, the agate rule prompted attention to typesetting's possibilities. Robert Bonner, owner of the competing *New York Ledger,* proved the most inventive, exploring (long before Warhol) the effects of repetition by reproducing a single ad for seven full six-columned pages. Bonner also used the combination of strategically placed capital letters and the *Herald*'s columns to create highly visible acrostics spelling out L-E-D-G-E-R. Ironically, the typographically austere Bennett was given to massive publicity stunts, like his reporter Henry Stanley's expedition to find the "lost" English missionary David Livingstone. Stanley's trip furthered the mapping of Africa, the filling in of spaces previously blank.

*APOLLINAIRE.*

Apollinaire's Calligrammes were certainly not the first, but remain the most famous examples of concrete poetry. More important, he saw how advertising would reorganize the relationship between language and typography. This insight began as a scandalous intuition of advertising's beauty: "You read prospectuses, catalogues, and posters which shout aloud / Here is poetry this morning and for prose there are the newspapers" ("Zone," 1913). Its subsequent formulation made his point more explicitly: "Our intelligence must get used to understanding synthetically and ideographically instead of analytically and discursively." By rapidly juxtaposing images of religion, business, and politics, his poetry effectively identified the twentieth century's three systems of social organization, each of which has generated a form crucial to the emergence of typography: the gloss, advertising, and propaganda.

B    *BOREDOM.*
Although writing and reading are conducted under the aegis of communication, both in fact are shadowed by the threat of boredom. Writers procrastinate because of the tedium involved in expressing plainly what occurred to them suddenly. They also must work to forestall the reader's *ennui,* anticipating it, heading it off, knowing that at any moment, the book (or magazine, or newspaper, or journal) may be closed. As children gradually move from books with only pictures to books with only type, boredom's menace increases. For several generations of Americans, the transition was the Hardy Boys series, a jumping-off place for forays into uncharted regions of pure type. These books contained only a single image, a drawing appearing as a frontispiece, but illustrating a crucial incident occurring far into the story. For young readers, this picture was an oasis, something to look forward to while trekking through the terrifyingly unillustrated pages: it sustained hope, and like a magnet, pulled readers through what might otherwise have been put aside. For adults, chapter breaks assume the same role: resting places where one can let down attention.

*BARTHES.*
Of all contemporary theorists, he was most haunted by what he called "panic boredom." He read less than other academics, but wrote more. Increasingly, he produced books that, by avoiding long stretches of unbroken type, responded to his own repudiation of the dissertation. His late work's apparent heterogeneity conceals a persistent effort to introduce typographic inventiveness. *S/Z, Roland Barthes, A Lover's Discourse, The Empire of Signs* all look strange: they contain italicized type, Roman type, words printed in all caps, numbered fragments, starred

paragraphs, marginal gloss, maps, photos, samples of handwriting, and so forth. The unparagraphed, conventionally punctuated page of type comes to seem, by its willed absence, its forced repression, a figure of death.

### BRECHT.

Like Barthes, he knew that pleasure and attentiveness were related. "From the first," he wrote in 1949, "it has been the theatre's business to entertain people, as it also has of all the other arts. It is this business which always gives it its particular dignity; it needs no other passport than fun, but this it has got to have" ("A Short Organum for the Theatre"). Working in the theater, he confronted a situation the exact reverse of the book: the spell of the uninterrupted tableaux enchanted, fostering not boredom but uncritical identification. As a solution, he introduced print (in titles preceding individual scenes), thereby replacing representation with formulation. Godard, by the time of his third feature film, *Une femme est une femme* (1961), had adopted the same tactic. As his hero and heroine argue, a series of comments appear on the screen:

> Emile takes Angela at her word because he loves her
> Angela lets herself be caught in the trap because she loves him
> Because they love each other, everything will go wrong for Emile and Angela
> They have made the mistake of thinking they can go too far
> Because their love is so mutual and eternal.

### C    CINEMA.

As a return to pictorial narrative, cinema inevitably redressed the modern ascendancy of print. Like books, movies marginalize the excluded mode, assigning it to fixed positions: while books often herd illustrations together into one or more special sections, commercial filmmaking restricts writing's appearance to the credits and an occasional establishing shot ("San Francisco," proclaims the overlay at the beginning of *The Maltese Falcon,* just in case the Bay is unfamiliar). More significantly, cinema popularizes collage, repeatedly demonstrating modern technology's limitless capacity to redistribute and recombine its representations. Indeed, although Hollywood moviemaking minimizes collage, its dominant form (montage) is the special case, achievable only by strictly adhering to a carefully policed continuity grammar, designed precisely to overcome the cinema's inherent capacity for spatial and temporal discontinuity. Retroactively, therefore, film exposes the mobility of print, its broken relationship with referent, author, and "original" context: the typesetter becomes the continuity girl, charged with controlling the letter's potential scattering.

### CONSTRUCTIVISM.

Of the early twentieth-century avant-gardes, the Constructivists displayed by far the most interest in typography, concerning themselves with posters, bookmaking, parade decorations, banners, films, and cartoons—all reconceived not only as forms of mass communication and Agitprop, but also as "art-objects." "Engineers create new forms," proclaimed the banner draped over Tatlin's famous Model for the Monument to the Third International, and the Constructivist redefinition of the artist-as-engineer expressed itself in an enthusiasm for technology. "His poems weren't spoken," Blaise Cendrars said of Mayakovsky, "his poems weren't written, they were designed." In "How to Make Verses," Mayakovsky himself encouraged poets to treat their work as film montage, by utilizing typographical experimentation to create a printed *mise-en-scène.*

### D    DANDYISM.

With its provocative manner, attention to surfaces (newly labeled "the signifier"), aestheticized disposition, and oppositional hedonism, post-structuralism can be understood as a later manifestation of dandyism, which as Baudelaire observed, "appears above all in periods of transition." Barthes, in particular, is the dandy *par excellence,* finally making explicit in autobiography and interviews his own chronic need for the new. "In a given historical situation—of pessimism and rejection—it is the intellectual class as a whole which, if it does not become militant, is virtually a dandy" (*Roland Barthes,* p. 106). Dandyism represents opposition *tout court;* while it may be enlisted by both left and right, it remains apolitical, characterizable only as profoundly undemocratic. Its target is always mass taste and that constituency's principal tool, assimilation. Thus in the late twentieth century, with books, newspapers, and magazines long established, dandyism flaunts alternate typographics: *Glas*'s two columns, *A Lover's Discourse*'s marginalia. In the mid-nineteenth century, by contrast, with mass printing still in its adolescence,

Baudelaire, surrounded by painters, restricted his costume to the most severe blacks, thereby making himself an icon of what still seemed radical: the rigor of print.

E    *ELECTRICITY.*

What happens when "alphabetic man" becomes "electrical man"? Will induction and deduction, made possible by writing (as Havelock, Ong, and Goody have shown), give way to conduction, thinking as a kind of transportation? In his preface to *Un Coup de Dés,* Mallarmé invoked precisely this metaphor, referring to his own sprinkled words whose appearance on the page anticipated the computer screen:

> [The poem is] without novelty except for the spacing out of the reading. The "whites" indeed take on an importance, are striking at first sight; ordinarily versification required them around like silence, to the extent that a lyrical piece or one of few feet occupies about a third of the leaf in the middle; I do not transgress this measure, only disperse it. The paper intervenes each time an image, of its own accord, ceases or withdraws, accepting the succession of others, and, as it is not a question, as it always is, of regular sonorous strokes or lines of verse rather, of prismatic subdivisions of the Idea, for the moment of their appearance and while their co-operation in some spiritual setting lasts, for reasons of verisimilitude it is in variable positions to, or far from, the latent *conductor wire* that the text asserts itself. (emphasis added)

*EPIGRAPHS.*

New techniques repressed by a culture often appear first in less well guarded marginal zones. Because it is regarded as less serious and its experiments less consequential, art thus moves more quickly than science. The university, on the other hand, perhaps because of its own responsible self-image, remains intransigently resistant to developments rapidly assimilated by the rest of society. Thus, while MTV, advertising, TV news, and pop music (especially rap and disco) have long since appropriated the collage aesthetic generated nearly a century ago by Cubism, most academic writing adheres to nineteenth-century discursive practices. In the last decade, however, the epigraph has flowered among even the most conservative critics. As quotations mount up at articles' beginnings and section breaks, collage juxtaposition begins to sneak in. When the chosen quotations, shining with the particular brightness of unmounted stones, begin to overwhelm the pallid texts they introduce, conventional dissertations have begun to undermine themselves. Epigraphing is the Trojan Horse of the traditional essay.

F    *FOOTNOTE.*
Dedication, acknowledgments, preface, table of contents, chapter headings, epigraphs, footnotes, appendices, bibliography, index—the paraphernalia of the text. What happens to writing when these assume greater importance? Historically, the attending apparatus increased in direct proportion to a text's sacralization, with the Bible prompting the most material. Only recently have secular writings (other than Greek and Latin works and a handful of classic authors like Shakespeare) seemed entitled to the massive annotation. At first, only "primary" writing (that is, literature) appeared worthy of it. Now, however, it gathers around even nonfiction, signaling its "prestige." For example, the University of Minnesota's Theory and History of Literature series typically aggrandizes its chosen texts with introductions and footnotes nearly equaling the works' own length: Peter Burger's slim 105-page *Theory of the Avant-Garde* comes equipped with 77 complete pages of foreword, notes, bibliography, and index. Barthes's *S/Z* parodies the accumulation of textual apparatus while also citing every word of *Sarrasine* at least twice. It violates one of commentary's last modesties, that while an analysis of a poem may exceed its object, an analysis of a novel should not. In its length alone, *S/Z* thus becomes a prophetic work, pointing toward something beyond even Borges's reviews of imaginary books: footnotes to unwritten texts.

*FRAKTUR.*
Typography-as-Ideology. The Nazi resurrection of Fraktur type, illegible, but prized for its "German-ness," symbolizes a totalitarian politics that encouraged attention to style rather than content. (The concluding lines to Benjamin's "The Work of Art in the Age of Mechanical Reproduction": "This is the situation of politics which Fascism is rendering aesthetic. Communism responds by politicizing art.") Just as Hitler's oratorical manner (and nighttime settings) distracted audiences from his message, Fraktur conveyed only a vaguely authentic folkishness. Almost never used to communicate important information, it was suppressed by the

German military and intelligence services in their own work. When early victories encouraged them to look beyond Germany's borders, the Nazis, quickly recognizing the usefulness of a plainer, more "European" style, banned Fraktur on January 3, 1941, as a "Jewish invention."

G    *GLOSS.*

While it begins as a gesture of reverence toward prized texts either sacred (the Scriptures) or secular (*The Aeneid),* glossing inevitably undermines the authority of the works it purports to serve. At first the treachery is graphic: the swelling commentary, appearing in the margins or even between the lines, crowds the object text and renders it increasingly illegible. More important, by demonstrating not only the possibility but the necessity of interpretation, glossing shifts attention from the revered work's silent decisiveness to its mute ambiguity. Inevitably, some Church leaders at the Council of Trent called for the suppression of the Bible itself, which was to be encountered only through approved commentaries. What would a civilization be like in which all primary texts had disappeared and only their glosses remained? This science fiction donnée in fact constitutes the working premise of psychoanalysis, which seeks to recover lost incidents inferable only from the patient's retroactive interpretations.

H    *HUMUMENT.*

Subtitled "A Treated Victorian Novel," Tom Phillips's book finds new narratives, fragments, dialogues, lyrics, and meditations by painting over (to leave only certain words exposed) W. H. Mallock's 1892 *A Human Document.* On the first page, Phillips, primarily a painter, leaves legible, scattered across Mallock's page where they happened to appear in entirely other syntaxes, these words: "The following sing I a book, a book of art of mind art and that which he hid reveal I." An allegory of every present's relationship to its past, which it rearranges, screens through the palimpsest of accumulated interpretations, memories, stories, amnesia, ideological revisions. For many people, what is Shakespeare now but a phrase ("To be or not to be") whose context has receded? The present as a treated book, read for purposes other than its author(s) intended.

I    *IDENTITY.*

Postmodernism's founding problem involves the copy, increasingly available from the modern technology that begins with print. Borges's Pierre

Menard reproduces portions of the *Quixote,* Duchamp signs a urinal identical to one found in a bathroom. Warhol issues Campbell's Soup cans, rap producers make "new" songs from sampled extracts of recognizable hits. Benjamin's "The Work of Art in the Age of Mechanical Reproduction" remains the most profound discussion of this development; poststructuralism, with its faith in citation, has only started to implement its ideas.

*INDEX.*
As Jack Goody has pointed out, certain written devices like the index and the list enable a kind of thinking impossible for a purely oral culture. Ironically, our own indexes do not always correspond to our most "advanced" knowledge. In structuralist books, for example, that boldly announce the death of the author, all but the most conscientiously produced indexes remained organized around not concepts, but proper names.

J    *JOURNAL OF TYPOGRAPHIC RESEARCH.*
Constraints Encourage Invention II. What would an article for a journal be like if it restricted its sources to work previously published in the same place? Some candidates from *Visible Language:* Typography without Words   Patterned Note-Taking: An Evaluation   Readable/Writable/Visible   One Second of Reading   Why Duchamp Loved Words   The Typography of El Lissitzky   At the Edge of Meaning   The Typographic Element in Cubism, 1911–1915   "No," says the signified: The "Logical Status" of Words in Painting   Biblioclasm: Derrida and His Precursors   Typography: Evolution = Revolution   Visible Language in Contemporary Culture   One Hundred Essential Sight Words   The Effects of Changes in Layout and Changes in Wording on Preferences for Instructional Text   The Changing Responsibilities of the Typographic Designer   Selected Theoretical Texts from Letterists   Poetry as a Means for the Structuring of a Social Environment   How Typewriters Changed Correspondence   Communication Theory and Typographic Research   The Future for Books in the Electronic Era   The Development of Visual Poetry in France   The Visual Editing of Texts.

Each of these titles seems at once optional and necessary: how can any one be eliminated? How can any article use them all? (*Roland Barthes,* p. 100: "Not to have read Hegel would be an exorbitant defect for a philosophy teacher, for a Marxist intellectual, for a Bataille specialist. But for me? Where do my reading duties begin?") The information explosion demands a shift from coverage to concept formation. What would happen if for one year, a journal required its authors to cite only from work published there? A forced economy, a moratorium on "new" ideas, an experiment in ecological recycling and combination?

*ST. JEROME.*
Simultaneously translating the Bible (into Latin) and inventing a punctuation system, he anticipated found poetry by breaking the given text into reading units, each lasting as long as either its sense or the imaginary reader's breath. This method is called stichometry, and strung out on a page, the resulting *weave* (one of Barthes's metaphors for writing) evokes that word's etymology: stitching. Fourteen centuries later, in the second half of the 1800s, American publicity changed profoundly with the introduction of lavishly illustrated, carefully designed newspaper ads created by the makers of sewing machines.

K    *KANJI.*
Saussurian linguistics insisted on each language's completion, its adequacy to its users' needs. Thus, even languages with much smaller vocabularies than English are regarded as no less finished, just as a game with only four possible moves is not defined as a stunted version of chess. No insight proved more central to the structuralist project, best exemplified by Lévi-Strauss's critique of "primitivism" as an ideological tool. What can we make, however, of a writing system whose hybrid difficulty seems to inhibit its users? As Edwin Reischauer argues, the Japanese had "the bad luck" to discover first a writing system (Chinese ideograms, called kanji in Japanese) designed for the exact opposite of their own highly inflected language. The result is the contemporary compromise: four writing systems, used interchangeably, often intertwined in a single text—kanji, the English alphabet, katakana (a phoneticized syllabic script), and hiragana (used primarily for grammatical distinctions). For Barthes (see *The Empire of Signs*), a lucky accident that continuously calls attention to the materiality, the elegance of the signifier, and thus the founding principle of Japanese civilization.

L    *LOUIE, LOUIE.*
The Kingsmen's 1963 hit version depended enormously on the evasion of printing. By not reproducing the lyrics on either the single or the album cover, the group ensured that a confused but imaginative listener

would hear as vaguely salacious what in fact was a clumsy attempt to imitate calypso's pidgin English ("Me catch the ship across the sea"). In doing so, the band had intuited a classic strategy of all intellectual vanguards: the use of tantalizing mystification. Lacan's "Imaginary" and "Symbolic," "the mirror stage," "The unconscious is structured like a language"; Derrida's "deconstruction," "grammatology," "différance," "There is no outside the text," and so forth—these terms and phrases, while committed to writing, remained elusive, inchoate, quasi-oral charms. As such they enticed, beckoned, fostered work. Lacan explicitly pointed to the paradox: at one moment in his year-long seminar on "The Purloined Letter," knowing full well that almost no one in the enormous lecture hall had actually read Poe's story (since by that time Lacan himself had become a celebrity, provoking curiosity among many people who had little interest in his subject matter), he turned and addressed his audience:

> We find ourselves before this singular contradiction—I don't know if it should be called dialectical—that the less you understand the better you listen. For I often say to you very difficult things, and I see you hanging on my every word, and I learn later that you did not understand. On the other hand, when one tells you simple things, almost too familiar, you are less attentive. I just make this remark in passing, which has its interest like any concrete observation. I leave it for your mediation.

**M/N**  MIDDLE? NO.

With its even number of letters, the 26-character Roman alphabet, the central organizing system of Western civilization, has itself no center. A sign of secularization? Significantly, most ancient alphabets afforded other possible calculations: the Phoenician (19 characters), old Hebrew (19), early Greek (21), and Etruscan (17). The modern writing systems, on the other hand, progenitors of philosophy, are centerless: classical Greek (20), early Latin (20), Arabic (28). In *The Empire of Signs*, Barthes points to the uneasiness engendered by quadrangular, centerless cities like Los Angeles and to the paradox of Tokyo: a metropolis organized around a center (the Emperor's palace) which remains forbidden, surrounded by walls and trees, openly imaginary.

Lest the reader think that this entry represents an evasion, a failure to come up with appropriate entries for **M** and **N** by themselves, the following adumbrations must suffice: *Morris, William:* (his typographic experiments, his belief that a beautiful house and a beautiful book are the most important goals of art, his furthering of the traditional connection between radicalism and printing). *Mr. Mxyzptlk:* (Superman's nemesis, a parody of the similarly consonantless name of God, JHVH). *Manifestos:* (Futurist/Constructivist manifestos as typographic pioneering, poststructuralist writing as assuming manifesto forms: hyperbole, volatility, graphic experimentation). *Memory:* (analogized both to writing, as in Freud's "mystic writing pad," and to its opposite, as in the ancient mnemonic of memory palaces that associated items to be remembered with images). *Navajo:* (the rare language used by American marines for radio broadcast in the South Pacific; known by fewer than two dozen non-Navajos, it avoided the need for further encoding; the Japanese never deciphered it). *Naming:* (Derrida's "signature effect," used as a research procedure in *Glas* and *Signsponge*). *Notation:* (musical versus written—their adequacy to oral forms of jazz and regional dialects).

O    *OULIPO.*

C nstraints Enc urage Inventi n III. Oulipo: an acronym for Ouvroir de Littérature Potentielle (Workshop for Potential Literature), a group founded in 1960 by Raymond Queneau and François Le Lionnais. Oulipo writers (among them Italo Calvino) insisted on the bankruptcy of traditional modes and experimented with fantastically rigorous generative devices which, according to Le Lionnais's first Manifesto, stimulated invention and discovery. Queneau also explained:

> What is the objective of our work? To propose new "structures" to writers, mathematical in nature, or to invent new artificial or mechanical procedures that will contribute to literary activity?—props for inspiration as it were, or rather in a way, aids for creativity.

The N + 7 composition method replaces every noun in a given text with the seventh noun occurring after it in a dictionary. With multiple-choice plots (fully developed by Calvino's *If on a winter's night a traveler*), the reader chooses at every fork which path to pursue: instructed at one juncture, "if you wish to know the rest, go to 20," he follows directions only to learn that "There is no rest and the story is finished." The most notorious Oulipo device, the Lipogram, which requires composition to

avoid one or more letters, resulted in the supreme example of Georges
Perec's *La Disparition,* a long novel deprived of the letter *e,* the fulfillment
of Borges's "prodigious idea of a book wholly impervious to chance."
More than simply a late version of Surrealism, Oulipo represents a
remotivation of traditional mysticism's obsession with the mathematics
of the alphabet. The Oulipo writers were not cabalists; they did not
expect their methods to reveal the universe's hidden truths. With them,
pseudo-science became practical aesthetics, a way of getting started, a
serious game without metaphysical consequences. Similarly, Derrida's
puns and coincidental etymologies serve only as sifting devices, vehicles
for filtering the massive wash of information for traces of possible
knowledge, a prospecting tool designed to locate that hidden region
where two apparently discrete discourses share a common vocabulary:
"Genet" as poet's name/"genet" as wildflower leads to "the flowers of
rhetoric" and botany *(Glas);* the single word "race" is discovered to connect
the problems of racism and the arms race ("No Apocalypse, Not Now").

P       *POSTERS.*
Of rock's three revolutionary moments (Elvis: 1954–1956; The Beatles:
1962–1964; and Punk: 1976–1978), each of which spawned hordes of
amateur garage bands, only the last occurred after the general dissemi-
nation of cheap photocopying. The poster advertising made possible by
this technology characteristically depended on a Warholian bricolage of
appropriated images and letters. For the bands who intuited the Constructivist lesson that revolutions must advertise, postermaking served
one vital function: it enabled musicians to play primarily original songs,
something that the two previous waves had not dared. Further, by calling
for skills normally developed in the visual arts, the new possibilities for
self-promotion attracted art students away from their traditional alliance
with literature into a new partnership with music. With every band
having its own graphic designer (in charge of posters, record covers, and
fliers), New Wave rock music achieved a postmodern *Gesamtkunstwerk.*

*PAYSAN DE PARIS.*
Aragon's surrealist memoir inspired Benjamin's *Arcades Project.* At first
glance, it seems tame by today's standards, but the sudden intrusion of
typographical difference, in the menus and wine lists and wall posters
inserted into the narrative, call attention to the book's frame, thereby

anticipating Derrida's interest in "margins" of every sort. Significantly, from the 55 woodblocks of Hiroshige's Tokaido, a child selects the one in which a snow-covered mountain breaks through the upper border.

Q    *QUESTIONNAIRE.*
Often used as a marketing tool, it could have flourished only in an age of commerce. Its success, however, depends on its being an exception to mass media's normal one-way communication. Appearing amidst sheets of uninterrupted print, the questionnaire's open spaces solicit a reader by providing a space for his reply, and by restricting its length (thereby eliminating the principal cause of writer's block, the purely blank page). It follows that all texts laid out with expansive margins seem friendly; they invite an exchange by opening the text to conversation: marginal questions, notes, objections. They convert reading and writing into a serious game, like the one Proust played with his friends: "Where would you like to live?" "Who is your favorite painter?" "What for you is the definition of happiness?"

R    *ROCHEFORT, JOSEPH.*
In February 1918, William F. Friedman, director of the U.S. Army's cryptography school, posed for a graduation picture with his students and colleagues, whom he had arranged into a cipher spelling out Bacon's aphorism "Knowledge is power." Coming up short by four people (in a system using heads facing front or sideways), Friedman had to stand in himself for the letter R. In 1920, Friedman published *Index of Coincidence and Its Applications in Cryptography,* called the most important book in the field's history; just before World War II, he managed to break the Japanese diplomatic code (Purple) produced by the J Machine or Alphabetical Typewriter. After Pearl Harbor, Friedman's missing four men and letter R appeared in a four-man team led by Rochefort, whose cracking of the Japanese naval cipher enabled the United States' victory at Midway, the decisive naval battle of the Pacific War. If, as anthropologist Dan Sperber has suggested, some ideas spread epidemically (they are "catching"), the success of semiotics derives from its adoption of the vocabulary of cryptography (Greek for "hidden writing"): encoding, decoding, message. A childhood fascination persisting into adulthood (where they appear principally in mystery and spy novels), codes and ciphers are the alphabetic equivalents of the fantasy of invisibility, of

power without responsibility, of escape from the censor. From the child's viewpoint, all writing represents an impenetrable code; acquiring literacy, he learns a system simultaneously efficient and useless, since it arrives "broken" and widely distributed. Only by becoming a cryptographer, or an avant-gardist working in not-yet-readerly codes, can the adult assume the status he had envied as a child. Hence, too, the appeal of jargon, which allows initiates to communicate to what Stendhal called "the happy few."

*RASÉ.*

By writing the notorious letters "L.H.O.O.Q." below a reproduction of the *Mona Lisa,* Duchamp confirmed Sontag's and Barthes's point that a caption is worth a thousand pictures: from a theoretical perspective, the added goatee was merely superfluous naughtiness. When, however, he subsequently issued an untouched postcard of the Mona Lisa, modified by only the single word *Rasé* ("shaved"), Duchamp managed something more radical: with the sequence of readymades, he effectively assumed ownership of Leonardo's image itself.

S  *S/Z.*

At the exact midpoint of his book about Balzac's Sarrasine and la Zambinella, Barthes pauses to examine the S which not only begins the hero's name, but also replaces its usual Z (*Sarrazine* = the conventional French spelling). Z as the "letter of mutilation," "an oblique and illicit blade" that "cuts, slashes" and appears in Balzac's name = "the initial of castration," the "geographical inversion" of S's curves. This Oulipoian moment represents Barthes's shift from structuralism's dream of exposing the hidden signified to the poststructuralist method of following the obvious signifier, a move initiated (and then aborted) by Saussure's investigation of the anagrams he found in Latin poetry. The premise: that language knows something: hence Derrida's essays generated by etymologies and puns, the traces left by meaning's adventures.

T  *TECHNOLOGY.*

As civilization's founding technology, writing inevitably attracted civilization's recurring objection: technology makes things too easy. Writing (as Plato argued) obviates memory. Similarly, photography evades the demands of painting, and the microphone those of the unamplified concert hall. In particular, twentieth-century technologies (film, video, audio recording) eliminate the need for the consecutive complete performance, replacing it as working unit with the "take," the fragment achievable at any point in the piece's making. Poststructuralism's embrace of the fragment, its preference for writing that can be taken up and stopped at different places, represents the equivalent of a recording studio's creation-by-tracks. Just as contemporary music never requires the presence of the whole band, contemporary writing no longer needs the single, elaborated thesis.

U    *UTOPIA.*
The coincidence of More's work with the first great innovations in printing and papermaking is telling. As a topos, "utopia" has always been rhetorical, the very word an effect of homophony: "utopia," Greek for "no-place," is pronounced the same as "eutopia," "good place." Utopians, therefore, have always been bookish, writing what could not yet be realized. Many have gravitated toward alphabetic, typographic, and spelling reforms: from More's Humanist Circle's Utopian Alphabet to Morris's Kelmscott Press to Shaw's new rules for English spelling, utopians have necessarily attended to the only medium in which their work exists. See Barthes on Fourier.

*THE UNCONSCIOUS.*
By positing the unconscious as behavior's prime cause, Freud furthered the "hermeneutics of suspicion" begun by Marx and Nietzsche. This symptomatic reading strategy regards all discourse as a code whose explicit meanings serve only as decoys. Barthes, Derrida, Foucault, Lacan, Althusser, Lévi-Strauss all practice symptomatic reading, looking for what apparently straightforward languages consciously or unconsciously repress. Freud's unconscious is a rebus, a site for the layering and mingling of words, images, and behavior: the Wolf Man's butterfly with yellow stripes switches homonymically from a pear with similar coloring (a "grusha") to a nursery maid with the same name who, by opening her legs, repeats both the movement of the butterfly's wings and the shape of the Roman V, the hour of the patient's chronic depression.

V    *VERTOV, DZIGA.*
The most important Constructivist filmmaker; his significance for contemporary theory's typographical experiments could well derive from a

single diary entry, dated April 1, 1941: "What conditions will guarantee success? Everything except the boring."

**W**   *WALL STREET JOURNAL, THE.*
By eschewing all illustrations (except graphs and sketched portraits) and by holding its advertisers to standardized forms (especially in the prominent notices of security issues, properly called "Tombstones"), it intends to convey high seriousness, a commitment to meaning. It shares this strategy with *U.S. News and World Report,* whose ads once showed famous models testifying to their preference for a magazine that has "no fashion, no flair, no style." Barthes once diagnosed this repudiation of art:

> On the one side the "thought," object of the message, element of knowledge, transitive or critical force; on the other the "style," ornament, province of luxury and leisure and thus futility; to separate the thought from the style is in some sort to relieve the discourse of its sacerdotal robes, to secularize the message.

*WHIMSEYS.*
A nineteenth-century parlor game that made poems (sometimes with rhymes and regular metric schemes) out of given texts, especially the Bible, but also Dickens). Thus, from *The Wall Street Journal:*

> John Mulhern, the arbitrager,
> Arrested for allegedly
> Threatening the life of former
> Takeover speculator Ivan F.
> Boesky, again agreed to the
> Government's deadline
> For obtaining an indictment.

Or, one more modern, *à la* William Carlos Williams:

> McGraw-Hill
>         surged 4½ to 68
> amid speculation
>         that a restructuring
> is in the works.

There were rumors
        circulating inside
    the company
that it would spin off
      all
    its
    operations
except
       *Business Week*
magazine

**X**    *X-ING A PARAGRAB.*

The structure of writing is the structure of crime and its detection. A deed is committed, followed by a delay: a reader appears to decode the mysterious marks left behind as a *memento mori*. Hence the inevitable association of the letter *X* with the mystery story. As the simplest letter to make, the mark of the child or the illiterate, it stands for all the others. More important, as the universal mark of cancellation, it represents alphabetic culture's murder of the author, and the resulting liberation of his words. One of Poe's strangest stories, "X-ing a Paragrab," implies a literal version of death-by-the-letter-*X*. Engaged in a competitive newspaper war, an editor is accused by his rival of excessive reliance on the letter *O*. He takes the bait and composes a long editorial using as many *O*s as possible. ("So ho, John! Told you so, you know. . . . Go home to your woods, old owl,—go! You won't? Oh, poh, poh, John, don't do so! You've *got* to go, you know!") Running out of *O*s, the typesetter makes the customary substitution for missing letters: "Sx hx, Jxhn! hxw nxw! Txld yxu sx, yxu knxw." The next morning, the town erupts in a furor, but the editorial's author, without explanation, has vanished, never to be seen again.

**Y**    *YAK.*

What do the following have in common: yak, vole, x-ray fish, ibis, umbrella bird, and newt? Answer: they exist almost entirely to accommodate children's alphabet books. (I except the perennials, the zebra and koala bear, which seem to have independent existence outside of such schema.) If the yak did not exist, would we have to invent it for the sake of alphabetic completion? To what extent does an alphabet cause objects, events, behavior, to come into being? If the letter *Q* exists, do we have to use it? Typographical Playfulness Leading to Scientific Truth I: a nonsense line from *Finnegans Wake,* "three quarks for Muster Mark," leads to a definition crucial to contemporary physics. Oddly, no actual quarks have ever been observed; "quark" in colloquial German means "nothing."

Z    *ZETTEL'S TRAUM.*

The novel-as-typescript, 1,334 pages, atlas size. Like *Ulysses,* Arno Schmidt's novel takes place during a midsummer day, but reduces Joyce's scope to four characters discussing Edgar Allan Poe. *Zettel* = the German translation of Shakespeare's Bottom (*A Midsummer Night's Dream,* the Schlegel version); the anatomical bottom = the German *Po. Zettel* also = the slips of paper on which Schmidt composed, in fragmentary fashion, his novels. *Zettel's Traum* resembles the Rosetta Stone: impenetrable, promising, demoralizing. With its footnotes, glosses, corrections, interlinear additions, multiple columns, drawings, maps, and so on, it seems intent on reproducing civilization's complete repertoire of graphic effects. Schmidt worked as a mapmaker, and his many essays and novels include a biographical study of Fouqué, the nineteenth-century French geologist who produced rocks and minerals artificially. Schmidt as alchemist, intent on using typography to transform the blank page into an image of the mind at work.

. . . . . . 2. The ABCs of Andy Hardy

> *Note:* In producing this set of fragments, I have frequently relied on the unpublished work of two University of Florida graduate students, Lesley Gamble and William C. Stephenson, whose brilliant experiments with Barthes's alphabetized form have stimulated my thinking about the Hardy movies. Sections entirely the product of one of these students I have labeled with the relevant name. With others, the results of my own expansions, rewritings, and modifications of their thoughts, I have affixed the contributor's (or collaborator's) initials.

A    *AUNT DORA.*

At the heart of the Andy Hardy series, the family drama described by Freud: the Oedipal Crisis, the assumption of gender roles, the accession to the Symbolic realm of language and custom (Lacan's Law of the Father). Hence the movies' obsession with defining "manhood" and "the woman's place" in terms whose slippage has stranded the plots depending on them. Contemporary culture has hardly abandoned such constructions; it simply no longer shares those of the Hardy world, themselves resting on an unsteady base: the Hardy characters appeared first in a 1925 play with the prophetic title *Skidding,* Lacan's term for the permanent instability of the signifier/signified relationship and for the neurosis's tendency to *slide* from symptom to symptom. Secure at home, the family roles break down away from Carvel in a pandemonium of sexual reversals and skids: in *Out West with the Hardys,* a daughter named Jake openly sabotages her father's prospective remarriage, Emily kisses her children on the mouth, Andy cries out "I want my Momma," and the children refer to their father's former girlfriend (who appears far younger than the Judge) as "Aunt Dora," thereby evoking Freud's most famous patient. Reversing Lacan's orderly assignment of signifier to signified,

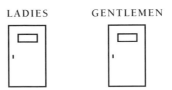

Jake puts the sugar in the salt jar and the salt in the sugar jar; she shoots, rides, tracks, and wisecracks better than Andy. Her last-minute repudiation of her own superiority (and her acceptance of "the woman's place") is *pro forma.* As Godard's heroine says in *Two or Three Things I Know about Her,* "In this room there is blue, red, and green. Yes, I'm sure of it. My sweater is blue. . . . Because I see that it's blue. And what if one had made a mistake from the beginning and called blue green? That would be serious."

*ANECDOTE.*

Here is a story: Late in the battle of Stalingrad, with the German army completely surrounded and facing extinction, an officer is selected to fly back to Berlin to plead for reinforcements or evacuation. Having endured months in "the pocket," the circle contracted daily by Russian offensives, the messenger represents a last chance to impress Hitler and the High Command with the situation's hopelessness. Arriving home in Berlin, he is wined and dined by friends and officers, reassured about the Stalingrad army's prospects, and treated as a hero. Hitler awards him a medal. He eats and drinks some more, sleeps in his own bed, feels comfortable for the first time in months. Gradually, day by day, hour by hour, he loses track of his reason for being in Berlin. Only on his return, over "the pocket," whose ring of devastation now stretches as far as his eyes can see, does he realize that he has failed his mission. He vows never again to allow a change of context to deter him from a duty, a promise he subsequently keeps.

As told by Alexander Kluge (in *The Battle*), this anecdote functions as an allegory of the larger concern: the irrationality of behavior. How, Kluge asks, can we account for the German invasion of Russia? How were several hundred thousand men moved to march across the border into the Russian winter, when history had conclusively demonstrated the folly of this move? No logical assessment can do justice to this behavior, which rests on myths mobilized to convince without logic. Thus, any analysis of the invasion that rests wholly on objective study will only fail. The anecdote becomes a representational tactic, a maneuver, designed to outflank the defenses embedded in all apparently irrational behavior. What anecdote can defend against the power of the movies?

B    *BOYS AND GIRLS.*

> *The Story of a Bad Boy* (Thomas Bailey Aldrich)
> "The Story of the Bad Little Boy"/"The Story of the Good Little
>     Boy" (Mark Twain)
> Huck Finn and Tom Sawyer
> Peck's Bad Boy
> *Little Women*

Horatio Alger
Penrod
*Ah, Wilderness!*
The Hardy Boys
Nancy Drew
Andy Hardy
Henry Aldrich
*Meet Me in St. Louis*
*It's a Wonderful Life* (George Bailey)
*Rebel without a Cause*
*Blackboard Jungle*
*American Graffiti*
*The Breakfast Club*

C    *CARVEL AS MANA.*
Rouverol's *Skidding* specifies Carvel as "a certain town in Idaho." What advantages accrue from the movies' negligence about locating the town in any state or region—a negligence so persistent that we must infer its opposite? Amidst the particulars of the Hardy house, the main street, the courtroom, the high school, the Benedict "mansion" (equipped with a butler, but set close enough to the street to disturb routine semiotic classification), a certain vagueness prevails. Carvel is a subject without a single predicate, and thus *available* for use by the spectator; like the shaman's *mana,* in Lévi-Strauss's analysis, the town functions as an empty constellation of signs which enable projection: each viewer fills in his own details, completing what in this case, MGM's sets, are literally facades.

*CRASH!*
From the interior of the Hardy series, images emerge, perceptible in the odd pulse of a laser disc's scan:

a hand reaches stealthily for a light switch
a couple stares anxiously through a rain-smeared windshield
a father spins out of control in a dilapidated car swept by a
    cloudburst, a windshield-wiper broken off in his hand
a woman turns a corner in a darkened hall.

In the films themselves, nothing will come of these possibilities, these hints of other, more disturbing narrative paths. Betsy Booth will turn on the jalopy's lights merely to announce her entrance *(Love Finds)*; Andy and Marion will reach home safely and find their mother recovered *(Judge Hardy and Son)*; both the Judge and Andy's car will survive this slapstick crash *(Private Secretary)*; and Emily will encourage her son to graduate after all *(Private Secretary)*.

The vivid persistence of these images, however, depends at least partially on their context, post-Thalberg MGM's preference for a shallowly focused, evenly lit *mise-en-scène,* perceived by Mayer as a means for distinguishing his studio's product from Warner's neo-expressionism, denigrated as "low-budget." Here, "class" results from a repudiation of the thriller, with its reliance (as in Feuillade's *Fantômas* serials) on a rapid succession of *intensities.* Subsequently, this genre can only recover respectability by distributing its attractions more parsimoniously, by surrounding them with long stretches of banal exposition (see Hitchcock). Nevertheless, these less interesting passages will gather stubbornly around their *raisons d'être,* the moments which Lacan would call (using the upholsterer's term for the buttons holding down a sofa's fabric) their *points de capiton*. Thus, these images, with their peculiar immediacy, represent the cinema's unconscious, its repressed infancy; and their return in movies so unlike the thriller suggests the medium's eidetic simulation of the mind, with its propensity for involuntary recall and (in Freud's useful term) for *screen memories*.

What would a filmmaking resemble which abandoned such pretensions, which contained *only* "intensities"? A dream? A collage like Chick Strand's *Loose Ends?* Or rather a movie structured by *the anecdote,* understood for the first time less as a narrative's outline than as its perfection.

D    *DÉCLASSÉ.*

The Hardy movies are dated, unfashionable, *déclassé,* a word meaning "abandoned," "obsolete" (as with certain weapons), and also "demoted," especially in social status. While the Hardy family is categorized as "middle class," the series' plots repeatedly turn on a potential (and threatening) class mobility: *The Hardys Ride High* raises the hopes of rising to the aristocracy (while trivializing the need to do so); *Out West with the Hardys* poses the opposite possibility—loss of savings, loss of house, loss of class itself. Significantly, movement in either direction upsets the family structure. While neither threat prevails, class structure and money haunt these movies which obsessively maintain their unimportance. Business failures, property foreclosures, financial swindles make up the rear projection in front of which Andy's romantic entanglements are played out. This arrangement is finally reversed by *It's a Wonderful Life,* which turns almost entirely around money.

E    *EDISON.*

Well, I doubt if Thomas Edison himself could have done better.

Judge Hardy, plugging in the Christmas tree lights *(Love Finds)*

You know, I'm mighty proud of that boy. He's a regular Thomas A. Edison.

Judge Hardy, complimenting Andy for his volcano in *Spring Fever*

At some point, as we retreat into history, the myth of Einstein (demythologized by Roland Barthes) gives way to that of Edison. The Edison legend shadows the Hardy series: the obsession with telegrams (Edison-as-telegrapher), the platitudes about hard work ("Genius is 1 percent inspiration and 99 percent perspiration"), the faith in the future. Those motifs, however, indicate a crucial distinction: while "Einstein" represents pure intelligence, the secret of the world reduced to a formula, "Edison" seems only a refashioning of the Alger myth. Thus, his story must begin in childhood (except for the bad math grade, Einstein's youth, by contrast, is unimportant). In MGM's *Young Tom Edison* (1940), Rooney demonstrates the interchangeability of the Andy/Edison roles, both dependent on high spirits misunderstood as mischief or stupidity. Significantly, the movie ends with Edison leaving Port Huron to make his fortune. "You want me to be successful in life, don't you?" Andy asks his father in *Debutante*. "I certainly do," the Judge replies.

F    *FAMILIES.*

> The Hardys
> *Father Knows Best*
> *Ozzie and Harriet*
> *Make Room for Daddy*
> *Leave It to Beaver*
> *The Courtship of Eddie's Father*
> *My Three Sons*
> *Bonanza*
> *Different Strokes*
> *The Partridge Family*
> *Alice*
> *Kate and Allie*
> *All in the Family*
> *The Brady Bunch*
> *Family*
> *Family Ties*
> *The Cosby Show*
> (W. Stephenson)

G    *GLAMOUR/GRAMMAR.*

In *Love Finds Andy Hardy,* Judy Garland (as Betsy Booth) sings "In Between," a song reflecting her actual situation at MGM, where she seemed too old for child parts, too young for romantic leads. For a brief period, the studio used her primarily to sing at birthday parties: in fact, her breakthrough occurred on February 1, 1937, when, at the age of 14, she serenaded the studio's biggest star at a reception in his honor. Harnessed to an old tune, "Dear Mr. Gable" (more recited than sung) became Garland's first hit, its apparent innocence belying a seamy allusion recognized by insiders: Gable had been receiving such formally addressed letters from a woman alleging his paternity of her child. Garland's acute self-consciousness during these grammar-school years left her vulnerable to MGM's pressures about her weight. In *Love Finds,* she laments that "I'm not allowed Clark Gable," diagnosing her own problems self-deprecatingly: "I'll never be able to get a man, much less hold him—no glamour, no glamour at all." This insecurity also appeared in real life:

> I went to the preview of my first picture, *Pigskin Parade.* . . . I thought I'd look as beautiful as Garbo or Crawford—that make-up and photography would automatically make me glamorous. Then I saw myself on screen. It was the most awful experience of my life. My freckles stood out. I was fat, and my acting was terrible. I burst into tears.

> My Dad says I should bother more
> About my lack of grammar.
> The only thing that bothers me
> Is my lack of glamour.
>   "In Between"

Glamour                                    Grammar

*Love Finds Andy Hardy*                    *Andy Hardy's Private Secretary*

As Betsy Booth (who appears in *Love Finds Andy Hardy, Andy Hardy Meets Debutante,* and *Life Begins for Andy Hardy*), Garland serves to resolve the series's founding oppositions:

| | |
|---|---|
| small-town reliability | big-city sophistication |
| friendship | sexual love |
| grammar | glamour |

True, Betsy *is* shy, selfless, awkward, and, above all, younger than Andy; but as a rich New Yorker, the daughter of a famous theatrical actress, and a hot singer in her own right, she is also, as Andy admits after the dance, "sensational." And her grammar is far better than his. In *Andy Hardy's Private Secretary,* he fails his final English exam, leaving his hopes of passing what the Judge refers to as "the most significant milestone in life" (high school graduation) up to a retest covering the distinctions between *lie* and *lay* and *who* and *whom,* and the recognition of misplaced modifiers, predicate adjectives, subordinate conjunctions, "infinitive phrases used as appositives," and "compound personal pronouns used self-reflexively": maturity represented as a function of grammar.

Etymologically, *glamour* is a late Scottish variant of *grammar,* both words referring to the secret knowledge required for casting spells. Hence, the terms' original connotations: illusion, concealment, initiation. In the middle ages ("in between"), grammar remained inaccessible, the province of priests who guarded the rules of writing and magic. Glamour, too, arose from notions of deception and control (see the history of cosmetics). *Glamour girls,* therefore, are really *grammar girls*— they both depend on rules.

No studio better understood the grammar of glamour than MGM. With its coveted cinematographers and set designers, its tireless publicists and press agents, its preeminent wealth and stability, the studio had everything needed to make a star. Why, then, did Garland baffle it? Like her character Betsy Booth, the grammar-school girl longing for glamour, Garland oscillates between two words/worlds. An enigma, she refuses the categories prescribed for her; she remains the "in between" identified by Baudrillard as the space of seduction. This ambiguity, this alternation, forms the basis of Garland's attraction, her unexpected power to *cast a spell.* (LG)

H    *HARRY.*

In *Andy Hardy's Private Secretary,* a unique hint of class-consciousness: going with his father to inquire why a classmate's check has bounced, Andy encounters Harry Land, bristling with resentment and anger: "You folks on the other side of town give me a pain." The Lands are poor, but the series cannot admit the true working class: Mr. Land, who speaks nine languages and "paints a little," is merely a bourgeois down-on-his-luck—his previously thriving Parisian travel agency has folded because of the War. Hence the restricted range of signifiers available for the portrayal of "poverty": the absence of a telephone, the inability to buy silk stockings.

Harry Land
*Andy Hardy's Private Secretary*

Harry Bailey
*It's a Wonderful Life*

This Harry's "rightness" seems unusually compelling, although it depends less on acting technique than on casting quirks: "Harry Land" is the same actor who will later play *It's a Wonderful Life*'s "Harry Bailey," George's football-playing, war-hero brother, the prodigal whose exploits cover for his abdication of family responsibility. Fifty years later, we inevitably reach the Andy Hardy series after having first met its more famous descendant. Thus, "Harry Land" appears as someone we already know, the sensation of realism enhanced by the coincidence of names. This "thickness" of allusion reaches its peak in *It's a Wonderful Life* (see "Unpacking"), but it does not always produce the same effect: when stars become more memorable than their roles, spectacle replaces realism.

I    *INTERIORS.*

The Kitchen

The Study

The Hall

The Dining Room

While certain parts of the Hardy family house appear regularly through-out the series—the Judge's study (scene of the man-to-man talks), the dining room, the front hall (with its staircase and all-important tele-phone), Andy's bedroom—other areas, while not entirely off-limits, are subject to only occasional sightings:

Marian's bedroom (*Spring Fever*)
the parents' bedroom (reserved for moments of crisis: Emily's near-
    fatal illness in *Judge Hardy and Son,* the Judge's financial panic in
    *Out West*)
Aunt Milly's bedroom
the living room

the kitchen
bathrooms
the attic

In part, this arrangement bespeaks the series' narrative hierarchy: the rooms on view will inevitably be those of the plots' prime movers, Andy and the Judge. But some other principle also seems to be operating, a censorship functioning to preserve feminine privacy: of the house's principal rooms, Marian's, Milly's, and Emily's are the most rarely seen. Furthermore, all areas of the house seem to shift in relationship to each other, thereby rendering the exact architecture uncertain. Does the Judge's study connect with the living room? Does Andy's bedroom open onto the stairs? Where are the bathrooms?

In 1969, having lost his nerve during a solo race around the world, Donald Crowhurst began to sail aimlessly up and down the coast of South America, forging progress by means of fake radio signals, bounced from satellites to indicate navigationally significant positions. Like Crowhurst's "voyage," the Hardy house is an effect of carefully orchestrated, but frequently contradictory, clues: it is, in other words, however imperfect, a working *simulation*.

Imagine, instead, another more rigorous arrangement, one in which the Hardys' rooms would appear according to a schedule determined by chance. The filmmakers draw numbers: over the course of sixteen films, Andy's room must be seen three times, Marian's twelve, the Judge's study only once, and so forth. Such constraints, used regularly by Oulipo, in fact seem merely an extension of the strict conditions already determining the series' shape: the established characters, the required entanglements, the familiar tropes (the opening courtroom scenes, the man-to-man talks, the closing embrace with Polly—"Woo! Woo!"). The Hollywood series and television sitcom become popular culture's versions of twelve-tone music: they are literally serial art.

J   *JALOPY.*

Andy's car, purchased on time from Peter Dugan's Garage in *Love Finds,* will last for five more movies until it becomes irreparable in *Private Secretary,* an obsolescence predicting the series' own. Like the word *jalopy* itself, which Andy carefully avoids, this vehicle has "no known origins." Ironically, it falls apart with the Judge at the wheel, thereby exacting revenge for his initial resistance to its purchase. Even before that transaction's completion, however, Andy has signed the car with his blazon, the *A.H.!* which decorates both doors. This marking rewrites *Ah, Wilderness!*, converting its universal sigh into an individual's signature, its conventionally placed exclamation point into the celebration of a single name.

*Love Finds Andy Hardy*                    *Love Finds Andy Hardy*

This maneuver, however, merely acknowledges the reality of the series: the steadily increasing emphasis on the Andy Hardy character, the rise of Mickey Rooney's box-office appeal. Nevertheless, the callow enthusiasm indicated by the punctuation cannot last: in *Blonde Trouble*, near the series' end, Kay Wilson (representing, perhaps, the audience's exasperation) will warn Andy that his trademark *Woo! Woo!* is "a little adolescent, don't you think?"

And yet: this concern for *maturity* has a more complex side. By replacing Andy's nondescript jalopy (a descendant of the Model T) with a stylized convertible, the series uses Andy's cars to display the maturing of American capitalism, its transition from an economy of production (Henry Ford) to an economy of consumption (GM's Alfred Sloan). The prophet of this "mature" capitalism, Werner Sombart, repudiated Max Weber's litany of austerity, thrift, and discipline, insisting instead on capitalism's grounding in expenditure, luxury, and desire. Anticipating this development, Andy employs his Fordist jalopy (the emblem of productive asceticism) as his primary site for lovemaking.

K    *THE KISS.*

With *Debutante*'s hansom sequence, we arrive, in Freud's terms, at the navel of the dream that is the Hardy series. Time: dawn, after Daphne Fowler's party. Place: Central Park, the interior of a horse-drawn cab. Situation: Andy has triumphed over Beezy and Polly by having his picture taken with Daphne, the celebrated New York debutante he has boasted of knowing. Betsy has dazzled Andy by singing "I'm Nobody's Baby." Now, a decision: should they kiss? Shyly, hesitatingly, they discuss the matter: should they or should they not? At last, Andy leans toward her and kisses her timidly, uncertainly, gently on the cheek, and she begins to cry. Betsy's tears, the most affecting moment in all of the Andy Hardy movies, seem to issue from absent circumstances, from a different scene which has disappeared—in other words, they are overdetermined. Their power to disturb derives initially from Garland's acting, more realistically expressive than this B-series can bear. Her performance reminds us that despite roots in presentational vaudeville, Garland as a singer is always as much actress as musician; hence, the movies (a representational form) are her ideal arena.

But like manifest dream content, this scene hides something else; it is a screen memory, a recurrence of an event from the series' past. In fact, it results from a restaging of *Love Finds Andy Hardy*'s conclusion: a fancy dress ball, Betsy's singing, the unexpectedness of Andy's pleasure, the startling transformation of a twelve-year-old tag-along into an object of desire. In the earlier film, Andy's reaction is more animated, evolving from an initial glumness (the novelty of little Betsy in an evening gown having largely worn off) into an anxiety about her offer to sing (what if she embarrasses him?). In *Love Finds Andy Hardy*, however, Betsy's performance brings him to a wild, rapturous joy, an excessive, hyperactive excitement. Ridiculously animated, stiffly at attention, physically inflated with pride, Andy may or may not have an erection, but he appears to be one. Hence the dejection during the ride home in Andy's car, an image of postcoital depression.

*Debutante* reworks this event. Andy's response to Betsy's singing is calmer, his feelings for her more complicated. Crowded next to each other in the hansom (as they had not been in his car), unavoidably touching, they have discovered the implications of mature desire, and Betsy's tears represent the series' dream of eternal adolescence capsizing.

The Kiss
*Andy Hardy Meets Debutante*

*Love Finds Andy Hardy*

*Andy Hardy Meets Debutante*

Garland's distress, of course, has a special poignancy: we know what will happen to her. But ultimately, the scene's resonance is diegetic. This kiss, like the Andy Hardy series itself, is haunted by the Judge's response to Andy's marriage proposal in *Spring Fever,* a warning describing the idyll whose abandonment the series must inevitably trace: "Are you prepared to give up your basketball and your baseball, your parties and little dances, our summer vacations together? Are you ready to give up all the happy things that young people of your age are entitled to? Now don't you be trapped into being an adult." (LG, WS)

L    *LIFE IMITATES ART (DEPARTMENT OF EASY IRONIES).*
Mickey Rooney, who will marry eight times, playing Andy Hardy, surveying his bureau's collection of photographs: "Gosh, how one's women do mount up!" (*Debutante*)

Extratextual knowledge of this sort, directly contradicting narrative tone, is fatal to a movie's diegetic effect, its power to absorb the viewer in a fictional world. Indeed, such knowledge is the beginning of camp. Recognizing this danger, studio publicity departments (none more resourceful than MGM's) vigilantly policed this terrain, working to ensure that information about performers' private lives would only enhance the roles they played. In emergencies, a powerful company could dictate the tenor of any resulting publicity: with Paul Bern's sudden death, for example, information reached the public as much from MGM (eager to protect its investment in Bern's widow, Jean Harlow) as from the Los Angeles Police Department. The studios' demise, however, abandoned films to the vagaries of intertextuality, exposing them to the disenchantment effected by the gap between fact and persona. See Charlie Chaplin and Woody Allen.

*LIKES/DISLIKES.*
*I like:* the schoolroom at night in *Spring Fever* (see Chapter 7); Betsy Booth; the rainstorm in *Judge Hardy and Son;* Jimmy McMahon's ham radio (W8XZR); the hansom cab ride (*Debutante*); Polly Benedict; the exploding volcano and the wandering moon (*Spring Fever*); Carvel; Polly's after-theater, early-summer-evening lawn party; Elvie Horton (*Judge Hardy and Son*); the train station in *Out West;* Marian's voice; Andy's car-door trademark, AH!; the ice cream parlor; the long walk home in *Ah, Wilderness!;* spring in Judge Hardy's courtroom; the living room

decorated for Christmas; the snowy ride home from the holiday ball (*Love Finds*).

*I don't like:* Emily's ignorance; Judge Hardy's lectures about Washington and Lincoln; Dr. Standish (Herbert Marshall) and Wainright College; Aunt Milly-as-old-maid; *Andy Hardy Comes Home*; Lionel Barrymore as Judge Hardy; *Out West*'s foreman; the Northcott ranch (*Out West*); the tour of New York's Hall of Fame (*Debutante*); Cynthia Potter (Lana Turner); Clarabelle Lee's exaggerated southern accent (*Judge Hardy and Son*); Andy's high school graduation.

**M**    *MATHEMATICS.*

> Judge Hardy [having learned that Andy intends marrying his teacher, Rose Meredith: *Spring Fever*]: Very nice young lady. But isn't there a considerable difference in your ages?
>
> Andy [unabashed]: Well, I'm pretty near 17—that makes me almost 21, really. She's 23, and that makes her just a little beyond 21. So what's all the fuss over a year's difference?

At the time of this scene, Mickey Rooney, playing a 16-year-old, is nearly 19, Lewis Stone (Judge Hardy), nearly 60. As 12-year-old Betsy Booth, Judy Garland completes *Love Finds* just three days before her sixteenth birthday. Thus, in reconfiguring his age, Andy merely follows the standard policy of a system in which facts are typically a liability. What is the effect of always pretending to be younger than you are? Is this role different from any other?

*MAYER.*

> "We were writing a script for Lubitsch called *Ninotchka*," Billy Wilder recalled, "and the windows gave onto a little bridge which connects this old building with the new Thalberg Building. We looked out the window because there was screaming going on, and Louis B. Mayer held Mickey Rooney by the lapel. He says, 'You're Andy Hardy! You're the United States! You're the Stars and Stripes. Behave yourself! You're a symbol!'"

*MISE-EN-ABYME I.*

Mise-en-abyme I
*Andy Hardy Meets Debutante*

Near the center of the series, in *Andy Hardy Meets Debutante,* a sign posted in the Carvel High newspaper office stages these movies' conditions-of-being:

> THIS SPACE FOR PICTURE OR DRAWING
> TO BE CHANGED EVERY MONTH.

Once fully under way, the series will provide an available frame for the starlets who pass through it: Judy Garland, Lana Turner, Kathryn Grayson, Donna Reed, Esther Williams. Only Garland will appear more than once (in *Love Finds, Debutante,* and *Life Begins for Andy Hardy*), but the newsroom scene cleverly finds another way to advertise Lana Turner, not seen since *Love Finds* five pictures before. Anticipating Hitchcock's *Lifeboat* ploy, Beezy offers a photograph of his girlfriend Cynthia Potter (Turner), proposing it for the next cover. Andy and Polly reject his suggestion (the cover's space will go to Daphne Fowler, the New York deb). But Beezy has intuited the Hardy machine's modular construction: narrative incidents and peripheral characters are fungible; what matters is the frame—the Hardy family, Andy's love interests—designed to accommodate an infinitude of situations. In such serial filmmaking, the studio production system most openly reveals its debt to its original model, the assembly lines of Henry Ford.

*MISE-EN-ABYME II.*
*Life Begins for Andy Hardy*—shot-reverse-shot sequence [Andy intercut with a billboard advertising "Golden Ham"].

Mise-en-abyme II
*Life Begins for Andy Hardy*

**MISE-EN-ABYME III.**

In 1938, MGM casts Mickey Rooney for the fourth time as Andy Hardy, paying him $650 a week. In *Love Finds,* Andy's friend Beezy pays Andy $8 plus expenses to feign enough interest in Cynthia Potter to keep the other boys away until he can return from a trip—in other words, he pays Andy to *act.* When Cynthia turns out to be Lana Turner, whom Rooney claims to have gotten pregnant two years before, the job turns out to be easier than expected.

N    **NOIR ANDY HARDY.**

Released in the same year as *The Maltese Falcon,* 1941's *Life Begins for Andy Hardy* has many attributes associated with *film noir:* a gritty New York rooming house, a *femme fatale* (secretary Jennitt Hicks), a sudden death (dancer Jimmy Frobisher's), and images of poverty, homelessness, and unemployment. Inevitably, therefore, to advanced students only casually interested in the Hardy movies, this film seems the most "serious" entry in the series. (Hence the basic questions about *film noir:* Why

Mise-en-abyme III
*Love Finds Andy Hardy*

does this fundamentally *sentimental* movement have such an abiding appeal for intellectuals? Why does "profundity" appear linked to *nostalgie de la boue?*) Despite the movie's *noir* features, however, it everywhere pulls its punches. An apparent suicide, Jimmy has in fact died from a "leaky mitral valve." And as Andy explains to Betsy, his down-and-out status is only an experiment: "Nothing serious's gonna happen to me. I've got a home to go back to." Furthermore, although the film occasionally anticipates *noir*'s chiaroscuro, its flat, even lighting more often anticipates the banal *mise-en-scène* of 1950s television.

Sensing Andy's immaturity as crucial to the series' survival, the Hardy movies stall his progress from high school graduation (in *Private Secretary*) to college matriculation (in *Blonde Trouble,* four films later). This effort requires the series to adopt a temporal continuity usually associated with serials: the trailer for *Life Begins* converts this exigency into a virtue, boasting that "for the first time in the movies [that is, in the Hardy movies], another story starts where the other finished. The graduation dance is over. Andy has taken Polly home. And now, here we go, into the brand new story!" Significantly, the plot of *Life Begins* returns Andy to his abandoned jalopy, now reconceived as a signifier of the childhood that neither the series nor his parents can allow him to abandon: as Andy works on the car in Dugan's garage, the Judge whispers on the telephone, "Now remember, Emily, nothing has happened. We've got our boy back again." The film's ending confirms this direction: reunited with Betsy and his parents, at the wheel of his "repaired" jalopy, Andy shifts triumphantly into third gear and finds the car moving rapidly, violently *backwards*.

In fact, however, this movement typifies *noir,* where *femmes fatales* develop hearts of gold and plot resolutions restore law's customary order: Sam Spade, after all, is not as crooked as he looks, and Brigid O'Shaughnessy will go to jail. In this context, *Life Begins'* Jennitt Hicks seems anomalous, a gold-digger who repudiates her own attempts to reform: "You've gotta learn, darling," she advises Andy. "A lot of people put on a big show about right thinking and right living and right this and right that. When you're young, you believe them; then when you grow up, you find that they preach one thing and do another." The movie will, of course, discredit these words, but they hang over the series like a prophecy, an epigraph for a film studies committed to "demystification" and circumscribed by the thinking described in Peter Sloterdijk's famous title, *Critique of Cynical Reason*.

O    *OPACITY.*

**Polly Benedict:** Why, Andrew Hardy, you kissed me last night by force!

**Andy:** Well, it's good that way, too!

   (*Love Finds Andy Hardy*)

**Andy:** Can I help it if I have irresistible charm?

**Polly Benedict:** That's not charm, that's polygamy, but oh, Andy, how we women love it!

   (*Andy Hardy Meets Debutante*)

These jokes, now properly forbidden, have, however, not yet become entirely opaque. We recognize the humor, but deplore its origins in gender codes we have forsworn. But to the extent that we still get the jokes, we propagate their ideology, becoming ourselves the means of its relay. As Foucault insisted, revolutionary change depends on *forgetting*: only when audiences can no longer imagine why anyone could find such scenes funny will the values they embody disappear.

P    *POLONIUS.*

A sample of Judge Hardy's maxims:

1. Half a woman's love is faith. (*Love Finds Andy Hardy*)
2. There's no new sorrow in the world, or trouble, that a lot of other people couldn't match. (*Love Finds*)
3. You'd be surprised at the number of people who define justice as something they think they'd *like* to get. (*Love Finds*)
4. I think a man's old enough to smoke when he's old enough to decide for himself that he's old enough to smoke. (*The Hardys Ride High*)
5. When there's trouble ahead, there's no use finding entertainment in the meantime. (*Andy Hardy Meets Debutante*)
6. I've learned the longer you put off something that's unpleasant, the harder it is when you finally have to face the music. (*Andy Hardy's Private Secretary*)

7. We're seldom called upon in this world to do things beyond human effort. Strangely enough, if you prepare for any contingency, you usually conquer it in a surprisingly easy fashion. (*Private Secretary*)
8. Marriage is the one happiness in the world today that can be spoiled by anticipating it. (*Life Begins for Andy Hardy*)

The Andy Hardy series turns on a basic problem: having established the Judge as the films' source of wisdom, it must protect his words from the scrutiny that would expose them as platitudinous. The first step involves the buffering effect of hackneyed phrases, which, when surrounding Judge Hardy's privileged discourse, render it less noticeably banal. Thus, in a single movie (*The Hardys Ride High*), the following expressions appear:

*all's fair in love and war*
*anybody knows that*
*back as far as Adam and Eve*
*believe it or not*
*dreams come true*
*Et tu, Brute*
*getting away with murder*
*a gilt-edged investment* (twice)
*the gist of the matter*
*honesty is the best policy*
*just put yourself in my place*
*man of the world*
*murder will out*
*no fool like an old fool*
*not a trouble in the world*
*the only two people in the world*
*orders is orders*
*stick-in-the-mud*
*take your hair down*
*thank your lucky stars*
*the wrong kind of people*
*you dish it out and I'll take it*
*you're just a wallflower*
*you're my right arm*

Second, the series relies on Lewis Stone, whose age, granite features, and orator's voice all legitimize Judge Hardy's counsel. These attributes, however, do not go unquestioned. Andy is always ready to argue that his father's age disqualifies him from ruling on contemporary mores. And consider the subtle parodies effected by *Andy Hardy Gets Spring Fever*, the first turning on the obvious similarities between the shape of Stone's face and that of a clown, whose picture on Andy's wall neatly bisects the image of father and son engaged in yet another man-to-man talk. (Leaving this scene, the Judge, in an isolated reaction shot, displays an odd grimace, inappropriate to the preceding action but furthering the resemblance.)

The Clown                                    *Andy Hardy Gets Spring Fever*

Later in the movie, infatuated with his drama teacher, Andy adopts a theatrical voice whose stentorian phoniness ("like molasses dripping downstairs," in Marian's description) seems another version of the impersonation which Rooney regularly used to tease Lewis Stone. Here the son devours the father and spits him out as a pretentious fool. As Judge Hardy becomes just another character in Rooney's repertoire (which includes Clark Gable and Herbert Marshall), the power of the father wanes, and the power of the son (high school hero, matinee idol) asserts itself, a transferral of authority whose evolution appears in the series' titles: although only two of the first eight titles (*Love Finds* and *Spring Fever*) mention Andy by name, none of the final eight will omit him. *Andy Hardy Comes Home* completes this process: the Judge has died, and Andy must officially replace him. But earlier in the series proper, Judge Hardy's diminished, infantilized status finds representation in an illness, which requires a tonsillectomy to restore what he has temporarily lost: his voice. (WS)

Q   QUOTAS.

Mickey Rooney: "During the '30s, Metro-Goldwyn-Mayer was geared to a schedule of fifty-two pictures a year: one movie a week. There were sets by the acre, directors by the dozen, writers by the score, and, as the studio advertised, 'More stars than there are in the heavens.'"

J. J. Cohn (executive producer of the Hardy series): "I loved working with W. S. Van Dyke—God, he was fast! He shot the last reel of *The Thin Man* in one day."

The best undergraduate presentation I have ever seen resulted from readings about MGM's production system. Having announced that they were in the business of "producing film criticism," and that they believed in the division of labor, the presenting students issued an assignment: *Within one minute, write a single sentence about Citizen Kane.* Group 1 would handle *mise-en-scène* issues; Group 2, editing; Group 3, lighting; Group 4, acting; Group 5 would assemble the parts. The result? "*Citizen Kane* uses deep-focus photography; its long takes alternate with rapid montage; in both lighting and acting, the film combines realism with a more expressionist style." "These are merely clichés," the presenters responded, doing their best to sound disappointed. "But we only had one minute," came the reply. "Only a minute? Now you understand why so few studio films, much less the Hardy series, did anything different. No one had the time." (WS)

R   RELATIVES.

The Hardy series' low-budget status reveals itself in the absence of relations. Betsy Booth, Polly Benedict, Cynthia Potter, Elvie Horton, Clarabelle Lee all appear to be only children, and of Andy's immediate circle, Beezy alone has a sibling: his sister surfaces in *Blonde Trouble,* primarily as a means of returning Andy's long-defunct car. The Hardys themselves are peculiarly lacking in relatives: no uncles, no cousins, no long-lost kin. They visit old friends but not family. Never appearing on screen, the one grandparent (Emily's mother) exists only as an excuse to call her daughter away, thereby increasing the holiday drama of *Love Finds* and enabling a Christmas Eve reunion which anticipates the finale of *It's a Wonderful Life*. Most significantly, the Judge's parents are wholly absent. For the Hardys, therefore, there is no law behind the Judge's law, no opportunity for a destabilizing conflict between James Hardy and *his* elders. Without roots, the Judge's rule becomes another version of Lacan's *nom du père,* authority-as-self-assertion, the solution to a vacancy. Despite the Judge's efforts to associate this law with America's official heroes (especially Lincoln), his authority is ultimately tautological. Thus, when Andy rejects his father's sermon about the Fathers of Our Country (*Debutante*), the Judge's reply represents ideology speaking to itself: "When a boy is stupid, he's just stupid, that's all."

In the Hardy series, the absence of relatives corresponds to a basic strategy of the *mise-en-scène:* the camera's typical confinement to a very restricted area—the Judge's courtroom and chambers, the bank's ground floor, a downtown street (including Dugan's garage), two exteriors (the Hardy and Benedict houses), and the interior of the Hardy house itself. This focus produces the secure sense of place which is the series' *comfort,* a sense which is cumulative, growing more pleasant with the accretion of installments. The setting's rightness and stability become so pervasive that when a scene suddenly shifts from Andy's boarding house room to Mother Hardy's kitchen (*Life Begins*), several seconds pass before we remember that Andy is not only no longer at home, but miles away in New York. Yet like the family's relatives, the Hardy house cannot exist. What, for example, is the spatial relationship between kitchen, dining room, living room, study, and hall? (See "Interiors.") Hence, this paradox: in a series celebrating the stability of home and family, the greatest sense of security is generated by fostering attachment to a utopia in the most literal sense—a no-place. (William Stephenson)

S    *SHOPPING.*

The Hardys, icons of the middle class, never engage in the most important of bourgeois functions: they never shop. The family appears instead to have a strangely constant store of goods, an arrangement of less advantage to the series' realism than to its continuity, a motive emphasized by *Spring Fever*'s pressbook:

A complete record is maintained by the producers of the Hardy pictures as to the progress, financial status, the additions to the home, etc., so that each production definitely will be a sequel to its predecessor.

In keeping with the family tradition, Andy doesn't look around for a car in *Love Finds*; rather, he makes a sudden and ill-advised deal which leads more to a situation than a sale: the complications resulting from his inability to complete the transaction drive the plot.

The Hardys cannot shop because doing so would specify their economic status: any purchases would wake to judgment a gaze that might never otherwise place an exact value on their visible property. By avoiding shopping, they remain vaguely middle-class, wealthy enough to admire, but not enough to envy. (This indeterminate status represents the characters' equivalent of Carvel's unspecified location: see "Carvel.")

Even in *The Hardys Ride High,* when Marian acquires an evening gown, Judge Hardy a silk hat, and Aunt Milly a whole new wardrobe, nothing is revealed. It is, after all, not the Hardys who are buying: "It wasn't really me," Marian explains to her father, apologizing for a guiltily concealed credit purchase. "It was the two million dollars that made me do such a dishonest thing." (William Stephenson)

*SPELLING.*

Her inconsistently spelled name (usually "Milly," but occasionally, especially in trailers, "Millie") suggests the maiden aunt's marginal status. Never appearing in the Hardy family photo that opens each film (she is, in fact, *not* a Hardy at all, but rather "Mildred Forest," Emily's sister), she alone of the principals can even be played by a different actress (in *Love Finds*) long after the rest of the cast has been established—with no damage to the movie's diegetic effect. (Buñuel will later experiment with this possibility by having two actresses play the same character in a *single* film, *That Obscure Object of Desire.*) Aunt Milly seems the series' token attempt to provide the Hardys with an *extended family,* an established signifier of the traditional values beloved by Mayer. Only in *The Hardys Ride High,* however, does her character provide plot material, and even then she appears foolish, mistaking for courtship what in fact is a salesman's ploy. While Studio Years Hollywood can portray attractive bachelors (for example, Joseph Cotten in *Since You Went Away*), spinsterhood nearly always implies neurosis. At best, the unmarried woman is merely repressed (the Mary in *Wonderful Life*'s Pottersville section). Aunt Milly, however, has a more disturbing *doppelgänger*: the Ambersons' Aunt Fanny.

*SURREALIST RECIPE.*

> *Andy Hardy Meets Debutante:* Aunt Milly enters the kitchen to find Emily distraught:
> **Emily:** Milly, I think I'm going insane.
> **Aunt Milly:** Oh, nonsense, now what is it, what's wrong?
> **Emily:** Well, there you are, "Recipe for a chocolate pudding" . . . read that.
> **Milly [reading]:** "Then remove the mix from the ice-box, add four eggs and (continued on next page, column 2), pour it down the sink."

These instructions represent continuity cinema's phobia, a bad match, this one resulting from a literal *cut:* Andy has torn out a magazine page picturing New York deb Daphne Fowler, thereby combining cuisine with plumbing and stalling his mother's cooking. In 1936, however, Joseph Cornell used a similar recipe to refashion Universal's 1931 B-picture *East of Borneo,* which, like *Spring Fever*'s "Adrift in Tahiti," had ended with an erupting volcano. Structured by both radical elision and obvious interpolations (of scientific footage), Cornell's short *Rose Hobart* anticipated Godard's jump cuts and docu-fiction collages. "In *Breathless,*" Godard wrote, "I took out everything . . . just to prove that it was possible." Oddly, as if affected by their own recipe, the Hardy filmmakers, in this one place, resolve Emily's dilemma with two unusually loose matches.

T    *THESIS.*

What would a "serious" treatment of the Hardy series look like?

### Subjectivity and the Screen Family: Representations of Self and Other in the Andy Hardy Movies

Order No. AH6106088    Szurgot, Brian Lynn, Ph.D.    Indiana University, 1988.    230pp.    Supervisor: Laura B. Bonde.

This dissertation is an analysis of the representation of subjectivity, the process of the construction of the subject within the family as described by psychoanalytic theory, in selected films of the Andy Hardy series (directed by George B. Seitz). The primary goal of this study is to consider a body of cinematic work that has not yet been an object of contemporary critical study in light of the advances in understanding of the positioning of the subject in discourse as enunciated by Jacques Lacan. The broad thesis of this study is that the Andy Hardy films, as an overlapping and essentially unified text, provide a mass cultural model for observing developing subjectivity within a family setting.

The study begins with a discussion of the crisis in the ideology of the individual. The second chapter is a history and summary of theories of the subject and their appropriation by film theory, most notably in the work of Christian Metz. The body of the dissertation consists of a textual analysis of four films: *Andy Hardy Meets Debutante, Out West with the Hardys, The Hardys Ride High,* and *Life Begins for Andy Hardy.* These individual analyses investigate respectively the relationship of language, sexual difference, narrative, and enunciation of subjectivity and the family. The specific formulation here is that the dynamics of the family structure determine the establishment of the coherence of the self.

The primary conclusion of this study is that these films refute the notion of the self as a unified, centered essence which controls discourse, and bring to the fore the fact of subjectivity—the radical discontinuity of the self, its unstable position as the product of signifying operations. Further, this study concludes that these films promote an ideology of the American family that its own representations of structures, within and between speaking subjects, undermine.

(See entry in *Dissertation Abstracts,* Vol. 47, No. 7; January 1987.) (William Stephenson)

*TRAVEL.*

| | |
|---|---|
| Catalina | *You're Only Young Once* |
| Washington, D.C. | *Judge Hardy's Children* |
| Arizona | *Out West with the Hardys* |
| Detroit | *The Hardys Ride High* |
| New York City | *Andy Hardy Meets Debutante* |
| New York City | *Life Begins for Andy Hardy* |
| Wainright College | *Andy Hardy's Blonde Trouble* |

In the Andy Hardy movies, referential accuracy about travel always yields to opportunities for visual spectacle: thus, in *Andy Hardy Meets Debutante,* the family's train trip to New York illogically provides them with their first glimpse of the city from the Staten Island Ferry.

More important, relocating the family to other locales, especially big cities, enables the series to dramatize its association of ideal values with small-town life. In all the Andy Hardy movies, New York is Carvel's implied antithesis (with Betsy Booth, who lives in both places, the resolving link). Not surprisingly, therefore, when New York becomes the actual narrative site (in *Life Begins*), the series' only death occurs.

U    *UNPACKING.*

All roads from Carvel lead to Bedford Falls. Like a dream, *It's a Wonderful Life* derives its effect from an allusiveness so dense as to require what Freud called "analysis interminable." A look at only the film's first few minutes yields the following:

1. The sign *You Are Now in Bedford Falls* reproduces the Hardy series' *Welcome to Carvel* (*A Family Affair*).
2. Clarence, the Angel, is played by Henry Travers, the janitor in MGM's *Edison the Man*.
3. Clarence carries *The Adventures of Tom Sawyer,* whose best friend was played by Mickey Rooney in MGM's 1939 *The Adventures of Huckleberry Finn.*
4. Bedford Falls: the small town, Christmas, snow. See Carvel in *Love Finds Andy Hardy.*
5. George Bailey's rescue of his brother from the ice = Young Tom Edison's rescue of the stationmaster's son from the railroad track (MGM/Mickey Rooney, 1940). Both Edison and George lose their hearing in their left ears, which are painfully handled by misunderstanding employers.
6. Mr. Potter is played by Lionel Barrymore, the original Judge Hardy; his character, however, derives from that of Taggart, the mean-spirited merchant in *Young Tom Edison.*
7. Mr. Gower when drunk, vulnerable and confused, descends from Tom Sawyer's Muff Peters, the victim of Injun Joe's frame-up.
8. *Love Finds Andy Hardy's* soda fountain becomes *It's a Wonderful Life's* drugstore counter. Violet Bick ("I like him"; Mary: "You like all the boys") is another version of both *Love Finds'* Cynthia Potter and *Blonde Trouble's* Lee Walker, about whom her twin sister comments, "As soon as you see a nice boy, you start to like him."
9. George's mention of Tahiti and his boast to Mary ("I'm going to have a couple of harems, maybe three or four wives") recall *Spring Fever's* "Adrift in Tahiti" and Polly's joke about polygamy (see "Opacity").
10. Mr. Gower's telegram about his son's death recalls both the telegram in *Love Finds* reporting the grandmother's stroke and the War Department messages in *The Human Comedy* (MGM, 1943).

*A Family Affair*

*It's a Wonderful Life*

*Young Tom Edison*

*It's a Wonderful Life*

*Young Tom Edison*

*It's a Wonderful Life*

*Love Finds Andy Hardy*

*It's a Wonderful Life*

*Love Finds Andy Hardy*

*It's a Wonderful Life*

*Andy Hardy's Blonde Trouble*

*It's a Wonderful Life*

11. The Sweet Caporals ad, advising George to "ASK DAD HE KNOWS," amounts to the Hardy series' epigraph.
12. The cab driver Ernie is played by the same actor (Frank Faylen) as the cabbie at the Wainright College train station (*Blonde Trouble*). Harry Bailey is *Private Secretary*'s Harry Land. Donna Reed (Mary) provides Andy's love interest in *The Courtship of Andy Hardy*.

V    *VICES*.

As would be expected, the Hardy series associates cigarettes and alcohol with city life and dissipation, most prominently in *The Hardys Ride High* and *Life Begins*. Neither the Judge, Emily, nor Aunt Milly is ever seen smoking or drinking, an unusual abstinence for the 1930s. In *The Hardys Ride High*, however, while pretending to Polly that his Detroit adventures have rendered him cosmopolitan, Andy feigns nicotine and alcohol addiction. What are the semiotics of lying? How does an actor convey to an audience that he is not telling the truth? This problem, masterfully handled by Mary Astor in *The Maltese Falcon*, is in fact central to the Hollywood studio system. What relationship exists between Andy Hardy's pretending to be sophisticated and Mickey Rooney's pretending to be Andy Hardy? How does Mickey Rooney, who does smoke and drink, pretend to be a character who does not pretending that he does? How can thrice-married Lewis Stone convincingly play Judge Hardy's warnings to Andy about infidelity: "The habit of transferring one's affections from one girl to another is very apt to destroy the ability to bestow those same affections permanently on your wife" (*Life Begins*)? At the heart of Hollywood's family movies lies a paradox: a sense of ordinariness resulting from performers leading the most extraordinary lives.

W    *WAR BONDS*.

In *Andy Hardy Meets Debutante*, on the eve of American entry into World War II, a discreet reminder of isolationism's advantages: a trust fund supporting Carvel's orphanage has been imperiled by non-American investments.

> **New York lawyer Underwood**: At the worst of the depression, Wyatt [president of the orphanage] demanded that we switch the *United States* securities in the orphanage trust fund to *European* bonds.

**Judge Hardy**: I see . . . recent European "developments" . . . those bonds are worthless.

X    *X MARKS THE SPOT.*

In *Love Finds Andy Hardy,* an unusual diegetic precision: Andy's calendar, with Christmas day circled (the country club ball) and the interim numbers steadily X'd out, limits the plot to thirteen days (only six fewer than the film's shooting schedule).

Andy's impatience, however, is misguided—time is both his and the series' enemy: neither can survive Mickey Rooney's inevitable maturation. In this case, therefore, the *X*, although deployed in youthful high spirits, in anticipation of first love and a holiday dance, returns to its traditional significance—as a warning of mortality.

Y    *YALE.*

On Andy's bedroom wall, only two pennants appear: *Carvel High* and *Yale.*

With the series making no other mention of it, this latter choice seems particularly arbitrary. Andy, after all, eventually follows his father's footsteps to "Wainright College," whose plentiful coeds, accessible teachers, and intimate size represent the Ivy League's opposite. Obvious answers, of course, present themselves: "Yale" as the best known college name, "Yale" as a signifier of "class." Then why not "Harvard" or "Princeton"? If we acknowledge instead another logic (more visual, more cinematic), we might begin to see "Yale" as an unusually valuable *design*—bold (the rare capital *Y*), concise (the shortest college name), memorable (the locks), available for multiple rhymes (including *hale,* the inevitable companion of *Hardy*). From this perspective, the Yale pennant signals a relaxation of filmmaking's referential drive, a turn toward Eisenstein's "montage of attractions" and the possibilities inherent in shapes, movements, and sounds: in the Hardy series, "Yale" suggests the cinema's revision of Mallarmé's famous warning to Degas—movies are not made with words, but with images.

*Or:* in the 1930s, Yale's two most famous alumni were probably Cole Porter (author of a school football cheer) and Rudy Vallee (popularizer of "The Whiffenpoof Song"). *Andy Hardy's Private Secretary* gives Porter's "I've Got My Eyes on You" to Kathryn Grayson, who uses it to satisfy Andy's requests (and the audience's) for something besides opera. But with his urbanity, dandyism, aristocratic wit, and cosmopolitan allusiveness, Porter is the Hardy series' antonym. Vallee's deportment, on the other hand—a studied juvenescence deployed to conceal a prima donna's ego—seems more like Rooney's own. In bursts of manic exuberance, Andy is given to expressions of self-satisfaction addressed to his bedroom mirror, pep talks descended from Franklin's *Autobiography.* Although the Hardy films unquestioningly accept Poor Richard's vulgarized legacy (chambers of commerce, boosterism, faith in "Progress"), those values will eventually be satirized even by popular culture, especially in 1961's *How to Succeed in Business Without Really Trying,* whose hero-on-the-make serenades his own mirror image with the show's hit, "I Believe in You." Making a Mickey-Rooney-style comeback, that play's costar, in the part of corporation president J. B. Biggley, was Rudy Vallee.

Z   *ZUZU'S PETALS.*
*It's a Wonderful Life:* the bank deposit misplaced, his business in ruins, his life an apparent failure, George Bailey comes home to find his youngest child sick with a cold. "Caught it coming home from school,"

Mary tells him matter-of-factly; "they gave her a flower for a prize and she didn't want to crush it so she didn't button up her coat." When Zuzu shows George her treasure, some of its petals loosen and fall. Turning his back to her, George pretends a repair, hiding the broken petals in his watch pocket, appeasing Zuzu.

Later in the film, restored to the present, but dazed by his vision of a world without him, George will require proof of being alive. He finds it, of course, in Zuzu's petals, which have magically reappeared in his pocket. Their significance is prophetic: in modern cultures, where notions of "the self" increasingly derive from popular culture, these petals are the movies, the remains of an illusion become the promise of an identity.

# Chapter Seven

## DERRIDA, *AUTEURISM*, AND THE SIGNATURE

"In that which I now propose, we will discard the interior points of this tragedy, and concentrate our attention upon its outskirts. Not the least usual error, in investigations such as this, is the limiting of inquiry to the immediate, with total disregard of the collateral or circumstantial events. It is the mal-practice of the courts to confine evidence and discussion to the bounds of apparent relevancy. Yet experience has shown, and a true philosophy will always show, that a vast, perhaps the larger portion of truth, arises from the seemingly irrelevant. It is through the spirit of this principle, if not precisely through its letter, that modern science has resolved to *calculate upon the unforseen*. But perhaps you do not comprehend me. The history of human knowledge has so uninterruptedly shown that to collateral, or incidental, or accidental events we are indebted for the most numerous and most valuable discoveries, that it has at length become necessary, in any prospective view of improvement, to make not only large, but the largest allowances for inventions that shall arise by chance, and quite out of the range of ordinary expectation. It is no longer possible to base, upon what has been, a vision of what is to be. *Accident* is admitted as a portion of the substructure. We make chance a matter of absolute calculation. We subject the unlooked for and unimagined to the mathematical *formulae* of the schools."

    Edgar Allan Poe, "The Mystery of Marie Rogêt"

### . . . . . . 1. The Intrigue

Sometime in 1939, while *The Hardys Ride High* and *Andy Hardy Gets Spring Fever* (the sixth and seventh pictures of the series) were in release, Mickey Rooney replaced Shirley Temple as the movies' biggest box-office attraction. This event, so mysterious in retrospect, might once have prompted an investigation relying on film scholarship's first tools: cultural history and the *auteur* theory. In the 1970s, however, those methods began to seem inadequate. At that point, literature and film scholars started responding like Borges's detective when confronted with a policeman's too straightforward explanation for a murder:

> "Possible, but not interesting," Lönnrot answered. "You'll reply that reality hasn't the least obligation to be interesting. And I'll answer you that reality may avoid that obligation but that hypotheses may not. In the hypothesis that you propose, chance intervenes copiously. Here we have a dead rabbi; I would prefer a purely rabbinical explanation, not the imaginary mischances of an imaginary robber." ("Death and the Compass")[1]

The rabbinical explanation settled on by the academic critical establishment became what David Bordwell has called "symptomatic interpretation,"[2] a practice (derived primarily from Freud, a kind of secular rabbi) devoted to *policing* texts for their political correctness. Directed by journeyman George B. Seitz, the Andy Hardy series has never attracted auteurists. But with their extravagant devotion to archaic gender roles, stereotyped characters, and simplistic homilies, the Hardy movies seem made for symptomatic interpretation. In fact, they are not. To display their skills, semiotic critics have always preferred subtler game: texts that offer themselves as having no politics, or even better, those that pretend to a leftism that analysis can discredit. The three masterpieces of this tradition are Barthes's *S/Z,* the *Cahiers du Cinéma*'s "John Ford's *Young Mr. Lincoln,*" and, less well known but equally brilliant, Charles Eckert's "The Anatomy of a Proletarian Film: Warner's *Marked Woman,*" three symptomatic readings which have stimulated an entire tradition of revolutionary scholarship.[3]

But criticism has never been particularly good at answering some of the most compelling questions about the movies, and especially about movies like the Andy Hardy series, whose mechanism, like the purloined letter, lies invisible while in plain sight. Why did these films achieve such popularity? How did Mickey Rooney become the biggest movie star in the world? These are mysteries, like the purloined letter's hiding place, that may not be solvable with the standard police procedures. But what is the alternative to critique?

In the context of this book's attempt to answer that question, we might begin to reimagine Derrida as less philosopher than avant-gardist.[4] Certainly, beginning with *Spurs* in 1972, he has relentlessly thrown into question the academic essay's conventional forms. With their exotic typographies, collagist quotations, and commitment to an investigative method relying on the accidents of language (puns, homonyms, etymologies), *Glas* (1974), *Signsponge* (1976), "Limited Inc abc" (1977), *La Carte postale* (1980), *Otobiographies* (1984), and "My Chances/*Mes Chances*" (1984) (to cite only the most obvious works) have had less and less to do with traditional philosophy. As with Barthes's late work, however, when these books and essays are mentioned at all, they are typically discussed for their "content," as if their unusual forms were at best only irritating impediments to arguments capable of being glossed in plainer language.[5] In fact, they seem to share an ambition I have mentioned in the Introduction to this book, the one that John Cage announced for his lectures: "My intention has been, often, to say what I had to say in a way that would exemplify it; that would, conceivably, permit the listener to experience what I had to say rather than just hear about it."[6]

Take, for example, "My Chances/*Mes Chances*: A Rendezvous with Some Epicurean Stereophonies."[7] Commissioned to lecture to the Forum on Psychiatry and the Humanities, Derrida begins by speculating about the *chance* that brings him to this place, that causes him to *fall* upon a particular topic, that enables his words to be used in ways beyond his control. "There," he announces after only six brief paragraphs; "I have just *enumerated* the themes of my lecture. They are all presented in what I have just said, including the theme of numbers" (p. 2). This proposition, worthy of Holmes or Dupin in their most confident (and least explanatory) moods, gives way to a meditation on the relationship of chance to the unpredictable swerve (*parenklisis*) of Epicurus's atoms, and to a question: why do words having to do with chance have etymological roots in terms for downward movement or *falling*? A particular example, the Greek *symptôma*, is typical, meaning both a sinking or depression (a *lapsus*, a "slip" or fall) and a coincidence or unforseen event.

Returning to Epicurus, Derrida observes how a certain view of the creation explicitly connects chance and falling in the theory of swerving, scattering, "destinerring" atoms. And then, *"First stroke of luck: Première chance"*: when Poe's narrator *slips* on a pile of street *stones*, Dupin imagines the associative logic that prompts him to arrive at the name

"Epicurus." In doing so, Derrida proposes, the detective anticipates Freudian analysis, whose texts, "when they deal with the question of chance, always revolve around the proper name, the number, and the letter" (p. 15). What is the chance, for example, that makes the French name "Pierre" be the same word that signifies the *stones* cut for cobblestone streets? And what is Derrida's "luck" to find that when Freud wants to understand the forgetting of a proper name, he tells this story:

> When I was examined in philosophy as a subsidiary student I was questioned by the examiner about the teachings of Epicurus, and after that I was asked if I knew who had taken up his theories in later centuries. I answered with the name of Pierre Gassendi, whom I had heard described as a disciple of Epicurus while I was sitting in a café only a couple of days before. To the surprised question how I knew that, I boldly answered that I had long been interested in Gassendi. The result of this was a certificate *magna cum laude,* but also unfortunately a subsequent obstinate tendency to forget the name Gassendi (p. 17).

By this point in Derrida's essay, the piling up of linguistic coincidence has become uncanny—and for an extraordinary effect, since "My Chances" ultimately turns on psychoanalysis's vexed relationship with chance. As Freud acknowledged, his own method hinged on its ability to account for what had previously seemed only accident: slips of the tongue, forgettings, dreams. But to deny randomness entirely, Freud knew, was the sign of paranoia, that compulsive sense of determinism and interpretability perfectly conveyed by the form of Derrida's essay.

When compared with the flourishing trade in canon revision, ideological critique, and theoretical self-scrutiny, the conspiracy of silence about Derrida's formal innovations confirms his own observation: "What this institution cannot bear, is for anyone to tamper with language. . . . It can bear more readily the most apparently revolutionary ideological sorts of 'content,' if only that content does not touch the borders of language and of all the juridico-political contracts that it guarantees."[8] The academy, in other words, will tolerate even radical ideas presented as a dissertation; departures from the *form* of the dissertation, however, it will not accept.

One of the best ways of understanding what Derrida has been up to is to see his work, like Barthes's, as a continuation of Surrealism.[9] The tolerance of chance, the investment in verbal games, the Mallarméan yielding of the initiative to words—these tactics seem less *sui generis* when placed in the tradition of the Exquisite Corpse, Dali's "paranoiac-critical activity," Ernst's frottage, the irrational enlargement of the object, and automatic writing. "You may think that I am juggling," Derrida admits in "My Chances," in a passage that could be mistaken for one of Breton's:

> For when chances increase steadily, and too many throws of the dice come to fall well, does this not abolish blind Chance *(le hasard)*? It would be possible to demonstrate that there is nothing random in the concatenation of my feelings. An implacable program takes shape through the contextual necessity that requires cutting solids into certain sequences (stereotomy), intersecting and adjusting subsets, mingling voices and proper names, and accelerating a rhythm that merely gives the feeling of randomness in those who do not know the prescription—which, incidentally, is also my case (p. 14).

As I have argued, Surrealism was above all an experiment in attentiveness, a set of strategies for noticing clues that would otherwise have been missed. If these clues did not exactly solve the mystery of how to live, they at least promised future revelation to an alternative logic developed to use them. From the start, Breton made explicit his debts to psychoanalysis, whose analytic situation (itself requiring a new kind of listening) depended simultaneously on the patient's free associations and the analyst's undirected, "evenly-hovering attention," both marked by their acceptance of chance. "Cases which are . . . destined at the start to scientific purposes and treated accordingly," Freud warned, "suffer in consequence; while the most successful cases are those in which one proceeds, as it were, aimlessly, and allows oneself to be overtaken by any surprises."[10]

Freud, of course, was a scientist. As I have suggested in Chapter 3, however, we have often neglected the extent to which Breton, himself a former medical student, conceived Surrealism in the spirit of scientific research. Denouncing the constraints on experimentation exacted by the criteria of "immediate utility" and "common sense," and pointing to the failure of "absolute rationalism," the *Manifesto of Surrealism* praised Freud for "enabl[ing] the explorer of the human mind to extend his investigations."[11] Further, psychoanalysis's initial strangeness awakened

Breton to the necessity of lifting the proscriptions which discouraged pure research:

> It is important to note that there is no method fixed *a priori* for the execution of this enterprise, that until the new order it can be considered the province of poets as well as scholars, and that its success does not depend upon the more or less capricious routes which will be followed.[12]

I have returned to this passage because this proposition could serve as the manifesto for all of Derrida's formal experiments, the hybrids of poetry and scholarship that Breton predicted fifty years ago. Certainly, the Derridean "signature experiment" practiced in *Glas* and *Signsponge* has seemed to many academics one of even poststructuralism's most capricious routes. In the context of Surrealism and Freud, however, it begins to appear as simply another method of *scanning,* a way of attending to a text that descends from automatic writing, irrational enlargements, Freudian free association, and the analyst's "freely hovering attention." Like Dupin, Derrida has learned how to notice precisely what the police ignore: the information, in this case the names, resting on the writing's surface, hidden in plain view. In performing the signature experiment, Derrida assumes the roles of both the patient who generates an associative discourse and the analyst who reads it. As a result, *Glas* and *Signsponge* produce a *shuttling* effect as they alternate between performing a decipherment and producing the very enigma to be solved. As a method of studying texts, therefore, the signature experiment satisfies Michael Taussig's goal for a nonreductive criticism, which I cited in my Introduction—a criticism that suggests the seductiveness of the object or behavior under analysis: *"to penetrate the veil while retaining its hallucinatory quality."*[13]

Taussig's formulation implies enlightenment's chronic dilemma: criticism, like the solution in detective stories, almost always proves less compelling than the mysterious circumstances it purports to explain. In his film *Clues*, Christian Keathley rephrases Taussig's challenge: "How to tell stories whose explanations are as exciting as their mysteries? How to relate knowledge so that an intellectual idea is as charged as a clue?"[14] The signature method may be one possible answer to both questions. By embedding his revelations within the very texts under investigation, by making suspense itself a kind of knowledge, Derrida has invented a new way of simultaneously studying something and re-presenting its appeal.

This capacity makes the signature method particularly useful for film criticism, whose objects of study, the movies, remain the most seductively mysterious cultural form yet discovered. The flickering images of beautiful men and women, projected at enormous size in darkened theaters—no police work so far has managed to explain this phenomenon away.

## . . . . . . 2. The Assignment

By chance (but what is chance? as Derrida asks), American academic film study developed out of a debate about the signature. The *auteur* theory, with its insistence on locating what Andrew Sarris called "the directorial signature," enabled an institution (the University) organized around single-authored works to begin talking about ones that resulted from efforts so thoroughly collaborative as presumably to prohibit the very attributions of responsibility on which criticism depended. After *auteurism,* however, film study would no longer be confined to communications departments; taking advantage of in-place technology, language professors could now discuss "Ford" and "Hawks" with the same methodologies designed for Keats and Faulkner.

In fact, the signature experiment, with its representation of *diffusion,* may be more appropriate to film study than its opposite, *auteur* theory. While *auteurism* centripetally (and misleadingly) gathers filmmaking's disparate work into one proper noun ("Hitchcock," "Capra"), a book like *Signsponge* works centrifugally, amending structuralism's "death of the author" by perversely using the author's name to scatter his effects. If names are the raw material, then a film scholar faces an overabundance of riches: anyone who stays to watch the almost endless scroll of names that now unrolls at the conclusion of every movie will begin to feel like the detective in Ellery Queen's *The Chinese Orange Mystery* who complains that "From the start, there were too *many* clues."

Where, indeed, would a cinematic signature experiment begin? With the name of the director? The producer? The scriptwriter? The cameraman? Even the people in the movie pose a problem. Do we use the names of the characters or of the actors? And if the latter, the real or the stage names? In this proliferation of possibilities, however, lies a great advantage: by providing multiple entrances into any single movie, the choice of names allows the signature experiment to spread feelers out in every direction. The metaphor is deliberate: a book like *Signsponge* enacts

Deleuze's and Guattari's theory of the rhizome that "always has multiple entrances," that "can be cracked and broken at any point" but "starts off again following one or another of its lines, or even other lines."[15] The rhizome, insist Deleuze and Guattari, is "*a map and not a tracing . . .* because its whole orientation is toward establishing contact with the real experimentally" (p. 25). As a form, the rhizome responds perfectly to film study's greatest responsibility, its need to comprehend the movies' simultaneous involvement in the ongoing histories of technology, economics, competing commercial forms, filmmakers, other media, politics, the audience, and sheer chance. "In a rhizome," Deleuze and Guattari point out, "semiotic chains of every kind are connected . . . according to very diverse modes of encoding, chains that are biological, political, economic, etc., and that put into play not only regimes of different signs, but also different states of affairs" (p. 11).

With its rhizomatic structure, the signature experiment offers an alternative to critique, a way of achieving a *hermeneutic effect* without practicing hermeneutics. For cinema studies, it has a particular advantage: when combined with other chance techniques, the signature approach provides a method of writing whose mingling of accident and determination exactly mirrors the conditions of filmmaking. I have experimented with this possibility in several classes, from graduate seminars to freshman introductory courses, by giving the following assignment:

1. *Drawing on your readings of* Signsponge *and the "Signature" chapter of* Text Book,[16] *write a text exploring the words and information that can be generated out of the names involved in* Andy Hardy Gets Spring Fever, *including those of characters, actors (real or stage), producers, directors, scriptwriters, and technicians.*[17] *As* Text Book *instructs (p. 267), your text should be "organized as much for aesthetic effect as for the exposition of your discoveries," but you should not avoid the goal of achieving knowledge about some aspect of the movies.*

2. *Combine this signature experiment with a specific procedure, influenced by or derived from Surrealism and John Cage, but proposed explicitly by Brian Eno with his cards* Oblique Strategies, *produced with painter Peter Schmidt. Here are their instructions:* These cards evolved from our separate observations of the principles underlying what we were doing. Sometimes they were recognized in retrospect (intellect catching up with intuition),

sometimes they were identified as they were happening, sometimes they were formulated.

They can be used as a pack (a set of possibilities being continuously reviewed in the mind) or by drawing a single card from the shuffled pack when a dilemma occurs in a working situation. In this case the card is trusted even if its appropriateness is quite unclear. They are not final, as new ideas will present themselves, and others will become self-evident.

*Below are 50 of* Oblique Strategies' *instructions. Cut them out, tape them to index cards, and draw at least five during the course of writing. Use the ones that you select as headings for sections of an essay and, while carrying out the signature experiment, follow their instructions.*

| | |
|---|---|
| Remove ambiguities and convert to specifics | State the problem in words as clearly as possible |
| Look at the order in which you do things | Discover the recipes you are using and abandon them |
| Be extravagant | Overtly resist change |
| Emphasize the flaws | Balance the consistency principle with the inconsistency principle |
| Is there something missing? | Only one element of each kind |
| Are there sections? Consider transitions | Don't stress one thing more than another |
| Just carry on | Make an exhaustive list of everything you might do and do the last thing on the list |
| Emphasize differences | Work at a different speed |
| Use an old idea | Disciplined self-indulgence |
| Think of the radio | Emphasize repetitions |
| Retrace your steps | Infinitesimal gradations |
| What mistakes did you make last time? | Assemble some of the elements in a group and treat the group |
| Look closely at the most embarrassing details and amplify them | Simple subtraction |

| | |
|---|---|
| Toward the insignificant | Tidy up |
| Consult other sources<br>   —promising<br>   —unpromising | Discard an axiom |
| Go to an extreme, move back to a more comfortable place | You don't have to be ashamed of using your own ideas |
| Once the search is in progress something will be found | Don't be afraid of things because they're easy to do |
| Honor thy error as a hidden intention | Give the game away |
| Cluster analysis | Only a part, not the whole |
| Reverse | Make a blank valuable by putting it in an exquisite frame |
| Use "unqualified" people | Define an area as "safe" and use it as an anchor |
| Imagine the piece as a set of disconnected events | Accept advice |
| Accretion | Change nothing and continue with immaculate consistency |
| Decorate, decorate | What is the reality of the situation? |
| The most important thing is the thing most easily forgotten | What are you really thinking about just now? |

What follows are the results of this investigation.

. . . . . . . 3. Taking Names

**Use an old idea:** *Signsponge*'s philosophical contribution (which will not much concern us here) involves, among other things, a demonstration of the profound instability of the syntactic unit we call the *proper* noun. Supposed to have no meaning in itself, to be able to designate even some*one* only in a given context, the proper name in fact finds itself perpetually drifting, slipping (by accident? by fate?) into becoming a noun of the *improper* kind. "Ponge," referring (and only when we already know it) to a particular French poet, steals away into "*éponge*," the ordinary word for "sponge," just as *Glas*'s "Hegel" and "Genet" threaten continually to vanish into "*aigle*" (eagle) and "*genêt*" (broomflower).[18] At stake in this oscillation is the power of any given language to control its signification, to delimit where meaning begins and where it leaves off.

Always determined to govern the meanings attributed to its product, Hollywood from the start worried about names. Studios routinely transformed Jane Peters into Carole Lombard, F. McIntyre Bickell into Fredric March, Phylis Isley into Jennifer Jones, Julius Ulman into Douglas Fairbanks, Constance Ockleman into Veronica Lake, Gladys Greene into Jean Arthur, and most famously, Marion Michael Morrison into John Wayne and Norma Jean Baker into Marilyn Monroe. Often, the change concealed an undesirable ethnicity: Marian Levy becomes Paulette Goddard, Julius Garfinkle gives way to John Garfield, Betty Joan Perske to Lauren Bacall, and Margarita Carmen Cansino to Rita Hayworth. But in other cases, the motivation seems aesthetic: the awkward mouthful G. G. Hallward transmutes into Gloria Grahame, the plain Lucy Johnson into Ava Gardner.

In the obsessive circles of studio publicity, all slippages between proper and improper names were to be anticipated and policed. "Lucille LeSueur" too closely resembled "sewer" and had to become "Joan Crawford." Even "Greta Garbo" barely survived MGM's fear that "Garbo" ("spirit" in Swedish) sounded too much like "garbage." "McMath" was too schoolmarmish for Ginger Rogers, and even Cary Grant could not have overcome "Archibald Leach." But other homonymic slides appear to have been encouraged: "Harlean Carpentier" seems safer than "Jean Harlow," but evoking the cluster of connotations attached to "harlot" was precisely the point. "Beery" is right for the character actor whose persona wouldn't have touched champagne, and "Astaire" (real name, Austerlitz) seems destined for the man who would dance down several.[19]

By coincidence, the beginning of *Andy Hardy Gets Spring Fever* (as always, the first scene occurs in the courtroom) offers a stern lesson regarding the proper: Judge Hardy lectures a man apparently in his twenties, "Seems ridiculous to me that a man of your age should be arrested for kissing a young lady in a parked car. This is not only a legal question; it's a question of good taste." Later, the movie will specifically conflate the use of a proper name with issues of propriety—Andy's attempt to call Miss Meredith "Rose" will be promptly checked by her admonishment:

Well, I'm sorry Andrew, of course we're friends, but if you called me Rose, it might slip out in class. . . . You know I'm a teacher, and you're my student. Neither of us must step over that line of teacher-student.

Rose Meredith
(Helen Gilbert)

Here, the movie merely displays the concerns which everywhere surround its production (and which its plot undercuts, since Rose has herself stepped over that line, having fallen in love with her professor): (1) Joseph I. Breen, head of Hollywood's self-censoring Production Code Administration (his name one letter away from signifying the sexual act most actively suppressed: "breed"), writes to MGM head L. B. Mayer after reviewing *Spring Fever*'s script: "Here and elsewhere," referring specifically to the play-within-a-play set in Tahiti, "please see that the persons of the various characters are adequately covered at all times." (2) But the studio has anticipated this concern for propriety: a week before, production supervisor J. J. Cohn writes to producer Lou Ostrow:

> While out with Mr. Van Dyke [*Spring Fever*'s director] on Lot 2, going over the sets, he very definitely and very vehemently said that he does not see Rose Meredith [the school teacher] living at an hotel, as:
> #1 Small town school teachers cannot afford to live in hotels;
> #2 School teachers never live alone so that they won't be talked about by the children;
> #3 They usually live or board with some small town old maid or family.

Behind the Andy Hardy series lies another court action that defines the proper name as *property:* the star of these movies, Joe Yule, Jr., disposed by patronym to holidays, had his first movie success at the age of six playing the *Toonerville Trolley* character Mickey McGuire. Having seen the success of fifty Mickey McGuire shorts (1926–1932), the studio insisted that Yule's name be changed to the character's. Already called Mickey by his mother (who herself had adopted McGuire for her last name), six-year-old Joe (previously called Sonny) was happy to oblige. But *Toonerville Trolley*'s author, Fontaine Fox, claimed the name as his own, and won his case in a two-year suit. When the actor's new employer, Universal Studios, found "Mickey Yule" unpleasing, the publicity man tried

> Mickey Maloney
> Mickey Downey
> Mickey Looney
> *Mickey Rooney.*[20]

What are the consequences of this shedding of identity, this assumption of a new fate? The shooting logs reveal that on some Hardy pictures, Joe Yule, Jr., will have only his own day off, working until 7:00 P.M. on Christmas Eve, and returning for duty the morning of the 26th. Having surrendered his name and the childhood freedoms that might have accompanied it, he will at one point during the series be instructed by MGM that a promotional visit to Omaha on behalf of the movie *Boys' Town* will be counted against his vacation time.

At the margins (or the center?) of every Andy Hardy movie is a story of property-in-crisis: Andy's debts, the family's potential ruin. In *Spring Fever,* Judge Hardy (Lewis Stone) innocently convinces his friends to invest in what he discovers to be a phony aluminum deal. Convinced that he has lost his family's savings, and probably their house, he worries about how *properly* to break the news to his friends. Endangered by capitalism, he is saved by property: his aqueduct land provides gravel (stones) which can be sold to the city. Exhilarated by this discovery, the Judge (for the first and only time in the series' sixteen films) breaks into a run, thereby prefiguring his own end and the fatality of the proper. In 1953, at the age of 73, and less hardy than he thought, Lewis Stone dies of a heart attack while chasing vandals, whom he had surprised in the act of assaulting his property with stones.

**What is the reality of the situation?** That chance plays a greater role in filmmaking than criticism has imagined. The Hardy series depends on Mickey Rooney, whose becoming established at MGM depended, by accident, on criminals: his first MGM movie, *Manhattan Melodrama*, poorly reviewed and going nowhere at the box office, happened to be the film from which John Dillinger emerged on July 27, 1934, when he was shot dead by the waiting Chicago police. Overnight, everyone wanted to see it, and when they managed to do so, they saw Mickey Rooney playing Clark Gable's character as a child. His next step depended on Hitler's rise to power in Germany, and the resulting emigration to America of theatrical director Max Reinhardt, who cast Rooney as Puck in the famous Hollywood Bowl version of *A Midsummer Night's Dream*, and then in the subsequent film.

In "My Chances/*Mes Chances*," looking for another example of psychoanalysis's relation to chance, Derrida falls upon an anecdote which, he points out, "is not a story about vacations":

> When he returns from vacation Freud thinks of the patients that he will see again and initially of an elderly, ninety-year-old woman . . . whom he has already given several years of medical treatment. Each year he wonders how much time remains for the old woman. One particular day, Freud, being in a hurry, hires a coachman who, like everyone else in the neighborhood, knew the address of the patient. He knew the destination. . . . The coachman—who knows the address, the correct one—stops, however, in front of another house, which has the same number (always a question of number) but on a parallel street. Freud reproves the man, who then apologizes. Is the error concerning the address simply an accident or does it actually mean something? Freud's answer is clear and firm, at least in appearance: "Certainly not to me, but if I were superstitious, I should see an omen in the incident, the finger of fate announcing that this year would be the old lady's last."[21]

Here is a story about how movies get made. One morning in 1933, MGM's story editor, Samuel Marx, arrived at his office to find scriptwriter F. Hugh Herbert waiting for him. Herbert had worked in Hollywood since the silent days, and loved MGM so much that he had been married in a church set on the back lot; but with the coming of sound, his career had waned, and although still on salary, he was rarely used. Marx tried to brush him off, but Herbert said that Thalberg himself had told him to come for an assignment. When did Thalberg say that? Marx asked skeptically. "Last night. He dropped in to see me at my house." Convinced that Herbert was inventing an excuse, Marx persisted: "How was he dressed?" "In a tuxedo." "And does he usually dress like that when he drops in on you?" Admitting that Thalberg had never paid him a visit before, Herbert nevertheless insisted that Irving had come calling around ten o'clock the previous night, and that after drinking some brandy, had asked whether Herbert was working. Told that he wasn't, Thalberg suggested that he go to Marx for a job. "When I woke up the next morning," Herbert confessed, "I thought I had dreamt it, so I went downstairs and there was the brandy bottle, with two glasses, on the dining room table." Still skeptical, Marx saw Thalberg later that day and asked him about Herbert's story, which, surprisingly, Thalberg confirmed: "I went to see someone who lives on the same street, but I rang the wrong doorbell. He asked me in and I couldn't refuse." "It seemed odd," Marx remembers, "he didn't explain what happened and go on to his planned destination." "Hughie's not a bad writer," Thalberg said. "See if you can find something for him." Marx bought a story from Herbert which became a B-movie, *The Women in His Life,* the first picture at MGM for George Seitz, the director of the Andy Hardy series.[22]

**Make an exhaustive list of everything you might do and do the last thing on the list:**

—discuss the sequence in the darkened classroom, the teacher (Rose Meredith) in silhouette, Andy watching, the grids of light and shadow made by the venetian blinds. What happened there in that room?

—Van Dyke's name, Seitz's name

—Andy's two girlfriends, Polly Benedict and Betsy Booth: their traitors' names

—Irving Thal*berg*, running MGM as if it were a small town (like the Hardy movies' Carvel), personally supervising every production, watching every foot of rushes, giving way to L. B. Mayer, who changed his first names (Eliezar Lazar) so that his new one would perpetually be arrogating power (*I'll be mayor*). Why then are Carvel's politicians, including its mayor, inevitably represented as corruptible, indifferent to Judge Hardy's moral positions?

—the letter, the mystery

—the name "Rose" (Meredith) and *Spring Fever*'s trailer, with its emphasis on flowers. The trailer form as the embodiment of Deleuze's and Guattari's call for a work made up entirely of plateaux, "a vibrant and continuous area of intensities that develops by avoiding every orientation toward a culminating point or external end."[23]

—the insignificance of Aunty Milly, given away by her name's minuscule decimal (*milli*: one thousandth). Milly as the Gaelic *mileag* (pronounced "milly"), "a freeloader." Milly as *mileid* or *millet grass*, which feeds from the roots of surrounding plants: it will not reproduce (Milly and the stereotype of "the old maid").

—the *jam* in Judge *James* K. Hardy: that the family gets into, that Emily preserves, that interferes with the short wave transmission in *Love Finds Andy Hardy*, that provides the colloquial (and comforting?) diminutive for the crisis that grips the world outside the movie theaters.

—"Lewis Stone" (Judge Hardy) as self-contradicting: a *lewis*, "an attachment for lifting heavy *stones*"—his first name eliminates his last. And a link to *Grand Hotel*, and his part as a doctor, face hideously burned in World War I—*lewisite*: "a poison gas for war use."

—the polymorphic possibilities with *Polly* (Benedict): the French *poli* (polite), but more important, the words formed from her-as-prefix (*poly*: "many, several, much, hyper, containing an infinite number"):

—*polyandrous:* "given to having more than one male mate at the
same time" (the character's fickleness), but also, "having an
indefinite number of stamens" (again, the Theme of Flowers,
picked up in *Andy Hardy Meets Debutante,* where Andy feigns an
interest in botany and meets Daphne Fowler, her last name an
anagram of the real concern)

Polly-as-Polynesian                    *Adrift in Tahiti*

—*Polynesian:* Polly's character in Tahula, in Andy's play, *Adrift in
Tahiti*
—the actress (Ann Rutherford) and the character (Polly)
anticipating the age to come: *rutherford* ("a unit of radiation"),
*poly* ("a polymorpho-nuclear leukocyte")
—*rose* as a type of compass, "a circular card with radiating lines";
Polly as similarly curved, in a *polyconic projection,* a type of map
—the visual rhyme with the French *hardes* ("old clothes"), a cliché
for "comfortable"
—draw another card

**Use "unqualified" people:** In the midst of the Depression, *Spring
Fever*'s unconscious betrays an obsession with food. From the paper of
an undergraduate, deemed "unqualified" by the institution in which his
work occurs:

The characters in *Andy Hardy Gets Spring Fever* can be seen as
having their actions delimited, or at least influenced, by their signatures. In specific, the character of Andy struggles under the

weight of the dual signatures of "Andy Hardy" and "Mickey Rooney," whose food-related connotations suggest his relations with Rose Meredith and Polly Benedict. "Andy Hardy" offers two main associations, the first a simple rhyme (Andy/candy), the second, a near homophone (Hardy/hearty) connoting Andy's appetite for both food and girls. "Mickey Rooney" is equally culinary, suggesting "macaroni."

At her introduction, Rose Meredith is identified by one of Andy's classmates as "a dish." Her first name combines with a fragment of her last to form *rosemary,* an extract from a shrubby mint which, as both seasoning and perfume, further blurs the line between amorous and epicurean interests. The saint bearing her name, Rosaline, was caught by her father taking food to the poor, but the food was turned into roses to disguise it. Suitably impressed, her father ordered that henceforth she might do whatever she thought best, a power that Judge Hardy similarly conveys to Rose Meredith in her dealings with his son. "Meredith" evokes the Spanish *merender,* "to snack," a meal often taken with a light wine or *rosé.* Furthermore, *arroz* means "rice," and we remember from *Romeo and Juliet,* the play whose plot Andy borrows for his own, that "arroz by any other name would smell as sweet."

In Polly Benedict's name appear other menu items. "Polly," of course, "wants a cracker," but perhaps more interesting would be *eggs benedict,* a dish associated at its origin with the very dissipation that the Hardy series either avoids or decries (it was invented by Samuel Benedict in 1894 when, having staggered into the Waldorf-Astoria Hotel after a wild night, he ordered the concoction as a cure for his hangover). The most relevant macaronic association with "Polly" is the Spanish *pollo* (chicken), suggesting that Andy's ideal meal, enabling him to avoid a difficult choice, would be chicken and rice, *arroz con pollo* (or Rose *with* Polly). After Rose rejects his proposal, however, Andy vows to become *a benedict,* a man who remains single for a long time before marriage (from the character in Shakespeare's *Much Ado about Nothing*).[24]

**Don't be afraid of things because they're easy to do:** In the mail comes a flier for John M. Ellis's *Against Deconstruction,* equipped with a blurb from Frank Kermode noting Ellis's conclusion that deconstruction "gives its adherents 'a routine way to a feeling of being excitedly shocking.' They get the feeling that might attend a genuine piece of original thinking, but *here it can be achieved without comparable effort"* (emphasis added). But hasn't this objection always been made to the avant-garde, whose point, at least since Duchamp's readymades, has been precisely to show that anyone can invent? And besides, do we need discoveries that will make thinking *harder?* Gregory Ulmer has demonstrated that Derrida's methods, however arcane their appearance, are in fact artificial intelligence machines as accessible as the computer games they sometimes mimic.[25] The signature experiment as readymade research technique—in Derrida's words, "what can be done with a dictionary" (*Signsponge*, p. 120).

**Toward the insignificant:** Barthes's "The Third Meaning" suggests that, like the psychoanalytic situation, film stills (and by implication, photographs)—the first stages of electronic culture—prompt an attention which often ignores the obvious informational (denotative) and symbolic (connotative) meanings. What if this different attention, which Barthes insists "compels an interrogative reading,"[26] represents a new kind of thinking derived from photography and film, one absolutely of a piece with the signature experiment? In fact, Derrida's uses of the accidents of language (the verbal equivalents of the details that strike Barthes—a lock of hair, an eyebrow's turn, a woman's kerchief) represent a particular, linguistic elaboration of Barthes's approach. *Signsponge*, therefore, is also cinematic, since it works from exactly the type of chance detail always available in photography. It practices a "third meaning strategy" resembling the one used by *Blow-Up*'s photographer, who begins his "interrogative reading" with the arresting details he cannot explain: the woman's ambiguous expression, the splotch of white in the hedges behind the fence. By coincidence, *Spring Fever* offers an anticipation of *Blow-Up*'s voyeurism in a troubling shot (significantly missing from television prints) of Andy hiding in the darkness, spying on Polly's rendezvous with the naval officer.

Once the search is in progress, something will be found: In the Hardy series, always multiple plots and the need to find the points of intersection. "This is the Judge's story . . .," "This is Marian's story . . .," "This is Andy's story . . .," writes script-supervisor and producer Carey Wilson in a memo outlining each of *Spring Fever*'s three strands. While Andy pursues Rose, the Judge digs for another quarry, bauxite. But concealed in *Rose* lies its anagram, *ores*, suggesting that even a woman can metamorphose, as in Andy's beloved Shakespeare: "Here's metal more attractive," Hamlet says, referring to Ophelia, mine-ing his claim. At the point where the two plots *meddle* (mix, mingle), Judge Hardy does not himself *meddle* (interfere). Happening upon Rose in the bank (a site crucial to the Depression, a place offering to guarantee paper money with precious metals), the Judge entrusts Andy's fate to Rose, certain that she will not (under)mine his future. The plots resolve in metallic rhyme, with Andy consoled by thinking of Rose as "a mile*stone* in my career," and the Judge (himself a *Stone*) saved by his aqueduct land's abundance of gravel, *stones* that can be sold to the city.[27]

**What are you really thinking about just now?** This scene—when the first rehearsal for *Adrift in Tahiti* ends at nine o'clock one night, the classroom empties. Andy sits down furtively, pretending (he is improvising) to be writing, unnoticed by Rose Meredith. Quietly rising, he turns to watch her as she switches off the lights. Still unaware of his presence, she walks slowly across the schoolroom, seen at a distance (Andy's point of view?) and in silhouette, moving in the darkness through a latticed network of shadows and light made by the half-opened venetian blinds behind her desk.

This shot, with its extraordinary chiaroscuro, its eerie surrealism (worthy of Joseph Cornell's *Rose Hobart*), is unique in the Andy Hardy series, movies characterized by high-key lighting and avoidance of long shots. At this moment, we might say, in its seventh film, the series has finally begun to operate under the signature of Rooney and his homonym: *rune*—mystery, magic.

The investigation points to W. S. Van Dyke II, *Spring Fever*'s director, whose name sticks out in the credits for a series whose other films were all directed by one man, George B. Seitz.[28] Having made *Trader Horn* (1931), *Tarzan, The Ape Man* (1932), *Manhattan Melodrama,* and *The Thin Man* (both 1934), Van Dyke is the only director associated with the Hardy series who might have any interest for *auteur* critics. MGM, of course, was never a director's studio. Its commitment to a strict division of labor, to extensive retakes shot by different crews, to the rotation of employees among different kinds and classes of productions, all diluted its directors' signatures, which disappeared into films memorable principally (and by design) for their stars.

Unlike Seitz, whose name suits a visual art, *Van Dyke* (appropriately for a Flemish master) offers only suggestions of *confinement, blocking:* "a barrier preventing passage," "a bank, usually of earth, constructed to control or confine water." For the scene in question, marked by an unusual darkness, we note that light has been impeded, checked from entering the area in front of the camera. But dikes leak (the story of the boy), and this Dyke has allowed some streams of light to slip through cracks in the venetian blinds. Around Van Dyke's name, therefore, cluster notions of water, impedimenta, light, and leakage.

At the beginning of Van Dyke's MGM career, he was sent to the real Tahiti as studio representative for a movie, *White Shadows in the South Seas,* which he had wanted to direct himself but which had been assigned to Robert Flaherty, *auteur* of *Nanook of the North* and among Andrew Sarris's "Pantheon Directors."[29] From the outset, the production was hampered by difficulties, *impedimenta:* Tahitian police arrested the unit's interpreter within twenty-four hours after his arrival (for a previous visit's behavior), and the natives' suspicion spread to the rest of the crew. Moreover, the movie's most important scene, to be shot under a *waterfall,* could only be filmed in a particular canyon, whose steep walls permanently *blocked* the sunlight needed for filming. Without portable lights and generators, then rarely sent on location, the cast refused to work in the waterfall, whose mysterious darkness made shooting dangerous. Flaherty resigned. Van Dyke replaced him and immediately ordered lights from Hollywood. The completed film established Van Dyke at MGM, where he became Mayer's own favorite director.

And what of *Andy Hardy Gets Spring Fever,* which Van Dyke has signed, whose classroom scene, with its restricted flows of light, so appropriate to his signature, seems nevertheless to recreate precisely the Tahitian canyon's semi-darkness whose negation had made his name? Here is a story, which is about names and about signing, and about what they have to do with filmmaking and with film criticism. By 1939, the extraordinary success of the Hardy movies had attracted L. B. Mayer's attention. The series' two previous films, *Out West with the Hardys* and *The Hardys Ride High,* had both been among the year's top twenty money-earners. It was time, Mayer concluded, to upgrade their production, and as part of that scheme he assigned his favorite A-budget director, Van Dyke, to *Spring Fever,* nominally still a B-movie. The night before shooting was to begin, cast members were called by the assistant director and told to report to the set an hour earlier than usual. Arriving the next morning for the first scene, Ann Rutherford and Mickey Rooney (as had been their habit working under Seitz) presented themselves in neither costume nor makeup to walk through the scene. No, they were told, Mr. Van Dyke is ready to shoot. Hurried into their clothes and into their positions on Polly's front-porch swing, they did a take, a close examination of which reveals Rutherford's haste: one arm has missed a sleeve. Having virtually co-directed his own scenes with Seitz (whom he called Uncle George), typically by suggesting bits of business that might be added in retakes, Rooney approached Van Dyke with advice. "Don't bother me, kid," Van Dyke said, as he ordered the cameras and lights moved to the next location.

"We worked this way for two weeks," Rutherford remembers, "until the picture's producers saw the rushes and decided that they weren't getting a Hardy movie."[30] Having begun his career at MGM by replacing Flaherty, Van Dyke was now himself replaced by Seitz, whose name, however, does not appear in the credits. At first glance an invalidation of *auteur* theory, *Andy Hardy Gets Spring Fever* in fact confirms Andrew Sarris's notorious proposition that "interior meaning is extrapolated from the tension between a director's personality and his material."[31] By flooding a waterfall with light, Van Dyke had allowed his signature to be subsumed in a movie whose title (*White Shadows in the South Seas*) prefigures the decisive elements of *Spring Fever*: the night scenes, the school play's Tahitian setting. By stopping light, by constricting its flow, he reaffirmed his own name and signed the most visually arresting shot in the Andy Hardy series. And for doing so, he was fired.

*Chapter Eight*

. . . . . . . . . . . . . . .

CODA:

*FLAUBERT'S PARROT*

I have proposed in this book what I know will be regarded as a controversial move: the appropriation of avant-garde experimentation for the purposes of humanities research. My proposal derives from a hypothesis, that the avant-garde's ready assimilation of new technology's consequences makes it an ideal means of enabling film scholarship to enter the electronic world. This strategy, in other words, would recast the way we think and write about the movies. For experimenting with this hypothesis, the Surrealist tradition (the twentieth century's most important avant-garde) offers obvious advantages: the emphasis on method, the tolerance of chance, the practical goals. Above all, Surrealism and its descendants took seriously photography's break with alphabetic culture, its introduction of new ways of meaning unanticipated by the camera's first users. As it *developed,* photographic practice confirmed Mallarmé's confidence in the benefits to be had from "yielding the initiative" to signifiers—a poem's words, an image's details, an argument's arrangement on the page.

This book amounts to a lab report, an account of the experiments my students and I have undertaken over the last five years. I have tried to convince with a combination of exposition, argument, and demonstration. But the best way to test my argument is to try it yourself. While any of the methods I have used remain available for further elaboration, I have investigated only a fraction of the avant-garde's possibilities. Other methods might yield spectacular results: the political line of Brecht, Godard, and Hans Haacke, with its concern for ideology's inflection of popular forms, seems particularly appropriate for cultural studies. What would "epic film criticism" be like? Or a new *Arcades Project?*

We might think about the avant-garde practice that I have proposed as a means of redeploying the three rhetorical principles of organization:

narration, exposition, and poetics. The traditional allocation, of course, assigns narration to the novel, exposition to the essay, and poetics to the poem, an arrangement ensuring that each of the traditional forms will be structured around a dominant mode. The avant-garde, on the other hand, demonstrates that an author producing a text always finds himself, like someone playing a video game, provided with three knobs, labeled *narrative, expository, poetic*. At any point during the text's creation, he can adjust the balance (as one would adjust a television's colors), thereby increasing (or reducing) the level of *any* of the three.[1] From this perspective, many avant-garde works begin to seem less strange: John Cage's lectures, after all, are only essays with the expository knob turned down and the narrative turned up; *Nadja* is merely a novel which increases exposition and poetics at the expense of narration.

Seventy years ago, in his famous call for "a montage of attractions," Eisenstein implied that poetics would inevitably become the dominant principle of cinematic and electronic thinking, and would provide an alternative logic of connections which Gregory Ulmer has named "conduction."[2] The advent of hypermedia, with its poetic organization of expository and narrative material, has validated that prophecy. So far, however, the liberal arts' uses of the new communications technologies have merely confirmed McLuhan's dictum that "The content of a new medium is always an old one." George Landow's enormously successful *Hypertext*, for example, simply demonstrates ways to harness the computer's power for scholarship's traditional interests—authors, periods, historical contexts.[3] A graduate student at the University of Florida tells the story of another hypertext programmer who, in response to a question about the possibilities of happening *by chance* upon something *unexpected* in one of his works, replied, "That's what I'm trying to ensure *doesn't* happen." In this model, hypertext (and, by implication, the other electronic/photographic technologies) become means of control, tools for dictating certain research paths. Thus, the urgent question: how can we establish links that will produce *information*, redefined as a function of surprise?

We might begin to think of the avant-garde tradition and its accompanying theoreticians as software designers proposing alternative ways of linking.[4] Freud, for example, appears in this analogy as someone whose "dream work" specifies connections between information and behavior that had not been apparent before. The Surrealists' games and automatic procedures, Derrida's etymologies and puns, Benjamin's *flânerie,* and Barthes's "third meanings" seem similarly designed to move one along unpredictable paths. Ong's description of electronic culture as a "secondary orality" implicitly predicts the return of the *two* modes that constituted pre-alphabetic culture: poetics and narration. This book's fragments and anecdotes represent one attempt to apply that forecast to a single field, film studies, and to suggest how those (pre/post-alphabetic?) forms might serve an electronic logic of "association" and "conduction."

As a way of concluding, I will mention one other model, Julian Barnes's *Flaubert's Parrot*[5]—part novel, part Flaubert biography, part literary criticism. I have used this book with great success in classes. Nearly all of my students, from freshmen to graduate students, like it enormously, and recently I have begun asking students to take the book as a manual for different ways of writing.

As a model, *Flaubert's Parrot* has the advantage of resembling a catalogue of experimental styles. Each of the fifteen chapters works from a different principle—a chronology, an examination, a legal brief, a bestiary (based on metaphors Flaubert applied to himself)—whose succession continuously adjusts the narrative-expository-poetic balance. Reading the book, therefore, resembles watching television while switching channels: every chapter offers a fresh start. As a way of presenting information, this method (which partakes of both collage and fragmentation) has particular advantages. Students read this book with more pleasure than they would ever experience in reading a conventional biography of Flaubert, much less a critical study of his work. In effect, Barnes has found a story nearly as good as Flaubert's own, one that is as much fun to read, but also one that never abandons the knowledge effect of criticism. Barnes, in effect, has strategically adopted Barthes's "novelesque," regularly drawing on fiction's resources: stories, images, details about the weather.

Here is an outline of the book's chapters which indicates the dominant rhetorical mode. I have also suggested potential names for the most interesting methods:

1. "Flaubert's Parrot": the narrator, a retired doctor and amateur Flaubert scholar, visits Rouen to search for the "real parrot" behind "Un Coeur Simple." Name: *The Referential Grail.* Mode: narrative.

2. "Chronology": three distinct chronological accounts of Flaubert's life. Mode: narrative and expository.

3. "Finders Keepers": a fictional account of the narrator's encounter with a man who claims to have owned, and destroyed, the most valuable documents a Flaubert scholar could imagine, his letters to Juliet Herbert, a British woman he frequently mentioned later in life. Name: *The Zapruder Fantasy*. Mode: narrative.

4. "The Flaubert Bestiary": metaphors used by Flaubert to describe himself. Mode: poetic.

5. "Snap!": three coincidences (see discussion below). Name: *The Paranoid Sublime*. Mode: narrative.

6. "Emma Bovary's Eyes": the narrator quarrels with Flaubert critic Enid Starkie. Mode: expository.

7. "Cross Channel": on a cross-channel voyage, the narrator recounts his problems in writing history and proposes a ban on ten narrative topics. Name: *Ad Hominem Philosophy, or Likes and Dislikes*. Mode: narrative and expository.

8. "The Train-spotter's Guide to Flaubert": eleven points about Flaubert and trains. Name: *Paleontology* (see below). Mode: poetic.

9. "The Flaubert Apocrypha": books that Flaubert might have written. Mode: expository.

10. "The Case Against": criticisms of Flaubert and the narrator's response. Mode: expository.

11. "Louise Colet's Version": an imaginary monologue in which Flaubert's most famous mistress defends herself. Mode: expository, narrative.

12. "Braithwaite's Dictionary of Accepted Ideas": a parody of Flaubert's own Dictionary. Name: *Imminent Criticism*. Mode: expository.

13. "Pure Story": the narrator's account of his wife and of her death. Mode: narrative.

14. "Examination Paper": a parody of a university exam on Flaubert. Mode: expository.

15. "And the Parrot . . .": narrator discovers that no "real" parrot can be identified. Mode: narrative.

Some of these chapters offer obvious approaches to the Andy Hardy series. *The Referential Grail* would encourage a search, perhaps, for Andy's jalopy or high school letter sweater, emblazoned with the enormous Carvel C. The chronologies, however, seem available for too many easy ironies: the juxtaposition of the public success (the box-office hits, the special Academy Award) with the backstage realities (Mayer's womanizing, Garland's drug addiction) has already motivated many accounts of MGM's triumphant years. But "Apocrypha" (*Milly Finds a Man? The Impeachment of Judge Hardy? Death Finds Andy Hardy?*) and "Examination Paper" ("Discuss the capitalistic implications of Marian's bleached-blonde hair") seem more promising. For my purpose here, however, two other chapters have more appeal, perhaps because they allow me to conclude this book with the forms most linked to "electronic thinking": the fragment and the anecdote.

"The Train-spotter's Guide to Flaubert" consists of eleven brief, numbered sections, each having something to do with Flaubert and trains. At first this approach, which is, after all, more poetic (organized around a motif) than expository (organized around an idea) or narrative (organized around a story), seems an unusually oblique entry into Flaubert's life and works. For trains figure in no prominent way in any of his books, occurring only in *The Sentimental Education,* and there merely as a passing reference. But as the chapter proceeds, we learn how much Flaubert's affair with Louise Colet depended on the railroad (which enabled them to meet regularly at Nantes, halfway between Paris and Croisset); how much Flaubert regarded the railway as a symbol for all his hatred for bourgeois myths of progress. So when we learn in section 11 that the penultimate sentence of Flaubert's life, uttered as he sensed the onset of his fatal stroke, was "It's lucky it should happen today; it would have been a great nuisance tomorrow, in the train," we feel that trains *are* the key to Flaubert's life and works.

Which, of course, they are not. We can call the rhetorical principle organizing this chapter *paleontological,* for as with the reconstruction of dinosaurs, even the most unimportant part can be used to construe the whole. As a mode of presentation, this style has the advantages of both the list (which has enormous popular appeal: see the success of the various Books of Lists) and the gag (with a great punchline). More important, it provides a different research strategy. If the traditional model's predictability finds its visual representation in the worn index cards of certain research paths (the trail of the author, the trail of the "important theme"), the paleontological approach corresponds to the new searches made possible by computers, which can be instructed to highlight any word, no matter how "unimportant."

Here is a section using "The Train-spotter's Guide," a combination of two students' essays:

### Communication Breakdown

1. In *Love Finds Andy Hardy*, the doorbell rings, and Emily answers it. Telegram for Mrs. Hardy. She looks at her husband, terrified of the small slip of paper. "Oh, James, I can't read it," she cries, reconfirming her series-long fear of technology. "Telegrams always bring bad news." "Mother, when we were young," he advises confidently, "telegrams were expensive and exciting. But today they're as ordinary as postal cards." Reassured that her fears are groundless, and grasping onto Judge Hardy for support, she opens the envelope. Her mother has had a stroke and is in a coma. She must go to her.

The telegram
*Love Finds Andy Hardy*

For the first time in the Andy Hardy series, the Judge has been wrong, and this scene, an echo of the future, prefigures the dark moment in his study when he turns away Andy's request for yet another man-to-man talk with intimations of his own death ("We must plan for it"). Atypically, Andy must do the consoling, taking his father to a friend's house to send a message to Emily, off at her stricken mother's house on a Canadian farm without a telephone.

When Jimmy McMahon's ham radio message gets through, and Mrs. Hardy's reply reaches the Judge, he offers to cancel an earlier decision against the boy in his court. But Jimmy, whose bandaged face seems less a reminder of his earlier car wreck than a foreshadowing of future casualties, modestly replies, "I had it coming to me." An impending crisis, a boy's resignation: in another rare moment of uncertainty, Judge Hardy replies, "Heaven only knows *what* this generation has coming."

*Love Finds Andy Hardy*

The eroding of authority, the collapse of the Father? No, just the markers of an imminent changing of the guard. Going back, we discover other prophetic clues: Emily's irrational fear of the gas being left on in her oven (*Debutante*), Betsy's "Won't we be something to dazzle the troops with" (*Life Begins*), Andy's discovery in *Debutante* that the human body, when reduced to its basic elements, is worth only 90 cents. The event these signs foretell will make telegrams, the notifications of death, the most feared means of communication.

2. Why are telegrams menacing in these movies, which appeared before World War II made their threat indexical? As both an advanced and a retrograde means of communication, the telegram stands between the letter and the telephone. The series' preoccupation with telegrams reaches its peak in *Private Secretary*, where Andy's modification of a man's wired acceptance of a job costs him the position.

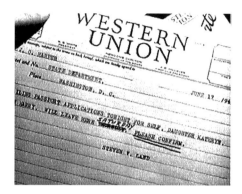

*Andy Hardy's Private Secretary*

But while this moment seems to confirm Plato's fear of the written word, *Blonde Trouble* will portray Andy as also able to commit forgery-by-telephone, when he perfectly imitates his faculty advisor.

3. Thomas Edison's break came when he saved a telegraph operator's son from being run over by a train, a mythic event transformed and doubled in *It's a Wonderful Life* by George's twin rescue of brother Harry and Mr. Gower's unseen patient. Eventually Edison found himself printing a newspaper leaflet called *The Weekly Herald,* containing advertisements, railroad information, and Civil War news received from railway telegraph offices along the line. Edison's experiments with the telegraph led him to invent the stock ticker, the mimeograph, the phonograph, and improvements for the telephone. His inventions made him famous, prompting books and movies, one of which, *Young Tom Edison,* starred Mickey Rooney.

4. In *The Human Comedy,* L. B. Mayer's favorite film, Mickey Rooney plays Homer McCauley, the telegram delivery boy who brings the War Department's fatal messages.

5. L. B. Mayer fired Judy Garland from *The Barkleys of Broadway* for constant tardiness, the first time she had ever been dismissed from a production. She got the news by telegram.

6. While filming at MGM, Mickey Rooney disguised himself as a Western Union messenger and walked into glamour girls' dressing rooms to deliver make-believe telegrams.

Lesley Gamble and Mary Polino

"Snap," the other chapter from *Flaubert's Parrot* that interests me, is essentially a treatise on coincidences. In its second section, "Desert

Island Discs," Barnes describes Flaubert's youthful summer romance with Gertrude Collier, an English girl with whom he maintained a lifelong, albeit intermittent, correspondence (he sent her a copy of *Madame Bovary;* she called it "hideous"). The section concludes with these two paragraphs:

> During the course of those long years (in 1847, to be precise, the year after Flaubert was recalling his Trouville sunsets to Louise) Gertrude had promised to love, honour and obey someone else: an English economist called Charles Tennant. While Flaubert slowly attained European fame as a novelist, Gertrude was herself to pub-lish a book: an edition of her grandfather's journal, called *France on the Eve of the Great Revolution.* She died in 1918 at the age of ninety-nine; and she had a daughter, Dorothy, who married the explorer Henry Morton Stanley. [The coincidences here, by the way, start becoming eerie. Rooney played Edison-the-boy, but Edison-the-man was Spencer Tracy, who also played Stanley.]
>
> On one of Stanley's trips to Africa, his party got into difficulties. The explorer was obliged gradually to discard all his unnecessary belongings. It was, in a way, a reverse, real-life version of "Desert Island Discs": instead of being equipped with things to make life in the tropics more bearable, Stanley was having to get rid of things to survive there. Books were obviously supernumerary, and he began jettisoning them until he got down to those two which every guest on "Desert Island Discs" is furnished with as a bare, civilised minimum: the Bible and Shakespeare. Stanley's third book, the one he threw out before reducing himself to this final minimum, was *Salammbô.* (p. 71)

We might call this method "the paranoid sublime," for it consists in releasing information in a novelistic way which, by suppressing logical connections, produces the uncanny effect of universal relationships. It has the appeal of being anecdotal and mysterious, and thus makes use of precisely the Proairetic and Hermeneutic codes which Barthes saw as providing the forward momentum for all readerly narratives. Here are my last two examples, which allow me to end as I began, with an anecdote. The first is by a University of Florida graduate student; I wrote the second.

## Peirce

Like the theory of evolution, structural linguistics has an uncertain parentage. But while Charles Darwin enjoys an unshakable prominence over his unfortunate doppelgänger Alfred Wallace, a man whose simultaneous and comparable work still goes largely unnoticed, it is difficult to speak of the modern study of signs without giving equal due to both of its founders. In fact, the discipline continues to be known by two different names. The one most common in Europe was coined by a Swiss academician named Ferdinand de Saussure. In his lecture notes, collected and published after his death by a group of loyal students, Saussure describes what he considers a science yet unborn. "A science that studies the life of signs within society is conceivable," he writes. "I shall call it semiology." Unaware of Saussure's work, an American named Charles Sanders Peirce developed his own theory of signification and called it "semiotics." His appellation remains current on this side of the Atlantic.

Like any truly revolutionary theory, semiotics remakes the world in a startling and controversial manner. Words, "signs," are arbitrary, it announces; they are by nature slippery, mutable, and untrustworthy. Yet we are utterly dependent on them, even as the connection between words and things becomes more and more tenuous, even if the physical and mental referents for our words, the meanings we intend and expect to convey, slide away and recede into an unreachable distance with every one we speak. Semiotics reveals human society as an endless world of talk, devoid of sure communication and shockingly unmoored from the material of existence. Or rather, the material of experience turns out to be signs, less solid than the finest tissue, no more substantial than a penstroke or a breath of air. In the world of semiotics, we are all tightrope walkers working without a net.

Yet, as Thomas A. Sebeok and Jean Umiker-Sebeok have shown in an interesting essay, Peirce did not believe that the unreliability of words precluded making good guesses about the world.[6] Once his overcoat and watch were stolen when he inadvertently left them behind in a steamship cabin. The watch held great sentimental and professional value for Peirce, and he was determined to get it back. He immediately engaged a Mr. Bangs, head of the New York Branch of the Pinkerton Agency, to help him recover it. Peirce had already demanded a line-up of boat employees that he thought suspicious. On the basis of a sudden intuition, he had pulled one man aside and accused him of the theft. The man, of course, denied his culpability, but Peirce was certain of his guilt. The philosopher told Bangs that the case could be concluded through a brief surveillance of his suspect. In no time, the thief would attempt to pawn his ill-gotten gain, and when he did, an operative could arrest him on the spot. With the goods in hand, his intentions clear, the culprit could hardly escape conviction. Peirce would recover his property; the law would mete out swift justice.

Bangs, however, an experienced professional with the nation's most famous detective agency, had no intention of following the hunches of an innocent professor. He pursued his own line of investigation and soon reached a dead-end. True to the victim's intuition, the watch, missing its chain, showed up a few days later in a local pawnshop. The proprietor described the customer who had brought it in: there was no doubt; it was Peirce's man. Disgusted, Peirce convinced a detective to accompany him to the thief's apartment. The Pinkerton man was afraid to enter without a search warrant, but Peirce barged in and confronted the occupants. Though the suspect had gone out, Peirce found his wife. He announced that her husband was certainly going to jail, but that he had come to retrieve his overcoat and chain. By observing nuances of voice and gesture as he led the woman and a friend through the rooms, all the while questioning them about the whereabouts of his belongings, the determined philosopher quickly discovered both items. In his search, he had made only two stops. Each was entirely accurate.

Peirce would call the success of his investigation a product of "abduction," the third branch of logic (supplementing the classical forms of induction and deduction), which he had previously described in his papers. Others, less sophisticated, might just call it good detective work.

In 1921, seven years after Peirce's death, and the breadth of a continent away from this forensic adventure, Dashiell Hammett ended his own career with the Pinkertons. He had solved a case a day too soon. Had he not revealed the discovery he had made in a steamship smokestack until after he and the boat were at sea, he would have won a trip to Australia and a much-needed rest. Had he not quit immediately in self-disgust, he might have stayed on with the San Francisco branch indefinitely, or at least for as long as his health held out. Instead, he began writing detective fiction in earnest. By the end of 1922, he was breaking into print. By 1929, he had published his third novel, *The Maltese Falcon,* and was famous.

In this novel, his fictional detective, Sam Spade, tells an apparently trivial story about a man named Flitcraft who discovers that life isn't nearly as stable as he had previously thought. Flitcraft had been a moderately successful businessman and a reliable husband and father, but a near scrape with tragedy instantly revealed to him the precariousness of his existence. When a beam fell from several stories above him and landed next to him on the sidewalk, close enough to send a chip of concrete slicing into his face, it was as if "somebody had taken the lid off his life and let him look at the works." What Flitcraft sees in the box is absolute contingency, an arbitrariness of fate that seems incompatible with his staid way of living. He has believed in a version of the world that can't be true if this new experience is also true. He has been living a lie. Without a word, he leaves town, leaves his family, starts a new life. Eventually Spade goes looking for him.

What Flitcraft observes in his brief encounter with chaos is the world that a detective like Sam Spade lives with every day, a place of sudden violence and pervasive lies, of guesswork and inadequate explanation. The Flitcraft tale is a story within a story about stories; it is a microcosm of a world in which nobody's word is wholly trustworthy, and fictions compete for authority in the absence of reliable facts. This is the version of reality that Hammett articulates over and over in his writings.

As for Flitcraft, he eventually gravitates back to normal life, a normal job, a normal family. It is his habit, and habits are hard to break. But he hasn't forgotten his vertiginous glimpse of the abyss. By the time Spade catches up with him, he has chosen another name: Charles Pierce.

William C. Stephenson

## Lights Out

In *Out West with the Hardys,* one of the series' most commercially successful entries (and, in fact, a top-five box-office hit in 1938), a scene occurs which, in the context of these movies, is exceptional for its explicit, albeit unexplained, emotional intensity. Emily has been frantically spring cleaning and seems overwrought. Since complaints from her are rare, her ill-temper is itself disturbing. She angrily announces that because she has no one to help her, dinner will consist only of bread and soup (the Depression meal), and the family warily gathers at the dinner table, attempting to reassure her while praising the qualities of what appears to be a very plain broth. Suddenly, the power fails, and with the house thrown into darkness, Emily collapses into an unprecedented crying jag, utterly unmotivated in terms of the plot, and furthermore left permanently unexplained. What is going on here? Why is this scene so troubling?

*Out West with the Hardys*

Partially, of course, because the series attends so little to its female characters or to the plights of domesticity, despite the films' family setting. Indeed, the Andy Hardy movies continue an American cultural tradition whose two nineteenth-century halves are Huck Finn (the complete nonconformist good/bad boy) and Horatio Alger (whose heroes began as social outcasts, but end, by virtue of utter commitment to the norm, as successes). Andy Hardy is both Huck Finn and an Alger boy, but already before him, American culture had produced a figure in whom these two opposites had combined: Edison, a nonconformist from the West who, having been expelled from high school for mischief-making, had become the icon of success-through-hard-work. The myth of Edison was everywhere in early twentieth-century culture, appearing in ways that we no longer recognize. Baum's Wizard of Oz got his name (and his independent crankiness) from the Wizard of Menlo Park, and George Bailey's deafness in *It's a Wonderful Life* occurs in the same ear as Edison's. Judy Garland, who appeared in three Andy Hardy movies, of course also starred in *The Wizard of Oz,* but more important, Mickey Rooney not only played Andy Hardy and Huck Finn; he also played *Young Tom Edison,* one half of a pair of 1940 MGM biopics completed by Spencer Tracy's *Edison the Man.*

And the lights in the Hardy dining room? When Edison died, President Hoover instructed America's cities to briefly shut off their power, in memory of the man who had given them the electric light bulb, the phonograph, and the movies.

*Notes*

*Acknowledgments*

*Illustration Credits*

*Index*

NOTES

## 1. Introduction: Reinventing Film Studies

1. Italo Calvino, *If on a winter's night a traveler,* trans. William Weaver (New York: Harcourt Brace Jovanovich, 1979).

2. In 1958 MGM made one last entry in the series, *Andy Hardy Comes Home.* It flopped commercially.

3. One exception to the rule of ignoring ordinary Hollywood product is David Bordwell, Janet Staiger, and Kristin Thompson, *The Classical Hollywood Cinema: Film Style and Mode of Production to 1960* (New York: Columbia University Press, 1985), a book which derives a description of the continuity style from a randomly generated sample of studio-years movies, most of which have been forgotten. My starting point, however, is somewhat different—ordinary films which became enormously *popular.*

4. For an analysis of *It's a Wonderful Life* (and other studio-years movies) from this American Studies perspective, see my *A Certain Tendency of the Hollywood Cinema, 1930–1980* (Princeton: Princeton University Press, 1985).

5. One exception is Thomas Schatz's *The Genius of the System: Hollywood Film-making in the Studio Era* (New York: Pantheon, 1989), pp. 256–261, which provides interesting material about several of the Hardy movies' scripting and production.

6. For a brief summary of the development of film studies, especially the Anglo-American branch, see my article "The Bordwell Regime and the Stakes of Knowledge," *Strategies* 1 (1988), pp. 142–181. For a different account of film studies' stagnation, see David Bordwell, *Making Meaning: Inference and Rhetoric in the Interpretation of Cinema* (Cambridge, Mass.: Harvard University Press, 1989).

7. See Meaghan Morris's similar, but more scathing diagnosis, proposed in an article significantly titled "Banality in Cultural Studies": "Sometimes, reading magazines like *New Socialist* or *Marxism Today* from the last couple of years, flipping through *Cultural Studies,* or scanning the pop-theory pile in the bookshop, I get the feeling that somewhere in some English publisher's vault there is a master-disk from which thousands of versions of the same article about pleasure, resistance, and the

politics of consumption are being run off under different names with minor variations. Americans and Australians are recycling this basic pop-theory article, too." *Discourse* 10, no. 2 (Spring-Summer 1988), p. 15.

8. Meaghan Morris diagnoses this remotivation as a function of critique's commodification and dislocation: "English pop-theory still derives at least nominally from a left populism attempting to salvage a sense of life from the catastrophe of Thatcherism. Once cut free from that context, as commodities always are, and recycled in quite different political cultures, the vestigial *critical* force of that populism tends to disappear or mutate." "Banality in Cultural Studies," p. 15.

9. Daniel S. Cheever, Jr., "Tomorrow's Crisis: The Cost of College," *Harvard Magazine,* November–December 1992, pp. 40–46.

10. Roland Barthes, "Change the Object Itself: *Mythology today,*" in *Image Music Text,* trans. Stephen Heath (New York: Hill and Wang, 1977), pp. 166–167.

11. Jonathan Culler, "At the Boundaries: Barthes and Derrida," in *At the Boundaries,* ed. Herbert L. Sussman, *Proceedings of the Northeastern University Center for Literary Studies,* vol. 1 (1983), p. 28.

12. Robert Benayoun, "Les Enfants du Paradigme," *Positif* 122 (December 1970), pp. 7–26. My source for this phrase is David Bordwell, *Making Meaning,* p. 84.

13. John Cage, *Silence* (Middletown, Conn.: Wesleyan University Press, 1973), p. 271.

14. Michael Taussig, *Shamanism, Colonialism, and the Wild Man: A Study in Terror and Healing* (Chicago: University of Chicago Press, 1987), pp. 369, 10. Taussig here is paraphrasing Frederick Karl, *Joseph Conrad: The Three Lives* (New York: Farrar, Straus and Giroux, 1979), p. 286.

15. Octavio Paz, *Marcel Duchamp,* trans. Rachel Phillips and Donald Gardner (New York: Seaver Books, 1978), pp. 154, 153.

16. As I mentioned in the Preface, Gregory Ulmer's work has provided me with this fundamental idea. See especially Ulmer's "The Object of Post-Criticism," in *The Anti-Aesthetic: Essays on Postmodern Culture,* ed. Hal Foster (Port Townsend, Wash.: Bay Press, 1983), pp. 83–110; "Textshop for Post(e)pedagogy," in *Writing and Reading Differently: Deconstruction and the Teaching of Composition and Literature,* ed. C. Douglas Atkins and Michael L. Johnson (Lawrence, Kans.: University Press of Kansas, 1985), pp. 38–64; and "Theory Hobby: 'How-To Theory,'" *Art and Text* 37 (1990), pp. 96–101. For full-length discussions of this idea about the avant-garde, see Ulmer's *Applied Grammatology: Post(e)-Pedagogy from Jacques Derrida to Joseph Beuys* (Baltimore: Johns Hopkins University Press, 1985), *Teletheory: Grammatology in the Age of Video* (New York: Routledge, 1989), and *Heuretics: The Science of Invention* (Baltimore: Johns Hopkins University Press, 1994).

17. Guillaume Apollinaire, "The New Spirit and the Poets," in *The Selected Writings of Guillaume Apollinaire,* trans. Roger Shattuck (New York: New Directions, 1971), p. 233.

18. Roland Barthes, *The Pleasure of the Text,* trans. Richard Miller (New York: Hill and Wang, 1975), p. 40.

19. Walter Benjamin, "One-Way Street," in *One-Way Street and Other Writings,* trans. Edmund Jephcott and Kingsley Shorter (London: NLB [New Left Books], 1979), p. 49.

20. Bertolt Brecht, *Brecht on Theatre,* trans. John Willett (New York: Hill and Wang, 1964), p. 229.

21. Emile Zola, excerpts from *The Experimental Novel,* in *Paths to the Present: Aspects of European Thought from Romanticism to Existentialism,* ed. Eugen Weber (New York: Harper and Row, 1960), p. 164.

22. Friedrich A. Kittler, *Discourse Networks 1800/1900,* trans. Michael Metteer, with Chris Cullens (Stanford: Stanford University Press, 1990).

23. See Rosalind E. Krauss, "The Photographic Conditions of Surrealism," in *The Originality of the Avant-Garde and Other Modernist Myths* (Cambridge, Mass.: MIT Press, 1985), pp. 103, 112–113.

24. Walter Ong, *Orality and Literacy: The Technologizing of the Word* (New York: Methuen, 1982).

25. Ibid., p. 51.

26. Barthes, *The Pleasure of the Text,* pp. 40–41.

27. In speaking of "potential criticism," I am thinking of the famous French avant-garde group OULIPO—the Ouvroir de Littérature Potentielle (Workshop of Potential Literature)—whose members included Raymond Queneau, Italo Calvino, and Georges Perec. See *OULIPO: A Primer of Potential Literature,* ed. Warren F. Motte, Jr. (Lincoln: University of Nebraska Press, 1986).

28. André Breton, *Nadja,* trans. Richard Howard (New York: Grove Press, 1960), p. 18: "I insist on knowing the names, on being interested only in books left ajar, like doors . . ."

29. Walter Benjamin, "The Work of Art in the Age of Mechanical Reproduction," in *Illuminations,* ed. Hannah Arendt (New York: Schocken Books, 1969), pp. 217–251.

30. Walter Benjamin, "The Author as Producer," in *Reflections,* ed. Peter Demetz (New York: Harvest/HBJ, 1978), p. 224.

31. For an especially interesting discussion of the academy's resistance to the formally experimental essay, see James R. Bennett, "The Essay in Recent Anthologies of Literary Criticism," *SubStance* 60 (1989), pp. 105–111. Bennett cites Winston Weathers's distinction between "Grammar A" (traditional forms) and "Grammar B" (alternative forms representing a different set of conventions: word play, fragmentation, collage, discontinuity). See Winston Weathers, *An Alternate Style: Options in Composition* (Rochelle Park, N.J.: Hayden, 1980).

32. When working with the Hardy films, I have given preference to the six films available on commercially released video cassettes: *Love Finds Andy Hardy, Andy Hardy Gets Spring Fever, Andy Hardy Meets Debutante, Andy Hardy's Private Secretary, Life Begins for Andy Hardy,* and *Andy Hardy's Double Life.* While this group includes the series' three best movies (*Love Finds, Spring Fever,* and *Meets Debutante*), it omits the three next-best (*Out West with the Hardys, The Hardys Ride High,* and *Judge Hardy and Son*). In fact, the release pattern seems dictated less by a particular film's quality

than by Rooney's co-stars: Judy Garland in *Love Finds* (along with Lana Turner), *Debutante,* and *Life Begins;* Kathryn Grayson in *Private Secretary;* and Esther Williams in the mediocre *Double Life.* Two laser-disc sets have also appeared, the first pairing *Love Finds* with *Debutante,* the second *Life Begins* with *Private Secretary.* Television's TNT occasionally shows the entire series, usually during the week of Rooney's birthday, September 23.

33. Roland Barthes, *"Longtemps, je me suis couché de bonne heure . . .,"* in *The Rustle of Language,* trans. Richard Howard (New York: Hill and Wang, 1986), p. 286.

34. Roland Barthes, *Roland Barthes,* trans. Richard Howard (New York: Hill and Wang, 1977), p. 74.

35. Barthes, *The Rustle of Language,* p. 289.

36. Cage, *Silence,* p. ix.

37. Barthes, *Roland Barthes,* pp. 80–81.

38. My colleague Gregory Ulmer provided me with this story.

39. Barthes, *Roland Barthes,* p. 63.

40. Ibid., p. 174.

41. Jacques Derrida, "My Chances/Mes Chances: A Rendezvous with Some Epicurean Stereophonies," in *Taking Chances: Derrida, Psychoanalysis, and Literature,* ed. Joseph H. Smith and William Kerrigan (Baltimore: Johns Hopkins University Press, 1984), pp. 20–25; Barthes, *Roland Barthes,* pp. 175–176.

42. Paul Auster, *The Art of Hunger* (New York: Penguin Books, 1993), pp. 304–305. This passage was called to my attention by Jonathan Rosenbaum's *Chicago Reader* review of *The Music of Chance,* a film made from one of Auster's novels.

43. Cage, *Silence,* pp. 263–264.

44. Ibid., p. 6.

45. Ulmer, "Textshop for Post(e)pedagogy," in *Writing and Reading Differently,* p. 39.

46. This story in fact happened not to me but to a graduate student at the University of Florida, Lesley Gamble. I have modified her account only slightly.

47. Cage, *Silence,* p. 107.

## 2. Snapshots: The Beginnings of Photography

1. Walter Benjamin, "N [Theoretics of Knowledge; Theory of Progress]," trans. Leigh Hafrey and Richard Sieburth, *The Philosophical Forum* 15, nos. 1–2 (1983–1984), p. 23.

2. Jean-Luc Godard, "Interview with Yvonne Baby," in *Breathless,* ed. Dudley Andrew (New Brunswick, N.J.: Rutgers University Press, 1987), p. 166.

3. Samuel Marx and Joyce Vanderveen, *Deadly Illusions: Jean Harlow and the Murder of Paul Bern* (New York: Random House, 1990), pp. 224–225.

4. See Noël Burch, "Film's Institutional Mode of Representation and the Soviet Response," *October* 11 (1979), pp. 77–96.

5. Benjamin, "N," p. 32.

6. Ian Jeffrey, *Photography: A Concise History* (New York: Oxford University Press, 1981), p. 240.

7. Dana Brand, "From the *Flâneur* to the Detective: Interpreting the City of Poe," in *Popular Fiction: Technology, Ideology, Production, Reading*, ed. Tony Bennett (London: Routledge, 1990), pp. 220–237.

8. Walter Benjamin, *Charles Baudelaire: A Lyric Poet in the Age of High Capitalism*, trans. Harry Zohn (London: NLB [New Left Books], 1973), p. 40.

9. Edgar Allan Poe, "The Man of the Crowd," in *The Portable Poe*, ed. Philip Van Doren Stern (New York: Viking, 1945), p. 107. See Dana Brand's comment on this passage in "From the *Flâneur* to the Detective," pp. 220–221.

10. *The Portable Poe*, p. 118.

11. Roland Barthes, *S/Z*, trans. Richard Miller (New York: Hill and Wang, 1974), pp. 172–173.

12. Richard Sieburth, "Same Difference: The French Physiologies, 1840–1842," *Notebooks in Cultural Analysis*, no. 1 (1984), pp. 163, 167.

13. Benjamin, *Charles Baudelaire*, p. 39.

14. Daniel Goleman, "'Useful' Modes of Thinking Contribute to the Power of Prejudice," *New York Times*, May 12, 1987, p. C10.

15. Jeffrey, *Photography: A Concise History*, pp. 12–13.

16. Sieburth, "Same Difference: The French Physiologies," p. 184.

17. *The Portable Poe*, p. 112.

18. Paul Willemen, "Cinematic Discourse—The Problem of Inner Speech," *Screen* 22, no. 3 (1981), p. 78.

19. Edward Tenner, "Revenge Theory," *Harvard Magazine*, March-April 1991, pp. 26–30.

20. E. C. Bentley, *Trent's Last Case*, in *Three Famous Murder Novels*, ed. Bennett A. Cerf (New York: The Modern Library, 1945), p. 1.

21. Arthur Conan Doyle, *The Complete Sherlock Holmes* (Garden City, N.Y.: Doubleday, 1927), p. 467.

22. "Because each photograph is only a fragment, its moral and emotional weight depends on where it is inserted. A photograph changes according to the context in which it is seen. . . . And it is in this way that the presence and proliferation of all photographs contributes to the erosion of the very notion of meaning." Susan Sontag, *On Photography* (New York: Farrar, Straus and Giroux, 1977), pp. 105–106.

23. James Lastra, "From the 'Captured Moment' to the Cinematic Image: Transformation in Pictorial Order," in *The Image in Dispute*, ed. J. Dudley Andrew (Austin: University of Texas Press, forthcoming). Arthur Conan Doyle, *The Unknown Conan Doyle: Essays on Photography*, ed. John Michael Gibson and Richard Lancelyn Green (London: Martin Secker and Warburg, 1982).

24. Roland Barthes, "The Third Meaning: Research Notes on Several Eisenstein Stills," in *The Responsibility of Forms: Critical Essays on Music, Art, and Repre-*

*sentation,* trans. Richard Howard (New York: Hill and Wang, 1985), pp. 41–62. In Chapter 5 I will discuss this essay in detail, extrapolating from it to develop a research method based on photographic details.

25. Roland Barthes, *Mythologies,* trans. Annette Lavers (New York: Hill and Wang, 1972), pp. 125, 127.

26. Willemen, "Cinematic Discourse," p. 64.

27. Quoted in *The Shadow and Its Shadow: Surrealist Writings on the Cinema,* ed. Paul Hammond (London: British Film Institute, 1978), pp. 42–43.

28. Barthes, "The Third Meaning," p. 59.

29. D. A. Miller, "Language of Detective Fiction: Fiction of Detective Language," in *The State of the Language,* ed. Leonard Michaels and Christopher Ricks (Berkeley: University of California Press, 1980), p. 482.

30. Roland Barthes, *Roland Barthes,* trans. Richard Howard (New York: Hill and Wang, 1977), p. 54–55.

31. Roger Cardinal, "Pausing over Peripheral Detail," *Framework* [London], 30/31 (1986), p. 124.

32. Susan Sontag, *Against Interpretation* (New York: Delta, 1966), p. 14: "In place of a hermeneutics we need an erotics of art."

## 3. Invention Finds a Method

1. Louis Aragon, *Paris Peasant* [*Le Paysan de Paris*], trans. Simon Watson Taylor (London: Jonathan Cape, 1971), pp. 130, 182, 128–129.

2. Cited in Richard Wolin, *Walter Benjamin: An Aesthetic of Redemption* (New York: Columbia University Press, 1982), p. 128.

3. See Dudley Andrew, "The Unauthorized *Auteur* and the Uncredited Image," in *The Image in Dispute,* ed. J. Dudley Andrew (Austin: University of Texas Press, forthcoming).

4. Walter Benjamin, "N [Theoretics of Knowledge; Theory of Progress]," *The Philosophical Forum,* vol. 15, nos. 1–2 (Fall-Winter 1983–1984), p. 5.

5. F. Gary Smith, "The Images of Philosophy," *The Philosophical Forum* 15, nos. 1–2 (Fall–Winter 1983–1984), p. iii.

6. Benjamin, "N," p. 241.

7. Walter Benjamin, "One-Way Street," in *One-Way Street and Other Writings,* trans. Edmund Jephcott and Kingsley Shorter (London: NLB [New Left Books], 1979), p. 47.

8. Quoted in Wolin, *Walter Benjamin,* p. 130.

9. *Aesthetics and Politics,* ed. Fredric Jameson (London: Verso, 1977), p. 129.

10. Benjamin, "N," p. 1.

11. André Breton, *Nadja,* trans. Richard Howard (New York: Grove Press, 1960), p. 19.

12. Benjamin, "N," pp. 1, 2, 5, 17, 21.

13. See David Macey, *Lacan in Contexts* (London: Verso, 1988), pp. 44–74; Elisa-

beth Roudinesco, *Jacques Lacan & Co.: A History of Psychoanalysis in France, 1925–1985,* trans. Jeffrey Mehlman (Chicago: University of Chicago Press, 1990), pp. 3–34, 101–128.

14. André Breton, *Manifesto of Surrealism* (1924), in *Surrealism,* ed. Patrick Waldberg (New York: Oxford University Press, 1965), p. 66.

15. Ibid., p. 66.

16. "There is no use being alive if one must work. The event from which each of us is entitled to expect the revelation of his own life's meaning—that event which I may not yet have found, but on whose path I seek myself—*is not earned by work.*" *Nadja,* p. 60.

17. Gregory L. Ulmer, *Heuretics: The Logic of Invention* (Baltimore: Johns Hopkins University Press, 1994), pp. 8–11.

18. André Breton, *Manifesto of Surrealism* (1924), in *Manifestoes of Surrealism,* trans. Richard Seaver and Helen R. Lane (Ann Arbor: University of Michigan Press, 1972), p. 29.

19. Susan Sontag, *On Photography* (New York: Farrar, Straus and Giroux, 1977), pp. 4, 22.

20. Bertolt Brecht, *The Messingkauf Dialogues,* trans. John Willett (London: Methuen, 1965), pp. 15–16. The model for Godard's *Le Gai Savoir, The Messingkauf Dialogues* consists of "four nights" of dialogue among the following characters: the Philosopher (a mouthpiece for Brecht's ideas, he "wishes to apply the theatre ruthlessly to his own ends"), the Actor (who "wishes to express himself. He wants to be admired"), the Actress ("interested in politics"), the Dramaturg (who "puts himself at the Philosopher's disposal"), and the Electrician ("a worker," "dissatisfied with the world"). Although critical theory has often represented the politicized Brecht as the antithesis of the aesthetic Breton, the two sound remarkably similar when talking about their goals:

**Brecht**

> THE PHILOSOPHER: It'd work like this: you'd just be artists whom I hired for an inartistic job. Finding myself unable to get hold of anybody else who was skilled in the exact imitation of active human beings, I would hire you for my purposes.
>
> THE DRAMATURG: What are these mysterious purposes?
>
> THE PHILOSOPHER *laughing:* Oh, I hardly like to tell you. You'll probably think they're terribly mundane and prosaic. I thought we might use your imitations for perfectly practical ends, simply in order to find out the best way to behave. You see, we could make them into something like physics (which deals with mechanical bodies) and so work out a technology (pp. 16–17).

**Breton**

> "Transform the world," Marx said; "change life," Rimbaud said. These two watchwords are one for us. "Speech to the Congress of Writers—1935," in *Manifestoes of Surrealism,* p. 241.

21. Breton, quoted in *The Autobiography of Surrealism,* ed. Marcel Jean (New York: Viking Press, 1980), p. 222.

22. Ibid.

23. For discussions of metaphor's importance to knowledge, see *Metaphor and Thought,* ed. Andrew Ortony (Cambridge: Cambridge University Press, 1979).

24. Breton, *Surrealist Manifesto,* in Waldberg, *Surrealism,* p. 66.

25. Ibid.

26. Lisa Gerber, undergraduate course paper, University of Florida.

27. Quoted in Rosalind Krauss, *The Originality of the Avant-Garde and Other Modernist Myths* (Cambridge, Mass.: MIT Press, 1985), p. 103.

28. Keith Quinones, undergraduate paper, University of Florida.

29. Mark D. Cohan, undergraduate paper, University of Florida.

30. "On Beginning the Treatment," in *The Freud Reader,* ed. Peter Gay (New York: Norton, 1989), p. 372. This passage is echoed (whether deliberately or not, I do not know) in John Cage's "Lecture on Nothing":

> As we go along
> an i-dea may occur in this talk.
> I have no idea whether one will
> or not. If one does, let it. Re-
> gard it as something seen momentarily, as
> though from a window, while traveling.
> If across Kansas, then, of course, Kansas.
> Arizona is more interesting.

Cage, *Silence* (Middletown, Conn.: Wesleyan University Press, 1973), p. 110.

31. "The technique . . . consists simply in not directing one's attention to anything in particular and in maintaining the same 'evenly-suspended attention' (as I have called it) in the face of all that one hears . . . as soon as anyone deliberately concentrates his attention to a certain degree, he begins to select from the material before him; one point will be fixed in his mind with particular clearness and some other will be correspondingly disregarded, and in making this selection he will be following his expectations or inclinations. This, however, is precisely what must not be done. In making this selection, if he follows his expectations he is in danger of never finding anything but what he already knows. . . .

"The rule for the doctor may be expressed: . . . 'He should simply listen, and not bother about whether he is keeping anything in mind'. . . .

"It is not a good thing to work on a case scientifically while treatment is still proceeding—to piece together its structure, to try to foretell its further progress, and to get a picture from time to time of the current state of affairs, as scientific interest would demand. Cases which are devoted from the first to scientific purposes and are treated accordingly suffer in their outcome, while the most successful cases are those in which one proceeds, as it were, without any purpose in view, allows oneself to be taken by surprise by any new turn in them, and always meets them with an open mind, free from any presuppositions." Freud, "Recommendations to Physicians Practicing Psycho-analysis," in *The Freud Reader,* pp. 357–359. The last sentence from this passage contains phrases that could serve as a manifesto for both *flânerie* and Surrealism as research practices:

*without any purpose in view*
*allows oneself to be taken by surprise*
*always meets them with an open mind.*

32. See The French Surrealist Group, "Data towards the Irrational Enlargement of a Film: *Shanghai Gesture,*" in *The Shadow and Its Shadow: Surrealist Writings on the Cinema,* ed. Paul Hammond (London: British Film Institute, 1978), pp. 74–80. For "interrogation of the object," see *The Autobiography of Surrealism,* pp. 298–300.

33. "For resistance is constantly altering its intensity during the course of a treatment; it always increases when we are approaching a new topic, it is at its most intense while we are at the climax of dealing with that topic, and it dies away when the topic has been disposed of. . . .

"How, then, do we account for our observation that the patient fights with such energy against the removal of his symptoms and the setting of his mental processes on a normal course? We tell ourselves that we have succeeded in discovering powerful forces here which oppose any alteration of the patient's condition; they must be the same ones which in the past brought this condition about." Sigmund Freud, *The Complete Introductory Lectures on Psychoanalysis,* trans. James Strachey (New York: Norton, 1966), p. 293.

34. See note 31.

35. Benjamin, "The Work of Art in the Age of Mechanical Reproduction," in *Illuminations,* trans. Harry Zohn (New York: Schocken Books, 1969), p. 240.

36. Man Ray, "Cinemage," in *The Shadow and Its Shadow,* p. 84.

37. Walter Benjamin, "Surrealism: The Last Snapshot of the European Intelligentsia," in *One-Way Street and Other Writings,* p. 237.

38. Louis Aragon, "On Décor," in *The Shadow and Its Shadow,* p. 29.

39. "The greatest intensity is shown by those elements of the dream for whose formation the most extensive *condensation-work* was required." *The Interpretation of Dreams,* trans. D. A. Brill (New York: The Modern Library, 1950), p. 220.

40. Ibid., p. 180.

41. Breton, *Manifestoes of Surrealism,* p. 32.

42. "When I was 'at the cinema age' . . . I never began by consulting the amusement pages to find out what film might chance to be the best, nor did I find out the time the film was to begin. I . . . appreciat[ed] nothing so much as dropping into the cinema when whatever was playing was playing, at any point in the show, and leaving at the first hint of boredom—of surfeit—to rush off to another cinema where

we behaved in the same way. . . . I have never known anything more *magnetising.*" Breton, "Into the Wood," in *The Shadow and Its Shadow,* pp. 42–43.

## 4. *Nadja* and Simulation

1. André Breton, *Manifesto of Surrealism* (1924), in *Manifestoes of Surrealism,* trans. Richard Seaver and Helen R. Lane (Ann Arbor: University of Michigan Press, 1972), p. 29.

2. Daniel S. Milo, "Towards an Experimental History, or Gay Science," *Strategies* 4/5 (1991), pp. 90–91.

3. Jacques Rivette, "Letter on Rossellini," in *Cahiers du Cinéma: The 1950s—Neo-Realism, Hollywood, New Wave,* ed. Jim Hillier (Cambridge, Mass.: Harvard University Press, 1985), p. 196.

4. Ibid., p. 199.

5. Breton, in *Manifestoes of Surrealism,* p. 26.

6. Friedrich A. Kittler, *Discourse Networks 1800/1900* (Stanford: Stanford University Press, 1990), p. 206.

7. Breton, in *Manifestoes of Surrealism,* pp. 27–28.

8. André Breton, *Nadja,* trans. Richard Howard (New York: Grove Press, 1960), pp. 13–14.

9. See Kittler, *Discourse Networks.*

10. Friedrich Nietzsche, *Philosophy in the Tragic Age of the Greeks,* trans. Marianne Cowan (South Bend, Ind.: Gateway Editions, 1962), p. 25 ("A Later Preface").

11. Carlo Ginzburg, "Clues: Roots of an Evidential Paradigm," in *Clues, Myths, and the Historical Method,* trans. John Tedeschi and Anne C. Tedeschi (Baltimore: Johns Hopkins University Press, 1989), pp. 96–125.

12. Holmes's proto-Surrealist formulation appears not in the actual novel, *The Hound of the Baskervilles,* but in the BBC television version, starring Jeremy Brett. For a contemporary elaboration of this epigram, see historian Robert Darnton's introduction to his *The Great Cat Massacre* (New York: Vintage, 1985), pp. 4–5: "There is no better way, I believe, than to wander though the archives [the *flâneur* research strategy]. One can hardly read a letter from the Old Regime without coming up against surprises—anything from the constant dread of toothaches, which existed everywhere, to the obsession with braiding dung for display on manure heaps, which remained confined to certain villages. What was proverbial wisdom to our ancestors is completely opaque to us. . . . When we cannot get a proverb, or a joke, or a ritual, or a poem, we know we are on to something. By picking at a document where it is most opaque, we may be able to unravel an alien system of meaning. The thread might even lead into a strange and wonderful world view." I will return to Darnton's method in Chapter 5.

13. This passage is quoted by Naomi Schor in her *Reading in Detail: Aesthetics and the Feminine* (New York: Routledge, 1987), p. 103. I have used Eleanor R. Morse's

translation: Salvador Dali, *The Tragic Myth of Millet's Angelus: Paranoiac-Critical Interpretation* (St. Petersburg: The Salvador Dali Museum, 1986), p. 1. In his introduction to this translation, A. Reynolds Morse dates the composition of this book to the mid-1930s. The manuscript was lost when Dali fled Paris, reappearing twenty years later. It was first published in France in 1962.

14. Schor, *Reading in Detail,* p. 105.

15. Ibid., p. 106.

16. Another connection: when *The Angelus* was slashed by a madman, Jacques Lacan was chosen to conduct the prisoner's examination. Lacan and Dali knew each other, sharing an interest in paranoia. As Dawn Ades points out, Dali's early (1933), brief discussion of Millet's painting, which appeared in the Surrealist journal *Minotaure,* immediately preceded Lacan's essay "The Problem of Style and the Psychiatric Conception of the Paranoiac Forms of Experience." *The Tragic Myth of Millet's Angelus,* p. 174.

17. André Breton, *What Is Surrealism?—Selected Writings,* ed. Franklin Rosemont (London: Plato Press, 1978), p. 136.

18. *The Autobiography of Surrealism,* ed. Marcel Jean (New York: Viking, 1980), pp. 275–278. See also *Surrealist Games,* ed. Mel Gooding (London: Redstone Press, 1991), pp. 22–23.

19. Walter Benjamin, "One-Way Street," in *One-Way Street and Other Writings,* trans. Edmund Jephcott and Kingsley Shorter (London: NLB [New Left Books], 1979), p. 229.

20. I am grateful to Allen Meek for this formulation, which appears in an unpublished seminar paper written at the University of Florida, 1993.

21. Marcos Novak, "Liquid Architectures in Cyberspace," in *Cyberspace: First Steps,* ed. Michael Benedikt (Cambridge, Mass.: MIT Press, 1992), pp. 230, 228. "Poetic thinking is to linear thinking as random access memory is to sequential access memory. Everything that can be stored one way can be stored the other; but in the case of sequential storage the time required for retrieval makes all but the most predictable strategies for extracting information prohibitively expensive" (p. 226). See Chapter 7 for an extrapolation of this idea.

22. Jean-Luc Godard, *Godard on Godard,* trans. Tom Milne (New York: Viking Press, 1972), p. 214.

23. Noël Burch, *Theory of Film Practice,* trans. Helen R. Lane (Princeton: Princeton University Press, 1981), pp. 111–112.

24. Gregory Ulmer, *Teletheory: Grammatology in the Age of Video* (New York: Routledge, 1989).

25. Jacques Derrida, "My Chances/Mes Chances: A Rendezvous with Some Epicurean Stereophonies," trans. Irene Harvey and Avital Ronell, in *Taking Chances: Derrida, Psychoanalysis, and Literature,* ed. Joseph H. Smith and William Kerrigan (Baltimore: Johns Hopkins University Press, 1984), p. 6.

26. *Godard on Godard,* p. 181.

27. Roland Barthes, *The Pleasure of the Text,* trans. Richard Miller (New York: Hill and Wang, 1975), pp. 53–54.

28. Roland Barthes, *Roland Barthes,* trans. Richard Howard (New York: Hill and Wang, 1977), p. 99.

29. Benjamin, *One-Way Street,* p. 47.

30. Walter Benjamin, *Illuminations,* trans. Harry Zohn (New York: Schocken Books, 1969), p. 262.

31. Walter Benjamin, "N [Theoretics of Knowledge; Theory of Progress]," trans. Leigh Hafrey and Richard Sieburth, *The Philosophical Forum* 15, nos. 1–2 (1983–1984), p. 1.

32. Benjamin, "Surrealism," in *One-Way Street,* p. 229.

33. Christopher Rawlence, *The Missing Reel: The Untold Story of the Lost Inventor of Moving Pictures* (New York: Penguin Books, 1990).

## 5. Roland Barthes: Fetishism as Research Strategy

1. Roland Barthes, *Roland Barthes,* trans. Richard Howard (New York: Hill and Wang, 1977), p. 54.

2. *"Longtemps, je me suis couché de bonne heure . . .,"* in *The Rustle of Language,* trans. Richard Howard (New York: Hill and Wang, 1986), p. 285.

3. "The Structuralist Activity," in Roland Barthes, *Critical Essays,* trans. Richard Howard (Evanston, Ill.: Northwestern University Press, 1972), p. 215: "One might say that structuralism is essentially an activity of *imitation,* which is also why there is, strictly speaking, no *technical* difference between structuralism as an intellectual activity, on the one hand, and literature in particular, art in general, on the other."

4. *Roland Barthes,* p. 74.

5. Barthes, *The Rustle of Language,* p. 289.

6. Ibid., pp. 278–279.

7. *Roland Barthes,* p. 90.

8. Roland Barthes, *Empire of Signs,* trans. Richard Howard (New York: Hill and Wang, 1982), p. 3.

9. Rosalind Krauss, "Poststructuralism and the 'Paraliterary,'" *October* 13 (1980), p. 40.

10. Roland Barthes, "The Theory of the Text," in *Untying the Text: A Post-Structuralist Reader,* ed. Robert Young (Boston: Routledge and Kegan Paul, 1981), p. 44.

11. "Lavish use of paradox risks implying (or quite simply: implies) an individualist position, and one may say: a kind of dandyism . . . in a given historical situation—of pessimism and rejection—it is the intellectual class as a whole which, if it does not become militant, is virtually a dandy. (A dandy has no philosophy other than a transitory one: a life interest: time is the time of my life.)" *Roland Barthes,* p. 106. And see this exchange in *The Grain of the Voice:*

*and you write in* Roland Barthes: *"In a given historical situation—a situation of*

*pessimism and rejection—it is the entire intellectual class that, if it does not become militant, is virtually given over to dandyism."*
Yes, everything that effectively consists in assuming an extremely marginal position becomes a form of combat. Once political progressivism is no longer simple or even possible, one must fall back on ruse and devious attitudes. Because at that point the principal enemy becomes what Nietzsche called the "gregarity" of society.
Barthes, *The Grain of the Voice: Interviews 1962–1980,* trans. Linda Coverdale (New York: Hill and Wang, 1985), p. 335.

12. Roland Barthes, *The Pleasure of the Text* (New York: Hill and Wang, 1975), p. 41.

13. Barthes, "The Theory of the Text," in Young, ed., *Untying the Text,* p. 44.

14. Quoted in Jerrold Seigel, *Bohemian Paris: Culture, Politics, and the Boundaries of Bourgeois Life, 1830–1930* (New York: Viking, 1986), p. 297.

15. For example, Benjamin to Gershom Scholem, August 9, 1935: "The work [the *Arcades Project*] represents . . . the philosophical application of surrealism." Quoted by Robert Alter, in *Necessary Angels: Tradition and Modernity in Kafka, Benjamin, and Scholem* (Cambridge, Mass.: Harvard University Press, 1991), p. 9.

16. "Surrealism," in Walter Benjamin, *One-Way Street,* trans. Edmund Jephcott and Kingsley Shorter (London: NLB [New Left Books], 1979), p. 229.

17. "One-Way Street," in *One-Way Street,* p. 91.

18. Louis Aragon, "On Décor," in *The Shadow and Its Shadow: Surrealist Writings on the Cinema,* ed. Paul Hammond (London: British Film Institute, 1978), p. 29.

19. *Roland Barthes,* pp. 54–55.

20. Barthes, *Empire of Signs,* p. 9.

21. "Propensity for division: fragments, miniatures, partitions, glittering details . . ." (*Roland Barthes,* p. 70).

"I have the antecedent (initial) taste for the detail, the fragment, the *rush* . . .

"Liking to find, to write *beginnings,* he tends to multiply this pleasure: that is why he writes fragments: so many fragments, so many beginnings, so many pleasures . . ." (*Roland Barthes,* p. 94).

22. "The Third Meaning," in Barthes, *Image Music Text,* trans. Stephen Heath (New York: Hill and Wang, 1977), pp. 61–62.

23. Ibid., pp. 64–65.

24. Ibid., p. 56.

25. Susan Sontag, *On Photography* (New York: Farrar, Straus and Giroux, 1977), p. 23.

26. For a discussion of this grammar, see my *A Certain Tendency of the Hollywood Cinema, 1930–1980* (Princeton: Princeton University Press, 1985), pp. 32–55.

27. The answer to either question depends upon the proairetic action's familiarity. In *Breathless,* for example, when editing a standard sequence of Belmondo arriving at an apartment house, ascending to the floor in question, entering an apartment, going to the bathroom, washing up, and finally emerging towel in hand, Godard could reduce the whole event to two quick shots of its beginning and end. Such

radical abridgment, of course, tests the viewer's inner speech, but it only represents an extreme version of continuity cinema's regular practice.

28. Daviau's remark appears in the video trailer for the PBS documentary *American Cinema*. The "marvelous minutes" observation, quoted earlier, is Man Ray's. See *The Shadow and Its Shadow*, pp. 8–9: "The worst films I've ever seen, the ones that send me to sleep, contain ten or fifteen marvelous minutes. The best films I've ever seen only contain ten or fifteen valid minutes."

29. Barthes, *S/Z*, p. 104.

30. See Walter Benjamin's point that "interruption is one of the fundamental methods of all form-giving. It reaches far beyond the domain of art. It is, to mention just one of its aspects, the origin of the quotation. Quoting a text implies interrupting its context. It will be readily understood, therefore, that epic theater, which depends on interruption, is quotable in a very specific sense." *Understanding Brecht*, trans. Anna Bostock (London: NLB, 1977), p. 19.

Photographer Cindy Sherman's *Untitled Film Stills*, cited in Chapter 2 (New York: Rizzoli, 1990), offers a different approach to the problem of the sequence's implication in received ideologies. "The Third Meaning" *suppresses* existing sequences (and their attendant formulas) in order to isolate fragments which can absorb one's attention in ways Eisenstein could not have predicted. Sherman's "stills" do just the reverse: her fragments are designed to *invoke* sequences which in fact have *never* existed. A diagram of these two methods would look like this:

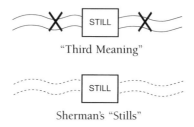

"Third Meaning"

Sherman's "Stills"

Both procedures are ideologically motivated. Barthes wants to evade *any* prescribed interpretation: ultimately, he views prescription itself, regardless of its political disposition, as reactionary. By encouraging a viewer to imagine the stock film narratives from which her "still" could have been extracted, Sherman wakes us to our own implication in the stereotypes we use to make sense of things.

31. Barthes, *The Pleasure of the Text*, p. 23.

32. *Roland Barthes*, pp. 63–64.

33. See *S/Z*, pp. 119–120: "Euphemism."

34. Barthes, *Image Music Text*, p. 62.

35. Ibid., p. 63.

36. See, for example, Section LIII ("Euphemism"), where Barthes substitutes an

explicitly erotic account of Sarrasine's theater visits for Balzac's straightforward version: "It follows that the meaning of a text lies not in this or that interpretation but in the diagrammatic totality of its readings, in their plural system. Some will say that the scene in the theater '*as told by the author*' has the privilege of literality and thus constitutes the 'truth,' the reality of the text. . . . '*The text and nothing but the text*': this proposition has little meaning except intimidation. . . . In fact, the meaning of a text can be nothing but the plurality of its systems, its infinite (circular) 'transcribability' . . ." (*S/Z*, pp. 119–120).

37. *Roland Barthes*, p. 148.

38. Here again, for reference, is Aragon's observation: "To endow with a poetic value that which does not yet possess it, to willfully restrict the field of vision so as to intensify expression: these are two properties that help make cinematic *décor* the adequate setting of modern beauty." *The Shadow and Its Shadow*, p. 29.

39. William Pietz, "The Problem of the Fetish—Parts 1, 2, and 3a," *Res* 9 (1985), pp. 5–17; *Res* 13 (1987), pp. 23–45; and *Res* 16 (1988), pp. 105–123.

40. Pietz, in *Res* 9, pp. 7–9.

41. Pietz suggests that the Africans' propensity to attach fetishistic value to the Europeans' "trifles" encouraged condescension: "While it was precisely such 'false' estimation of the value of things that provided the desired huge profit rates of early European traders, it also evoked a contempt for a people who valued 'trifles' and 'trash'" (*Res* 13, p. 41). Compare this attitude to the one in Hollywood screenwriter Herman Mankiewicz's famous telegram to Ben Hecht: "WILL YOU ACCEPT THREE HUNDRED PER WEEK TO WORK FOR PARAMOUNT PICTURES? ALL EXPENSES PAID. THE THREE HUNDRED IS PEANUTS. MILLIONS ARE TO BE GRABBED OUT HERE AND YOUR ONLY COMPETITION IS IDIOTS. DON'T LET THIS GET AROUND." Thomas Schatz, *The Genius of the System: Hollywood Filmmaking in the Studio Era* (New York: Pantheon, 1988), p. 71.

42. Cited by Pietz, *Res* 9, p. 12. Strikingly, one of Leiris's examples of such a "crisis moment"—"some snatches of song murmured at random"—corresponds exactly to Benjamin's question: "What form do you suppose a life would take that was determined at a decisive moment precisely by the street song last on everyone's lips?" "Surrealism," in *One-Way Street*, p. 229.

43. Gregory Ulmer has explicitly argued this point: "The first stage of Barthes's strategy is the simulation of fetishism." "Fetishism in Roland Barthes's Nietzschean Phase," *Papers on Language and Literature* 14 (1978), p. 350. See also this summarizing proposition: "Barthes's writings manifest at every level—theme, style, critical method—all the features of fetishism. . . . The ultimate benefit of Barthes's example . . . for the study of letters is the development of an alternative mode of reading and writing" (p. 354).

44. Cited by Carlo Ginzburg, "Clues: Roots of an Evidential Paradigm," in *Clues, Myths, and the Historical Method*, trans. John Tedeschi and Anne C. Tedeschi (Baltimore: Johns Hopkins University Press, 1989), p. 98.

45. Barthes, *Image Music Text*, p. 53.

46. "On 10 August 1925 an overpowering visual obsession led me to discover the technical means which gave me a wide range for putting Leonardo's lesson ["one is bound to see bizarre inventions in . . . a smudge"] into practice. Departing from a childhood memory in the course of which a false mahogany panel facing my bed played the role of optical *provocateur* in a vision of near-sleep, and finding myself one rainy day in an inn by the seacoast, I was struck by the obsession exerted upon my excited gaze by the floor—its grain accented by a thousand scrubbings. I then decided to explore the symbolism of this obsession and, to assist my contemplative and hallucinatory faculties, I took a series of drawings from the floorboards by covering them at random with sheets of paper which I rubbed with a soft pencil. When gazing attentively at these drawings, I was surprised at the sudden intensification of my visionary faculties and at the hallucinatory succession of contradictory images being superimposed on each other with the persistence and rapidity of amorous memories.

"As my curiosity was now awakened and amazed, I began to explore indiscriminately, by the same methods, all kinds of material—whatever happened to be within my visual range—leaves and their veins, the unravelled edges of a piece of sackcloth, the brushstrokes of a 'modern' painting, thread unrolled from the spool, etc. etc. . . .

"I collected the first results of this *frottage* process . . . under the title *Natural History.*

"I emphasize the fact that in the course of a series of spontaneously exposed suggestions and transmutations . . . drawings obtained by *frottage* lose more and more of the character of the material explored (wood, for example) to take on the aspect of unexpectedly precise images whose nature probably reveals the initial cause of the obsession or a semblance of that cause." From Max Ernst, *Au-delà de la peinture* (1936), in *Surrealism,* ed. Max Waldberg (New York: Oxford University Press, 1965), pp. 96–97.

47. Robert Darnton, *The Great Cat Massacre and Other Episodes in French Cultural History* (New York: Vintage, 1985).

48. Note that Cindy Sherman requires something similar of her readers, but for her "stills," the stories (which never existed) must be *invented.*

49. Sophie Calle, *Suite vénitienne*/Jean Baudrillard, *Please Follow Me,* trans. Dany Barash and Danny Hatfield (Seattle: Bay Press, 1988).

50. Among the book's *Nadja*-like coincidences is Henri B.'s reason for visiting Venice, which Calle learns only near her project's conclusion: he is scouting locations for a film.

## 6. The Alphabet

1. Roland Barthes, *S/Z,* trans. Richard Miller (New York: Hill and Wang, 1974), p. 21.

2. Marcos Novak, "Liquid Architecture in Cyberspace," in *Cyberspace: First Steps,* ed. Michael Benedikt (Cambridge, Mass.: MIT Press, 1991), p. 231.

## 7. Derrida, *Auteurism*, and the Signature

1. Jorge Luis Borges, *Labyrinths* (New York: New Directions, 1964), p. 77.

2. David Bordwell, *Making Meaning: Inference and Rhetoric in the Interpretation of Cinema* (Cambridge, Mass.: Harvard University Press, 1989), pp. 71–104.

3. The *Cahiers du Cinéma* and Eckert articles are most readily available in, respectively, *Movies and Methods,* vols. I and II, ed. Bill Nichols (Berkeley: University of California Press, 1976 and 1985).

4. I am aware, of course, that this proposition is controversial. Since its beginnings in nineteenth-century France, the avant-garde has repeatedly been criticized as lapsing into a formalism that serves conservative interests. In film studies, that position appears in its most strident form in Noël Burch's famous "Foreword" (a self-repudiation, written twelve years after the text it precedes) to his own *Theory of Film Practice* (Princeton: Princeton University Press, 1981). On the other hand, every twentieth-century totalitarian regime has banned the avant-garde arts, seeing in them a threat to the established order. Derrida has, characteristically, observed the relationship between these two extremes. While warning against an "obscurantist irrationalism" that, as a posture, "is completely symmetrical to, and thus dependent upon, the principle of reason," he has also encouraged an academic commitment to experimental research, which by admitting a "margin of randomness," would "interrogate the essence of reason and of the principle of reason" ("The Principle of Reason: The University in the Eyes of Its Pupils," *Diacritics* 13, no. 3 [Fall 1983], pp. 14–15, 16). "'Thought,'" Derrida concludes, "requires *both* the principle of reason *and* what is beyond the principle of reason, the *arkhe* and an-archy" (pp. 18–19).

In the traditional avant-garde spirit, however, Derrida has not refrained from assuming the role of *provocateur.* In *Signsponge,* for example, he sounds the customary *épater-le-bourgeois* note: "We must decide to scandalize those illiterate scienticisms, those tiresome and obscurantist advocates of poetics—impotent censors above all—shocked by what can be done with a dictionary. . . . We have to scandalize them, make them cry out still louder—in the first place because it is fun to do so, and why deny ourselves the pleasure?" Derrida, *Signéponge/Signsponge,* trans. Richard Rand (New York: Columbia University Press, 1984), p. 120.

5. For an example of this tendency, see Christopher Norris, *Derrida* (Cambridge, Mass.: Harvard University Press, 1987). Norris's frequent updates on Derrida's work in the *London Review of Books* display the same reluctance to admit form as a contributing element of Derrida's meaning. Someone, for example, knowing only Norris's review of *Signsponge* (*London Review of Books,* February 20, 1986, pp. 10–12) would have almost no notion of that book's fundamental strangeness.

6. John Cage, *Silence* (Middletown, Conn.: Wesleyan University Press, 1973), p. ix.

7. In *Taking Chances: Derrida, Psychoanalysis, and Literature,* ed. Joseph H. Smith and William Kerrigan (Baltimore: Johns Hopkins University Press, 1984), pp. 1–32.

8. "Living on: Borderlines," in *Deconstruction and Criticism* (New York: Seabury, 1979), pp. 94–95.

9. Whether Derrida would acknowledge this connection I cannot say. A passing remark made in *Spurs,* a revision of Lautréamont's famous dictum, amounts to a subtle acknowledgment of debt: "One doesn't just happen onto an unwonted object of this sort in a sewing-up machine on a castration table." Derrida, *Spurs: Nietzsche's Styles,* trans. Barbara Harlow (Chicago: University of Chicago Press, 1979), pp. 129, 131.

In the past two decades, any explicit embrace of Surrealism would have encountered the criticisms of that movement's misogyny, romantic spiritualism, and theoretical diffidence. See, for example, Rosalind Krauss and Jane Livingston, *L'Amour fou: Photography and Surrealism* (New York: Abbeville Press, 1985) and Daniel Cottom, *Abyss of Reason: Cultural Movements, Revelations, and Betrayals* (New York: Oxford University Press, 1991). This prevailing intellectual climate may have accounted for Barthes's and Derrida's reticence about Breton. On the other hand, while Walter Benjamin anticipated many of the recent critiques, warning of Surrealism's proximity to "the humid backroom of spiritualism," he also insisted on its systematic "substitution of a political for a historical view of the past" and its determined "pushing the 'poetic life' to the utmost limits of possibility." Benjamin, "Surrealism: The Last Snapshot of the European Intelligentsia," in *One-Way Street and Other Writings,* trans. Edmund Jephcott and Kingsley Shorter (London: NLB [New Left Books], 1979), pp. 228, 230, 226.

10. "Recommendations for Physicians on the Psychoanalytic Method of Treatment" (1912), in *Therapy and Technique,* trans. Joan Riviere (New York: Collier Books, 1963), p. 120.

11. In Patrick Waldberg, *Surrealism* (New York: Oxford University Press, 1965), p. 66.

12. Ibid.

13. Michael Taussig, *Shamanism, Colonialism, and the Wild Man: A Study in Terror and Healing* (Chicago: University of Chicago Press, 1987), p. 10.

14. *Clues* is an as yet unreleased hour-long film, made at the University of Florida.

15. Gilles Deleuze and Félix Guattari, *On the Line* (New York: Semiotext(e), 1983), pp. 26, 17–18.

16. Robert Scholes, Nancy R. Comley, and Gregory L. Ulmer, *Text Book: An Introduction to Literary Language* (New York: St. Martin's Press, 1988), pp. 236–285. This chapter is by far the best way to introduce even advanced students to the signature experiment, and the model student essay, James Michael Jarrett's "A Jarrett in Your Text," the most accessible example.

17. Like nearly all the movies in the series, *Andy Hardy Gets Spring Fever* begins in the Judge's courtroom, where he acknowledges Spring by suspending sentence on a man arrested for romantic parking. Irritated by taxes due on his aqueduct land ("that pile of gravel"), the Judge is ripe for two men's proposition to extract that property's 8 percent bauxite, a mineral necessary for aluminum production. Driving home with the news of this windfall, the Judge passes Andy, outfitted (as he is

throughout the movie) in his Carvel letter sweater, en route to girlfriend Polly Benedict's house. But Polly is entertaining an older man, Navy Lieutenant Charles Copley, sent to oversee Carvel's road building. Snubbed, Andy goes home to sulk. Judge Hardy, however, is delirious with the anticipation of profits. His good mood makes him receptive to daughter Marian's desire for a job, and he dictates so she can practice shorthand.

At school the next day, Andy is handed a letter from Polly Benedict advising that she no longer wishes to see him. Planning a reply of his own, he is distracted by the introduction of the substitute drama teacher, Rose Meredith, who proposes that the class write and produce its own play, preferably one modeled on a classic. For Andy, it is love at first sight, and Polly is forgotten. While the Judge meets with the two businessmen, agreeing to raise (with his friends) the $17,000 necessary to build an aluminum plant, Andy is at home composing his play, *Adrift in Tahiti* (a cross between *Romeo and Juliet* and *Madame Butterfly*), which Miss Meredith chooses as the one to be performed. At rehearsal, however, Andy (playing a naval officer) becomes too embarrassed to kiss Polly (playing a native girl, Tahula, who is to throw herself into a flaming volcano after Andy rejects her). Remaining after practice, Andy catches Rose crying, but she refuses to explain.

By now, tipped off by Marian (who has been working as an unpaid secretary), Judge Hardy is aware that he has been swindled, that the surface of the earth everywhere contains 8 percent bauxite. He goes to the bank to alert its president, Polly's father, and there runs into Rose. He asks for her help in dealing with Andy's infatuation, and she promises to do the correct thing. But back home, in a man-to-man talk, he learns that Andy has proposed to Rose, and that she will give him her decision the next night, after the play. In despair, less at this news than his financial ruin, the Judge tells his wife, Emily, that he has lost everything. But the next morning, he accidentally overhears that the city is buying the very gravel which his aqueduct property has so much of. He and his friends are saved.

That same evening, just before going onstage, Andy sees Rose kissing a strange man. His anger and jealousy motivate his performance, which is undercut, however, by a malfunctioning moon and a misfiring volcano. Afterwards, Rose explains that the man is her fiancé, her former professor, separated from her by financial pressures. Reconciled to losing Rose, Andy arrives a hero at the cast party where, as always, he makes up with Polly.

> Judge James K. Hardy (Lewis Stone)
> Emily Hardy (Fay Holden)
> Andy (Mickey Rooney)
> Marian (Cecilia Parker)
> Aunt Milly (Sara Haden)
> Polly Benedict (Ann Rutherford)
> Rose Meredith (Helen Gilbert)

18. Jacques Derrida, *Glas*, trans. John P. Leavey, Jr., and Richard Rand (Lincoln: University of Nebraska Press, 1986).

19. See Christopher Finch and Linda Rosenkrantz, *Gone Hollywood: The Movie Colony in the Golden Age* (New York: Doubleday, 1979), pp. 207–210.

20. Arthur Marx, *The Nine Lives of Mickey Rooney* (New York: Berkley Books, 1986), pp. 18–27.

21. Smith and Kerrigan, eds., *Taking Chances,* pp. 20–21.

22. Samuel Marx, *A Gaudy Spree: Literary Hollywood When the West Was Fun* (New York: Franklin Watts, 1987), pp. 75–76.

23. Deleuze and Guattari, *On the Line,* p. 49.

24. From Scott Thompson, "Andy Hardy and Signature Theory" (unpublished course paper, the University of Florida), with contributions from Thomasine Cobb and Vivian Menge.

25. See Gregory L. Ulmer, *Applied Grammatology: Post(e)-Pedagogy from Jacques Derrida to Joseph Beuys* (Baltimore: Johns Hopkins University Press, 1985), pp. 3–153; and *Teletheory: Grammatology in the Age of Video* (New York: Routledge, 1989).

26. Roland Barthes, "The Third Meaning," in *Image Music Text,* trans. Stephen Heath (New York: Hill and Wang, 1977), p. 53.

27. From Amy Slaughter, "Disciplined Self-Indulgence" (unpublished undergraduate paper).

28. Seitz died in 1944. The two postwar Andy Hardy movies, *Love Laughs at Andy Hardy* (1946) and *Andy Hardy Comes Home* (1958), were directed by Willis Goldbeck and Howard W. Koch, respectively.

29. Andrew Sarris, *The American Cinema: Directors and Directions 1929–1968* (New York: Dutton, 1968).

30. Information about Van Dyke's work on *Spring Fever* comes from an interview with Ann Rutherford. See her similar account in Walter Wagner, *You Must Remember This* (New York: Putnam, 1975), p. 199. For information about Van Dyke's career, see Robert C. Cannom, *Van Dyke and the Mythical City Hollywood* (New York: Garland, 1977).

31. "Notes on the Auteur Theory in 1962," in *Film Theory and Criticism,* ed. Gerald Mast and Marshall Cohen (New York: Oxford University Press, 1979), p. 663.

## 8. Coda: *Flaubert's Parrot*

1. I am grateful to my colleague Gregory Ulmer for this analogy.

2. Sergei Eisenstein, "The Montage of Film Attractions," in *Eisenstein: Writings 1922–1934,* ed. Richard Taylor (Bloomington: Indiana University Press, 1988), pp. 39–58. The best discussion of this aspect of Eisenstein's thought is Chapter 9 of Gregory Ulmer's *Applied Grammatology: Post(e)-Pedagogy from Jacques Derrida to Joseph Beuys* (Baltimore: Johns Hopkins University Press, 1985). For Ulmer's discussion of "conduction," see Chapter 2 of his *Teletheory: Grammatology in the Age of Video* (Baltimore: Johns Hopkins University Press, 1989).

3. George P. Landow, *Hypertext: The Convergence of Contemporary Theory and Technology* (Baltimore: Johns Hopkins University Press, 1992).

4. I am indebted to University of Florida graduate student Michelle Glaros for this idea.

5. Julian Barnes, *Flaubert's Parrot* (New York: Alfred A. Knopf, 1985).

6. Thomas A. Sebeok and Jean Umiker-Sebeok, "'You Know My Method': A Juxtaposition of Charles S. Peirce and Sherlock Holmes," in *The Sign of Three: Dupin, Holmes, Peirce,* ed. Umberto Eco and Thomas A. Sebeok (Bloomington: Indiana University Press, 1983), pp. 11–19.

## ACKNOWLEDGMENTS

An experimental book of this sort, even when signed by a single author, inevitably results from a sustained period of collaboration. In my case the debts are many, especially to the undergraduate and graduate students at the University of Florida who participated in the Andy Hardy projects which informed my work. My thanks go especially to William Stephenson, Lesley Gamble, Michelle Lekas, Julie Howe, and John Long, some of whose work appears in this book.

I am grateful to Thomas Schatz for generously sending me detailed information about the location of archival material regarding the Andy Hardy films, and to Ned Comstock, the archival assistant managing the MGM collections at the University of Southern California.

By awarding me an Obermann fellowship at the University of Iowa, Dudley Andrew provided me with an idyllic means for trying out and refining the ideas that have made their way into this book. I have profited especially from my conversations at Iowa with Andrew, Dana Benelli, James Lastra, Estera Milman, Robert Newman, John Peters, and Lauren Rabinovitz. I also want to thank Jay Semel and Lorna Olson at Iowa's Center for Advanced Studies for their hospitality.

Anthony Rue, a University of Florida graduate student, has patiently and skillfully demonstrated electronic technology's new capacities by producing the film stills used in this book.

James Naremore (Indiana University) and Craig Saper (University of Pennsylvania) have provided me with forums for this project's early stages. Their comments and suggestions have, as always, helped me enormously.

Portions of this book have appeared (often in preliminary versions) in the following places: *Visible Language* 22, no. 4 (Autumn 1988); *Modernity and Mass Culture,* ed. James Naremore and Patrick Brantlinger (Bloomington: Indiana University Press, 1991); *Film Criticism* 17, no. 2-3 (Winter/Spring 1993); and *Deconstruction and the Visual Arts: Art, Media, Architecture,* ed. Peter Brunette and David Wills (Cambridge: Cambridge University Press, 1994; reprinted with the permission of Cambridge University Press). Chapter 2 was originally commissioned for *Photo-Textualities: Reading Photographs and Literature,* ed. Marsha Bryant (Newark: University of Delaware Press, 1995), where it appears in somewhat different form. I would like to thank the editors of these journals and books for both their support and their permission to reprint this material.

In reviewing the manuscript of this book, Marjorie Perloff and Charles Maland generously took the time to specify where and how I could improve, clarify, and correct it. Their support for this project, and their scrupulous interest in its refinement, far exceeded their duties as "reviewers." I owe similar thanks to my editors at Harvard University Press, Lindsay Waters and Alison Kent, who enthusiastically championed this experimental venture and skillfully brought it to press. And I have had the exceptional good luck of benefiting from the corrections, suggestions, and advice of manuscript editor Mary Ellen Geer, art director and designer Marianne Perlak, and production coordinator David Foss.

My regular conversations with Christian Keathley have informed this book's writing in dozens of ways, particularly by reminding me of the filmmaker's perspective, whose attitude toward the details of everyday life, observed by chance, so often differs from the modes of Walter Ong's "alphabetic literacy."

My chief thanks go to an unlikely pair: first, to Ann Rutherford, Andy Hardy's Polly Benedict, who flew across the country to address my classes in a way so stimulating that my students wanted the University of Florida to hire her; and finally, and principally, to my colleague Gregory Ulmer, whose work and friendship have prompted such a great part of this book.

·  ·  ·  ·  ·  ·  ·  ·  ·  ·  ·  ·  ·  ·  ·  ·

## ILLUSTRATION CREDITS

*Golconde* by René Magritte (1953) is from the Menil Collection, Houston, Texas, reproduced courtesy of Giraudon/Art Resource, New York.

*Le Mois des Vendages* by René Magritte (1959) is reproduced courtesy of Giraudon/Art Resource, New York.

*The Menaced Assassin* by René Magritte (1926), oil on canvas, 150.4 X 195.2 cm, is reproduced by permission of The Museum of Modern Art, New York. Kay Sage Tanguy Fund. Photograph © 1995 The Museum of Modern Art, New York.

*L'Angélus* by Jean François Millet, The Louvre Museum, Paris, is reproduced courtesty of Photographie Giraudon/Art Resource.

*Untitled Film Stills #39* is reproduced by permission from Cindy Sherman, *Film Stills* (New York: Rizzoli, 1990).

A STRANGE DAY IN JULY and CAPTAIN TORY are reproduced from *The Mysteries of Harris Burdick,* copyright © 1984 by Chris Van Allsburg. Reprinted by permission of Houghton Mifflin Co. All rights reserved.

# INDEX